SERMONS
and Memoirs
of
Christmas Evans

Christmas Evans preaching

SERMONS
and Memoirs
of
Christmas Evans

Memoirs by
Joseph Cross

Foreword by
Warren W. Wiersbe

KREGEL PUBLICATIONS
Grand Rapids, Michigan 49501

Sermons and Memoirs of Christmas Evans by
Christmas Evans. Copyright © 1986 by Kregel
Publications, a division of Kregel, Inc. All rights
reserved.

Translated from the Welch by Joseph Cross.

Library of Congress Cataloging-in-Publication Data

Evans, Christmas, 1766-1838.
  Sermons and Memoirs of Christmas Evans.

  Reprint. Originally published: New York: Leary &
Getz, 1856.
  1. Baptists—Sermons
  2. Sermons, English.
  3. Evans, Christmas, 1766-1838.
I. Cross, Joseph. II. Title.
BX6333.E4S38   1986   252'.061   86-7108
ISBN O-8254-2522-0

Printed in the United States of America

CONTENTS

MEMOIRS AND PORTRAITURE

FOREWORD

He was called "the Bunyan of Wales" because of his gift of sanctified imagination. He transformed ideas into pictures and pictures into powerful tools to build the church, and into weapons to fight the devil.

The New International Dictionary of the Christian Church calls him "one of the three greatest figures in the history of the nation's [Wales] preaching." "Christmas Evans ranks among the most remarkable preachers of his age," wrote Edwin C. Dargan in his classic *History of Preaching.* "Wales has produced many able preachers," wrote F.R. Webber, "but none greater than Christmas Evans" *(A History of Preaching In Britain and America).*

He was born the year the Stamp Act was repealed. He was ordained the year the Constitution of the United States was adopted. He died the year Queen Victoria was crowned. He ministered during the era of Napoleon, the Monroe Doctrine, and the ministries of men like Robert Murray McCheyne, John Henry Newman, F.W. Robertson, and Henry Ward Beecher.

The American authority on preaching, Dr. John A. Broadus, called Evans "a notable example of untutored eloquence." Yes, Evans did not have the advantages of formal ministerial training, but he gave all that he had to God and the Spirit used him to turn many to righteousness. Even Broadus admitted that education probably would have "hampered the wings of soaring fancy and made him really less effective."

I rejoice that this rare volume is now back in print. For one thing, we need to recover and treasure every piece of homiletical literature that we can; for today's preachers can learn much form the giants of the past. Until we dig again the old wells, we can never benefit as we should from these ministries that were so signally blessed of God. Not that we should imitate them, but that they should inspire and instruct us as we seek to minister today.

But the main reason I rejoice at the publication of this particular volume is that it brings to the fore the importance of imagination in preaching. Not every preacher has the gifts that Christmas Evans possessed, but all of us can make better use of the gifts we have. Again, I am not suggesting that we imitate his dramatic retelling of Bible events, or his vivid descriptions of Bible people; but I am suggesting — yes, *urging* — that we start using the imagination as we study the Bible, prepare our messages, and present them to the people.

Most modern biblical preaching is saturated with information and explanation, but it lacks imagination. Our preaching is predictable and, therefore, it is not as powerful as it could be. We are guilty of what Emerson said was wrong with a series of lectures he had given in Boston: "A cold mechanical preparation...fine things, pretty things, wise things — but no arrows, no axes, no nectar, no growling, no transpiercing, no loving, no enchantment."

Allow these messages to penetrate your heart and stimulate your mind. You will not be the same!

WARREN W. WIERSBE

SERMONS

of

CHRISTMAS EVANS

INTRODUCTION

In presenting to the public a selection from the sermons of Christmas Evans, we find ourselves embarrassed by two circumstances:

First.—It is impossible to exhibit on paper the peculiarly forcible elocution of the author. Some of the most effective discourses ever delivered seem comparatively powerless when perused afterward in private. This observation is verified in the case of the two most remarkable pulpit orators of modern times, George Whitefield and John Summerfield. Their spoken eloquence was like the breathings of the seraphim, but their printed sermons are of no very extraordinary character. Like them, Mr. Evans was much indebted, for his success, to a very popular and powerful delivery. His appearance in the pulpit was fine and commanding; his voice, one of unrivalled compass and melody; his gesticulation, always easy, appropriate, and forcible; and when he warmed under the inspiration of his theme, his large bright eye shot fire through the assembly. But the sermons are now divested of all these auxiliary accompaniments; and without the prophet before us, we may wonder at the effects attributed to his message. The following selections will give the reader at least a tolerable idea of Mr. Evans' modes of thought and illustration; but if he would have any adequate conception of the splendid phantasmagora in process of exhibition, he must imagine the burning lamp within the scenes.

But the greater difficulty is the impossibility of a perfect translation. Genius is proverbially eccentric. Mr. Evans' style is altogether unique. The structure of his sentences is very original. None of his countrymen approximated his peculiar mode of expression. It would be exceedingly difficult for any man, however well qualified to translate other Welsh authors, to render him into English, with the preservation, everywhere, of his spirit. The writer at first thought of publishing a selection from his sermons, as translated by J. Davis; but upon examination, that translation was found so faulty, that it was deemed expedient, if possible, to produce a new. In pursuance of this purpose he obtained the aid of a friend, whose excellent literary taste, and accurate acquaintance with both languages, constitute a sufficient guarantee for the general correctness of the following translation. It lays no claim to perfection, though it is at least free from the most obvious and glaring faults of Mr. Davis' version. Some of the nicest shades of thought are inevitably lost, and many of the startling metaphors and splendid allegories have doubtless suffered some diminution of their original force and beauty; but the writer trusts that enough of the author's spirit is retained to furnish a pretty correct idea of his talents, and render the book acceptable to the reader.

With these apologetic remarks, we commit the sermons of Christmas Evans to the press; praying that they may be accompanied with something of the same Divine unction, as when, in their original delivery by the author, they " set the land of Cambria on fire!"

JOSEPH CROSS

Sermon 1

THE TIME OF REFORMATION

Until the time of reformation (Hebrews 9:10).

THE ceremonies pertaining to the service of God under the Sinaic dispensation were entirely typical in their character; mere figures of Christ, the " High-priest of good things to come, by a greater and more perfect tabernacle, not made with hands;" who, " not by the blood of goats and calves, but by his own blood, has entered once into the holy place, having obtained eternal redemption for us." Sustaining such a relation to other ages and events, they were necessarily imperfect, consisting " only in meats and drinks, and divers washings, and carnal ordinances," not intended for perpetual observance, but imposed upon the Jewish people merely " until the time of reformation," when the shadow should give place to the substançe, and a Greater than Moses should " make all things new." Let us notice the time of reformation, and the reformation itself.

I. Time may be divided into three parts; the Golden Age before the fall, the Iron Age after the fall, and the Messiah's Age of Jubilee.

In the Golden Age, the heavens and the earth were created; the garden of Eden was planted; man was made in the image of God, and placed in the garden to dress and to keep it; matrimony was instituted; and God, resting from his labor, sanctified the Seventh Day, as a day of holy rest to man.

The Iron Age was introduced by the temptation of a foreigner, who obtruded himself into Paradise, and persuaded its happy denizens to cast off the golden yoke of obedience and love to God. Man, desiring independence, became a rebel against Heaven, a miserable captive of sin and Satan, obnoxious to the Divine displeasure, and exposed to eternal death. The law was violated;

the image of God was lost, and the enemy came in like a flood. All communication between the island of time and the continent of immortality was cut off, and the unhappy exiles saw no hope of crossing the ocean that intervened.

The Messiah's Age may be divided into three parts; the time of Preparation, the time of Actual War, and the time of Victory and Triumph.

The Preparation began with the dawning of the day in Eden, when Messiah came in the ship of the Promise, and landed on the island of Time, and notified its inhabitants of his gracious intention to visit them again, and assume their nature, and live and die among them; to break their covenant allegiance to the prince of the iron yoke; and deliver to them the charter, signed and sealed with his own blood, for the redemption and renovation of their island, and the restoration of its suspended intercourse with the land of Eternal Life. The motto inscribed upon the banners of this age was,—"He shall bruise thy heel, and thou shalt bruise his head." Here Jehovah thundered forth his hatred of sin from the thick darkness, and wrote his curse in fire upon the face of heaven; while rivers of sacrificial blood proclaimed the miserable state of man, and his need of a costlier atonement than mere humanity could offer. Here also the spirit of Messiah fell upon the prophets, leading them to search diligently for the way of deliverance, and enabling them to "testify beforehand of the sufferings of Christ, and the glory that should follow."

Then came the season of Actual War. "Messiah the Prince" was born in Bethlehem, wrapped in swaddling-bands, and laid in a manger. The Great Deliverer was "made of a woman, made under the law, to redeem those that were under the law, that we might receive the adoption of sons." With an almighty hand, he laid hold on the works of the devil, unlocked the iron furnace, and broke the brazen bands asunder. He opened his mouth, and the deaf heard, the blind saw, the dumb spake, the lame walked, and the lepers were cleansed. In the house of Jairus, in the street of Nain, and in the burial-ground of Bethany, his word was mightier than death; and the damsel on her bed, the young man on his bier, and Lazarus in his tomb, rising to second life, were but the earnests of his future triumph. The diseases of sin he healed, the iron chains of guilt he shattered, and all the horrible caves of human corruption and misery were opened by the Heavenly Warrior. He took our yoke, and bore it away upon his own shoulder, and cast it broken into the bottomless pit. He felt in his hands and his feet the nails, and in his side the spear. The iron entered into his soul, but the corrosive power of his blood destroyed it, and shall ultimately eat away all the iron in the kingdom of death. Behold him hanging on Calvary, nailing upon his cross three bills; the handwriting of the law which was against us, the oath of our allegiance to the prince of darkness, and the charter of the " everlasting covenant;" fulfilling the first, breaking the second, and sealing the third with his blood!

Now begins the scene of Victory and Triumph. On the morning of the third day, the Conqueror is seen " coming from Edom, with dyed garments from Bozrah." He has " trodden the wine-press alone." By the might of his single arm, he has routed the hosts of hell, and spoiled the dominions of death. The iron castle of the foe is demolished, and the hero returns from the war, " glorious in his apparel, travelling in the greatness of his strength." He enters the gates of the everlasting city, amid the rejoicing of angels, and the shouts of his redeemed. And still he rides forth in the chariot of his grace, " conquering, and to conquer." A two-edged sword issues from his mouth, and in his train follow the victorious armies of heaven. Lo! before him fall the altars of idols, and the temples of devils; and the slaves of sin are becoming the servants and sons of the living God; and the proud skeptic beholds, wonders, believes, and adores; and the blasphemer begins to pray, and the persecutor is melted into penitence and love, and the wolf comes and lays him down gently by the side of the lamb. And Messiah shall never quit the field, till he has completed the conquest, and swallowed up death in victory. In his " vesture dipped in blood," he shall pursue the armies of Gog and Magog on the field of Armageddon, and break the iron teeth of the beast of power, and cast down Babylon as a millstone into the sea, and bind the old serpent in the lake of fire and brimstone, and raise up to life immortal the tenants of the grave. Then shall the New Jerusalem, the metropolis of Messiah's golden empire, descend from heaven, adorned with all the jewelry of creation, guarded at every gate by angelic sentinels, and enlightened by the glory of God and of the Lamb; and the faithful shall dwell within its walls, and sin, and sorrow, and death, shall be shut out for ever!

Then shall time be swallowed up in eternity. The righteous shall inherit life everlasting, and the ungodly shall find their portion in the second death. Time is the age of the visible world; eternity is the age of the invisible God. All things in time are changeful; all things in eternity are immutable. If you pass from time to eternity, without faith in Christ, without love to God, an enemy to prayer, an enemy to holiness, "unpurged and unforgiven," so you must ever remain. Now is the season of that blessed change, for which myriads shall sing everlasting anthems of praise. "To-day, if ye will hear his voice, harden not your hearts." To-day the office is open; if you have any business with the Governor, make no delay. Now he has time to talk with the woman of Samaria by the well, and the penitent thief upon the cross. Now he is ready to forgive your sins, and renew your souls, and make you meet to become partakers of the inheritance of the saints in light. Now he waits to wash the filthy, and feed the hungry, and clothe the naked, and raise the humble, and quicken the spiritually dead, and enrich the poor and wretched, and reconcile enemies by his blood. He came to unloose your bands, and open to you the gates of Eden; condemned for your acquittal, and slain for the recovery of your forfeited immortality. The design of all the traveling from heaven to earth, and from earth to heaven, is the salvation of that which was lost, the restoration of intercourse and amity between the Maker and the worm. This is the chief of the ways of God to man, ancient in its origin, wise in its contrivance, dear in its accomplishment, powerful in its application, gracious in its influence, and everlasting in its results. Christ is riding in his chariot of salvation, through the land of destruction and death, clothed in the majesty of mercy, and offering eternal life to all who will believe. O captives of evil! now is the accepted time; now is the day of salvation; now is the year of jubilee; now is the age of deliverance; now is "the time of reformation!"

II. All the prophets speak of something within the veil, to be manifested in due time; the advent of a Divine agent in a future age, to accomplish a glorious "reformation." They represent him as a prince; a hero; a high-priest; a branch growing out of dry ground; a child toying with the asp and the lion, and leading the

wolf and the lamb together. The bill of the reformation had been
repeatedly read by the prophets, but its passage required the descent
of the Lord from heaven. None but himself could effect the change
of the dispensation. None but himself had the authority and the
power to remove the first, and establish the second. He whose
voice once shook the earth, speaks again, and heaven is shaken.
He whose footsteps once kindled Sinai into flame, descends again,
and Calvary is red with blood. The God of the ancient covenant
introduces a new, which is to abide for ever. The Lord of the
temple alone could change the furniture and the service from the
original pattern shown to Moses in the mount; and six days before
the rending of the veil, significant of the abrogation of the old ceremonial, Moses came down upon a mountain in Palestine to deliver
up the pattern to him of whom he had received it on Sinai, that he
might nail it to his cross on Calvary; for the " gifts and sacrifices"
belonging to the legal dispensation " could not make him that did
the service perfect, as pertaining to the conscience; which stood
only in meats, and drinks, and divers washings, and carnal ordinances, imposed on them until the time of reformation."

This reformation signifieth " the removal of those things that are
shaken, as of things that are made, that those things which cannot
be shaken may remain;" the abrogation of " carnal ordinances,"
which were local and temporal in their nature, to make room for a
spiritual worship, of universal and perpetual adaptation. Henceforth
the blood of bulls and goats is superseded by the great reconciling
sacrifice of the Lamb of God, and outward forms and ceremonies
give place to the inward operations of a renovating and purifying
Spirit.

To the Jewish church, the covenant of Sinai was a sort of starry
heaven. The Shekinah was its sun; the holy festivals, its moon;
and prophets, priests, and kings, its stars. But Messiah, when he
came, shook them all from their spheres, and filled the firmament
himself. He is our " Bright and Morning Star;" the " Sun of
Righteousness," rising upon us " with healing in his wings."

The old covenant was an accuser and a judge, but offered no
pardon to the guilty. It revealed the corruption of the natural
heart, but provided no renovating and sanctifying grace. It was a
national institution, for the special benefit of the seed of Abraham.
It was a small vessel, trading only with the land of Canaan. It

secured to a few the temporal blessings of the promised possession, but never delivered a single soul from eternal death; never bore a single soul over to the heavenly inheritance. But the new covenant is a covenant of grace and mercy, proffering forgiveness and a clean heart, not on the ground of any carnal relationship, but solely through faith in Jesus Christ. Christianity is a personal concern between each man and his God, and none but the penitent believer has any right to its spiritual privileges. It is adapted to Gentiles as well as Jews, "even as many as the Lord our God shall call." Already has it rescued myriads from the bondage of sin, and conveyed them over to the land of immortality; and its voyages of grace shall continue to the end of time, "bringing many sons to glory."

"Old things are passed away, and all things are become new." The circumcision of the flesh, made with hands, has given place to the circumcision of the heart by the Holy Ghost. The Shekinah has departed from Mount Zion, but its glory is illuminating the world. The sword of Joshua is returned to its scabbard; and "the sword of the Spirit, which is the word of God," issues from the mouth of Messiah, and subdues the people under him. The glorious High-priesthood of Christ has superseded the sacerdotal office among men. Aaron was removed from the altar by death before his work was finished; but our High-priest still wears his sacrificial vestments, and death has established him before the mercy-seat, "a priest for ever, after the order of Melchisedec." The earthquake which shook mount Calvary, and rent the veil of the temple, demolished "the middle wall of partition" between Jews and Gentiles. The incense which Jesus offered fills the temple, and the land of Judea cannot confine its fragrance. The fountain which burst forth in Jerusalem, has sent out its living streams into every land; and the heat of summer cannot dry them up, nor the frosts of winter congeal.

In short, all the vessels of the sanctuary are taken away by the Lord of the temple. The "twelve oxen," bearing the "molten sea," have given place to "the twelve apostles of the Lamb," proclaiming "the washing of regeneration and renewing of the Holy Ghost." The sprinkled mercy-seat, with its overshadowing and intensely-gazing cherubim, has given place to "the throne of grace," stained with the blood of a costlier sacrifice, into which the angels desire to look. The priest, the altar, the burnt-offering the table of shew-bread, and the golden candlestick, have given place to the better things of the new dispensation introduced by the Son of God, of which they were only the figures and the types. Behold, the glory is gone up from the temple, and rests upon Jesus on mount Tabor; and Moses and Elias are there, with Peter, and James, and John; and the representatives of the old covenant are communing with the apostles of the new, and the transfigured Christ is the medium of the communication; and a voice of majestic music, issuing from "the excellent glory," proclaims—"This is my beloved Son; hear ye him!"

"God, who at sundry times and in divers manners spake unto our fathers by the prophets, hath in these last days spoken unto us by his Son." Behold him nailed to the cross, and hear him cry— "It is finished!" The voice which shook Sinai is shaking Calvary. Heaven and hell are in conflict, and earth trembles at the shock of battle. The Prince of Life expires, and the sun puts on his robes of mourning. Gabriel! descend from heaven, and explain to us the wondrous emblem! As set the sun at noon on Golgotha, making preternatural night throughout the land of Palestine; so shall the empire of sin and death be darkened, and their light shall be quenched at meridian. As the Sun of Righteousness, rising from the night of the grave on the third morning, brings life and immortality to light; so shall "the day-spring from on high" yet dawn upon our gloomy vale, and "the power of his resurrection" shall reanimate the dust of every cemetery!

He that sitteth upon the throne hath spoken—"Behold, I make all things new!" The reformation includes not only the abrogation of the old, but also the introduction of the new. It gives us a new Mediator, a new covenant of grace, a new way of salvation, a new heart of flesh, a new heaven and a new earth. It has established a new union, by a new medium, between God and man. "The Word was made flesh and dwelt among us, and we beheld his glory, the glory as of the Only Begotten of the Father, full of grace and truth." "Forasmuch as the children were partakers of flesh and blood, he also himself likewise took part of the same." "God was manifest in the flesh, justified in the spirit, seen of angels, preached unto the Gentiles, believed on in the world, received up into glory." Here was a new thing under the sun; the "Son of man" bearing the "express image" of the living God; bearing it untarnished through the world; through the temptations and sorrows of such a wilderness as humanity never trod before; through the unknown agony of Olivet, and the supernatural gloom of Golgotha, and the dark dominion of the king of terrors; to the heaven of heavens; where he sits, the adorable representative of two worlds, the union of God and man! Thence he sends forth the Holy Spirit, to collect "the travail of his soul," and lead them into all truth, and bring them to Zion with songs of everlasting joy. See them, the redeemed of the Lord, flocking, as returning doves upon the wing, "to the heavenly Jerusalem, the city of the living God; and to the spirits of just men made perfect; and to an innumerable company of angels; and to Jesus, the Mediator of the new covenant; and to the blood of sprinkling, that speaketh better things than that of Abel!"

O, join the joyful multitude! The year of jubilee is come. The veil is rent asunder. The way into the holiest is laid open. The blood of Jesus is on the mercy-seat. The Lamb newly slain is in the midst of the throne. Go ye with boldness into his gracious presence. Lo, the King is your brother, and for you has he stained his robe with blood! That robe alone can clothe your naked souls, and shield them in the day of burning. Awake! awake! put on the Lord Jesus Christ! The covenant of Sinai cannot save you from wrath. Descent from Abraham cannot entitle you to the kingdom of heaven. "Ye must be born again;" "born, not of the flesh, nor of the will of men, but of God." You must have a new heart, and become a new creation in Christ Jesus. This is the promise of the Father.

"This is the dear redeeming grace,
    For every sinner free!"

Many reformations have expired with the reformers. But our Great Reformer "ever liveth" to carry on his reformation, till his enemies become his footstool, and death and hell are cast into the lake of fire. He will finish the building of his church. When he laid the "chief corner-stone" on Calvary, the shock jarred the earth, and awoke the dead, and shook the nether world with terror; but when he shall bring forth the top stone with shoutings of "grace!" the dominion of Death and Hades shall perish, and the last captive shall escape, and the song of the bursting sepulchre shall be sweeter than the chorus of the morning stars! Even now, there are new things in heaven; the Lamb from the slaughter, alive "in the midst of the throne;" worshipped by innumerable seraphim and cherubim, and adored by the redeemed from earth; his name the wonder of angels, the terror of devils, and the hope of men; his praise the "new song," which shall constitute the employment of eternity!

Sermon 2
THE TRIUMPH OF CALVARY

Who is this that cometh from Edom, with dyed garments from Bozrah? This that is glorious in his apparel, travelling in the greatness of his strength? I that speak in righteousness, mighty to save. Wherefore art thou red in thine apparel, and thy garments like him that treadeth in the winefat? I have trodden the winepress alone; and of the people there was none with me: for I will tread them in mine anger, and trample them in my fury; and their blood shall be sprinkled upon my garments, and I will stain all my raiment. For the day of vengeance is in mine heart, and the year of my redeemed is come. And I looked, and there was none to help; and I wondered that there was none to uphold; therefore mine own arm brought salvation unto me; and my fury, it upheld me. And I will tread down the people in mine anger, and make them drunk in my fury, and I will bring down their strength to the earth (Isaiah 63:1-6).

THIS passage is one of the sublimest in the Bible. Not more majestic and overwhelming is the voice of God issuing from the burning bush. It represents "the Captain of our salvation," left alone in the heat of battle, marching victoriously through the broken columns of the foe, bursting the bars asunder, bearing away the brazen gates, and delivering by conquest the captives of sin and death. Let us first determine the events to which our text relates, and then briefly explain the questions and answers which it contains.

I. We have here a wonderful victory, obtained by Christ, in the city of Bozrah, in the land of Edom. Our first inquiry concerns the time and the place of that achievement.

Some of the prophecies are literal, and others are figurative. Some of them are already fulfilled, and others are in daily process of fulfilment. Respecting this prophecy, divines disagree. Some think it is a description of Christ's conflict and victory, without the gates of Jerusalem, eighteen centuries ago ; and others understand it as referring to the great battle of Armageddon, predicted in the Apocalypse, and yet to be consummated before the end of the world.

I am not willing to pass by mount Calvary, and Joseph's new tomb, on my way to the field of Armageddon ; nor am I willing to pause at the scene of the crucifixion and the ascension, without going farther on to the final conquest of the foe. I believe Divine inspiration has included both events in the text; the victory already won on Calvary, and the victory yet to be accomplished in Armageddon; the finished victory of Messiah's passion, and the progressive victory of his gospel and his grace.

The chief difficulty, in understanding some parts of the word of God, arises from untranslated words; many of which are found in our own version, as well as in that of our English neighbors. For instance—in Mat. ii. 23, it is said, " He came and dwelt in a city called Nazareth, that it might be fulfilled which was spoken by the prophet, He shall be called a Nazarene." Where in the prophets is it predicted that Christ shall be called a Nazarene? Nowhere. When the proper names are translated, the difficulty vanishes. "He came and dwelt in a city called *plantation*, that it might be fulfilled which was spoken by the prophet, He shall be called *the Branch*." This name is given him by Isaiah, Jeremiah, and Zechariah. Now this is precisely the difficulty that occurs in our text, and the translation of the terms unties the knot:—" Who is this that cometh from Edom," *red earth*—" with dyed garments from Bozrah," *tribulation*?

The former part of the text has reference to the victory of Calvary; the latter part anticipates the battle and triumph of Armageddon, mentioned in Rev. xvi. 16. The victory of Calvary is consummated on the morning of the third day after the crucifixion. The Conqueror comes up from the earth, exclaiming:—" I have trodden the winepress alone on Calvary; and I will tread them in mine anger, and make them drunk in my fury, at the battle of Armageddon. I will overtake and destroy the beast, and the false prophet, and that old serpent the devil, with all their hosts."

When the tide of battle turned, on the field of Waterloo, the Duke of Wellington mounted his horse, and pursued the vanquished foe. So Isaiah's Conqueror, having routed the powers of hell on Calvary, pursues and destroys them on the field of Armageddon. Here he is represented as a hero on foot, a prince without an army; but John, the revelator, saw him riding on a white horse, and followed by the armies of heaven, all on white horses, and not a footman among them.

The victory of Calvary is like the blood of atonement in the sanctuary. The cherubim were some of them looking one way, and some the other, but all were looking on the atoning blood. Thus all the great events of time—all the trials and triumphs of God's people—those which happened before, those which have happened since, and those which are yet to happen, are all looking toward the wrestling of Gethsemene, the conflict of Golgotha, and the triumph of Olivet. The escape from Egypt, and the return from Babylon, looked forward to the cross of Christ; and the faith of the perfect man of Uz hung on a risen Redeemer. The Christian martyrs overcame by the blood of the Lamb, and all their victories were in virtue of one great achievement. The tomb of Jesus is the birthplace of his people's immortality, and the power which raised him from the dead shall open the sepulchres of all his saints. "Thy dead men shall live; together with my dead body shall they arise. Awake and sing, ye that dwell in the dust; for thy dew is as the dew of herbs, and the earth shall cast forth her dead."

Christ offered himself a sacrifice for us, and drank the cup of God's righteous indignation in our stead. He was trodden by Almighty justice, as a cluster of grapes, in the winepress of the law, till the vessels of mercy overflowed with the wine of peace and pardon, which has made thousands of contrite and humble spirits "rejoice with joy unspeakable and full of glory." He suffered for us, that we might triumph with him. But our text describes him as a king and a conqueror. He was, at once, the dying victim and the immortal victor. In "the power of an endless life," he was standing by the altar, when the sacrifice was burning. He was alive in his sacerdotal vestments, with his golden censer in his hand. He was alive in his kingly glory, with his sword and his sceptre in his hand. He was alive in his conquering prowess, and had made an end of sin, and bruised the head of the serpent, and spoiled the principalities and powers of hell, and turned the vanquished hosts of the prince of darkness down to the winepress of the wrath of Almighty God. Then, on the morning of the third day, when he arose from the dead, and made a show of them openly—then began the year of jubilee with power!

After the prophets of ancient times had long gazed through the mists of futurity, at the sufferings of Christ and the glory that should follow, a company of them were gathered together on the summit of Calvary. They saw a host of enemies ascending the hill, arrayed for battle, and most terrific in their aspect. In the middle of the line was the law of God, fiery and exceeding broad, and working wrath. On the right wing, was Beelzebub with his troops of infernals; and on the left Caiaphas with his Jewish priests, and Pilate with his Roman soldiers. The rear was brought up by Death, the last enemy. When the holy seers had espied this army, and perceived that it was drawing nigh, they started back, and prepared for flight. As they looked round, they saw the Son of God advancing with intrepid step, having his face fixed on the hostile band. "Seest thou the danger that is before thee," said one of the men of God. "I will tread them in mine anger," he replied, "and trample them in my fury." "Who art thou?" said the prophet; He answered: "I that speak in righteousness, mighty to save." "Wilt thou venture to the battle alone?" asked the seer. The Son of God replied: "I looked, and there was none to help; and I wondered there was none to uphold; therefore mine own arm shall bring salvation unto me; and my fury it shall uphold me." "At what point wilt thou commence thy attack?" inquired the anxious prophet. "I will first meet the Law," he replied, "and pass under its curse: for lo! I come to do thy will, O God. When I shall have succeeded at the centre of the line, the colors will turn in my favor." So saying he moved forward. Instantly the thunderings of Sinai were heard, and the whole band of prophets quaked with terror. But he advanced, undaunted, amidst the gleaming lightnings. For a moment he was concealed from view; and the banner of wrath waved above in triumph. Suddenly the scene was changed. A stream of blood poured forth from his wounded side, and put out all the fires of Sinai. The flag of peace was now seen unfurled, and consternation filled the ranks of his foes. He then crushed, with his bruised heel, the old serpent's head; and put all the infernal powers to flight. With his iron rod he dashed to pieces the enemies on the left wing, like a potter's vessel. Death still remained, who thought himself invincible, having hitherto triumphed over all. He came forward, brandishing his sting, which he had whetted on Sinai's tables of stone. He darted it at the Conqueror, but it turned down, and hung like the flexible lash of a whip. Dismayed, he retreated to the grave, his palace, into which the Conqueror pursued. In a dark corner of his den, he sat on his throne of moldering skulls, and called upon the worms, his hitherto faithful allies, to aid him in the conflict; but they replied—"His flesh shall see no corruption!" The scepter fell from his hand. The Conqueror seized him, bound him, and condemned him to the lake of fire; and then rose from the grave, followed by a band of released captives, who came forth after his resurrection to be witnesses of the victory which he had won.*

John in the Apocalypse did not look so far back as the treading of this winepress; but John saw him on his white horse, decked with his many crowns, his eyes like flames of fire, a two-edged sword in his hand, in the van of the armies of heaven, going forth conquering and to conquer. This is the fulfilment of his declaration in our text:—"For I will tread them in mine anger, and trample them in my fury." This is the beginning of the jubilee, the battle of Armageddon, wherein all heathen idolatry and superstition shall be overthrown, and the beast and the false prophet shall be discomfited, and the devil and his legions shall be taken prisoners by Emmanuel, and shut up in the bottomless pit. He who hath conquered principalities and powers on Calvary, will not leave the field, till he make all his enemies his footstool, and sway his scepter over a subject universe. Having sent forth the gospel from Jerusalem, he accompanies it with the grace of his Holy Spirit; and it shall not return unto him void, but shall accomplish that which he pleaseth, and prosper in the thing whereto he hath sent it.

The victory of Armageddon is obtained by virtue of the victory of Calvary. It is but the consummation of the same glorious campaign; and the first decisive blow dealt on the prince of darkness is a sure precursor of the final conquest. "I will meet thee again at Philippi!" said the ghost of Julius Cæsar to Brutus. "I will meet thee again at Armageddon!" saith the Son of God to Satan on Calvary—"I will meet thee in the engagement between good and evil, grace and depravity, in every believer's heart; in the contest of Divine Truth with human errors, of the religion of God with the superstitions of men; in every sermon, every revival, every missionary enterprise; in the spread and glory of the gospel

---

* This paragraph is one of the celebrated "Specimens of Welsh Preaching," printed in England some years before the publication of any of these sermons. We give the first English version verbatim. Ed.

in the latter day, I will meet thee ; and the heel which thou hast now bruised, shall crush thy head for ever!"

Man's deliverance is of God. Man had neither the inclination nor the power. His salvation originated in the Divine Love, and burst forth like an ocean from the fountains of eternity. Satan, as a ravenous lion, had taken the prey, and was running to his den with the bleeding sheep in his mouth ; but the Shepherd of Israel pursues him, overtakes him, and rends him as if he were a kid. The declaration of war was made in Eden :—" I will put enmity between thee and the woman, and between thy seed and her seed ; thou shalt bruise his heel, and he shall bruise thy head." It shall be fulfilled. The league with hell, and the covenant with death shall not stand. The rebellion shall be quelled, the conspiracy shall be broken, and the strong man armed shall yield the citadel to a stronger. The works of the devil shall be destroyed, and the prey shall be taken from the teeth of the terrible. The house of David shall grow stronger and stronger, and the house of Saul shall grow weaker and weaker, till the kingdoms of this world shall become the kingdom of our God and of his Christ, and Satan shall be bound in chains of darkness, and cast into the lake of fire. All the enemies of Zion shall be vanquished, and the forfeited favor of God shall be recovered, and the lost territory of peace and holiness aud immortality shall be restored to man.

This campaign is carried on at the expense of the government of heaven. The treasury is inexhaustible ; the arms are irresistible ; therefore the victory is sure. The Almighty King has descended ; he has taken the city of Bozrah ; he has swayed his scepter over Edom ; he has risen victoriously, and gone up with a shout, as the leader of all the army. This is but the pledge and the earnest of his future achievements. In the battle of Armageddon, he shall go forth as a mighty man ; he shall stir up jealousy as a man of war ; and he shall prevail against his enemies. They shall be turned back—they shall be greatly ashamed, that trust in graven images—that say unto molten images, " Ye are our gods!" Then he will open the blind eyes, and bring the prisoners from the prison, and them that sit in darkness out of the prison-house. He will make bare his holy arm—he will show the sword in that hand which was hidden under the scarlet robe—he will manifest his power in the destruction of his enemies, and the salvation of his people. As certainly as he hath shed his blood on Calvary, shall he stain all his raiment with the blood of his foes on the field of Armageddon. As certainly as he hath drained the cup of wrath, and received the baptism of suffering, on Calvary, shall he wield the iron rod of justice, and sway the golden sceptre of mercy, on the field of Armageddon. Already the sword is drawn, and the decisive blow is struck, and the helmet of Apollyon is cleft, and the bonds of iniquity are cut asunder. Already the fire is kindled, and all the powers of hell cannot quench it. It has fallen from heaven; it is consuming the camp of the foe; it is inflaming the hearts of men; it is renovating the earth, and purging away the curse. " The bright and Morning Star" has risen on Calvary; and soon " the Son of Righteousness" shall shine on the field of Armageddon; and the darkness that covers the earth, and the gross darkness that covers the people, shall melt away; and Mohammedism, and Paganism, and Popery, with their prince, the devil, shall seek shelter in the bottomless pit!

After a battle, we are anxious to learn who is dead, who is wounded, and who is missing from the ranks. In the engagement of Messiah with Satan and his allies on Calvary, Messiah's heel was bruised, but Satan and his allies received a mortal wound in the head. The head denotes wisdom, cunning, power, government. The devil, sin, and death have lost their dominion over the believer in Christ, since the achievement of Calvary. There is now no condemnation, no fear of hell. But the serpent, though his head is bruised, may be able to move his tail, and alarm those of little faith. Yet it cannot last long. The wound is mortal, and the triumph is sure. On Calvary the dragon's head was crushed by the Captain of our salvation; after the battle of Armageddon, his tail shall shake no more!

There is no discharge in this war. He that enlisteth under the banner of the cross must endure faithful until death—must not lay aside his arms till death is swallowed up in victory. Then shall every conqueror bear the image of the heavenly, and wear the crown instead of the cross, and carry the palm instead of the spear. Let us be strong in the Lord, and in the power of his might, that we may be able to stand in the evil day; and after all the war is over, to stand accepted in the Beloved, that we may reign with him for ever and ever'

II. It remains for us to explain, very briefly, the glorious colo-
quy in the text—the interrogatives of the church, and the answers
of Messiah.

How great was the wonder and joy of Mary, when she met the
Master at the tomb, clothed in immortality, where she thought to
find him shrouded in death! How unspeakable was the astonishment and rapture of the disciples, when their Lord, whom they had
so recently buried, came into the house where they were assembled,
and said—" Peace be unto you!" Such are the feelings which the
church is represented as expressing in this sublime colloquy with
the Captain of her salvation. He has travelled into the land of
tribulation; he has gone down to the dust of death; but lo, he
returns a conqueror, the golden sceptre of love in his left hand, the
iron rod of justice in his right, and on his head a crown of many
stars. The church beholds him with great amazement and delight.
She lately followed him, weeping, to the cross, and mourned over
his body in the tomb; but now she beholds him risen indeed, having destroyed death, and him that had the power of death—that is,
the devil. She goes forth to meet him with songs of rejoicing, as
the daughters of Israel went out to welcome David, when he
returned from the valley, with the head of the giant in his hand,
and the blood running down upon his raiment. The choir of the
church is divided into two bands; which chant to each other in
alternate strains. The right hand division begins the glorious
colloquy—" Who is this that cometh from Edom?" and the left
takes up the interrogative, and repeats it with a variation—" with
dyed garments from Bozrah?" " This that is glorious in his
apparel?" resumes the right-hand company—" glorious notwithstanding the tribulations he hath endured?" " Travelling in the
greatness of his strength?" responds the left—" strength sufficient
to unbar the gates of the grave, and liberate the captives of corruption?" The celestial Conqueror pauses, and casts upon the company of the daughters of Zion a look of infinite benignity; and with
a voice of angel melody, and more than angel majesty, he replies—
" I that speak in righteousness, mighty to save!" Now bursts the
song again, like the sound of many waters, from the right—
" Wherefore art thou red in thine apparel?" and the response rolls
back in melodized thunder from the left—" And thy garments like
him that treadeth in the wine-fat?" The Divine hero answers:—

" I have trodden the wine-press alone; and of the people there was none with me. Even Peter has left me, with all his courage and affection; and as for John, to talk of love is all that he can do. I have triumphed over principalities and powers. I am wounded, but they are vanquished. Behold the blood which I have lost! behold the spoils which I have won! Now will I mount my white horse, and pursue after Satan, and demolish his kingdom, and send him back to the land of darkness in everlasting chains, and all his allies shall be exiles with him for ever. My own arm, which has gained the victory on Calvary, and brought salvation to all my people from the sepulchre, is still strong enough to wield the golden sceptre of love, and break my foes on the field of Armageddon. I will destroy the works of the devil, and demolish all his hosts; I will dash them in pieces like a potter's vessel. For the day of vengeance is in mine heart, and the year of my redeemed is come. My compassion is stirred for the captives of sin and death; my fury is kindled against the tyrants that oppress them. It is time for me to open the prisons, and break off the fetters. I must gather my people to myself. I must seek that which was lost, and bring again that which was driven away. I must bind up that which was broken, and strengthen that which was weak; but I will destroy the fat and the strong; I will feed them with judgment; I will tread them in mine anger, and trample them in my fury, and bring down their strength to the earth, and stain all my raiment with their blood!"

Let us flee from the wrath to come! Behold, the sun is risen high on the day of vengeance! Let us not be found among the enemies of Messiah, lest we fall a sacrifice to his righteous indignation on the field of Armageddon! Let us escape for our lives, for the fire-storm of his anger will burn to the lowest hell! Let us pray for grace to lay hold on the salvation of his redeemed! It is a free, full, perfect, glorious, and eternal salvation. Return, ye ransomed exiles from happiness, return to your forfeited inheritance! Now is the year of jubilee. Come to Jesus, that your debts may be cancelled, your sins forgiven, and your persons justified! Come, for the Conqueror of your foes is on the throne! Come, for the trumpets of mercy are sounding! Come, for all things are now ready!

THE SMITTEN ROCK

For they drank of that spiritual rock that followed them, and that rock was Christ (1 Corinthians 10:4).

In this chapter the apostle solemnly cautions his brethren against apostasy, and consequent shipwreck of their spiritual privileges. His admonitions are educed from important events in the history of the journey of the Israelites from Egypt to the land of Canaan. He speaks of the march of the twelve tribes out of the scene of their bondage, under the uplifted banner of God; of their baptism unto Moses in the cloud and in the sea, when Jehovah gloriously lisplayed his power in preserving their lives between the watery ramparts which shut them in like the solid walls of the sepulchre, while the cloud rested upon them through the deep night, like the marble covering of the tomb; of their safe emerging on the other side of the flood, a type of the resurrection, leaving Pharaoh and his host to sleep in the waters till the morning of the last day, when they shall rise without their chariots and their horses; of their miraculous supply in the wilderness, with bread from heaven, and water from the smitten rock, which he calls spiritual meat and spiritual drink, because of their typical reference to the sacrificial death of Christ, which is the spiritual life of the world ; and of their subsequent ingratitude and forgetfulness of God, notwithstand-ing.these great deliverances and mercies, their murmurings, idola-tries, fornications, and tempting of Christ, for which they were destroyed by the plague, slain by fiery serpents, smitten by the angel of the Lord, and fell to the number of three and twenty thousand in one day. " Now all these things," he adds, " hap-oened unto them for ensamples, and are written for our admonition, upon whom the ends of the world are come ; wherefore, let him that thinketh he standeth, take heed lest he fall." Thus he opens the graves of ancient sinners, and brings before his brethren the carcases of those " who fell in the wilderness ;" brings them into our solemn assemblies, and hangs them up over the pulpit, the baptistry, and the communion-table, terrible warnings against departing from the living God ; even as the censers of Korah, Dathan, and Abiram were beaten up, and made a covering for the altar, for a perpetual sign and memorial to Israel, to keep them from the sin of those men, that they might not share their fate.

In speaking of the smitten rock, which the apostle authorizes us to regard as a type of Christ, we shall consider :—*First*, Its smiting by Moses ; and *Secondly*, The consequent flowing of the waters.

I. The smitten rock was a type of Christ. Messiah is the " Rock of Ages" to his church. He is the foundation of her hope, sure and steadfast, and her protection in times of danger and of dread. The armor and the prowess of Egypt constituted no rock like this rock. Edom, and Moab, and Philistia, and the seven nations of Canaan, had their gods and their heroes ; but their rock was not able to shelter them from the wrath of Jehovah, when it came upon them like a tempest of hail. The gods that made not the heavens and the earth are far off in the day of trouble ; but the God of Israel is " nigh at hand," and his arm is strong to deliver. He is the rock that stood firm and immovable, for the defence of his people, amid the ragings of the Red Sea. Messiah is the man, who is predicted as " a hiding-place from the wind, and a covert from the tempest, and the shadow of a great rock in a weary land." He can shield, not only from the scorching sun and the scathing simoom of the desert ; but also from the fiery torments of remorse, and the ruinous judgments of heaven. Our Lord is a rock, also, on account of the blessings which flow from him, for the refreshment of his Israel ; as " the droppings of honey from the rock ;" as " springs of water in a dry place ;" as " living streams in the desert," and " rivers from the mountains of Lebanon."

There are two accounts of the smiting of the rock ; one in the seventeenth chapter of Exodus, and the other in the twentieth chapter of Numbers. From a comparison of these two accounts, it appears that the rock was smitten at two different times ; the first, as is supposed, about a year after the egress from Egypt, and the other about a year before the entrance into Canaan; making an intervening period of about thirty-eight years. The war with Amalek succeeded the first; the embassy to Edom followed the second. At the first, Miriam was alive; just before the second is the record of her death.

It seems that the people murmured bitterly against Moses, spoke of their superior fare in Egypt, and accused him of bringing them out into the wilderness to kill them with thirst. This is ever the spirit of backsliding. Those who are under its influence are apt to complain of the burdens imposed upon them by their religion, and the injuries occasioned to them by their brethren; and to speak uncharitably of their spiritual leaders, instead of crying to God for help. To ask, "Is the Lord among us?" when his word and his works, indicating either his pleasure or his displeasure, testify that he is, is tempting God, with a dreadful presumption.

It does not appear that Moses sinned the first time he smote the rock; but the second time, the servant of God was evidently off his guard, and the meekest of men " spake unadvisedly with his lips;" on account of which, both he and Aaron were shut out of the promised land. His sin consisted in entering into a quarrel with the people, instead of asking God for water to quench their thirst. It appears that their chidings had provoked him to anger, and he had lost the spirit of sympathy for their sufferings, and his hard feelings stood like a thick wall between him and the miracle which God was about to work for his own glory and his people's relief. Neither did he as God commanded him; for instead of simply speaking to the rock, as he was bidden, he smote it twice, with evident agitation of mind; and at the same time, bitterly reproached the people with their rebellion.

Every minister of the gospel is a " drawer of water," to his congregation, from the " Spiritual Rock" which follows the church. He must be clothed with meekness from Heaven, or the provocations of the people will be apt to embitter his spirit. God would have us minister mercy, in the spirit of his own mercy. " The servant of God must not strive, but be gentle toward all men; in meekness instructing those that oppose themselves, if, peradventure, God would grant them repentance unto the acknowledging of the truth: and that they might recover themselves out of the snare of the devil, who are taken captive by him at his will."

The smiting of the rock was intended to open it, that the water might flow. This prefigured the smiting of Christ, " the Rock of Ages," and " the Shepherd of the sheep." The shedding of the blood of lambs, and goats, and calves, and bullocks, for the space of four thousand years, faintly shadowed forth the sacrificial passion of our blessed Lord. Their groans and struggles under the slaughtering knife ; the sound of the blood, falling into the golden basins, and poured into the flames upon the altar; the noise occasioned in cutting up the victim, and piling the pieces upon the fire; and the smoke and vapor ascending from the consuming sacrifice to heaven; all, all, in their own way, foreshadowed the necessity of mangling the body and shedding the blood of Messiah, that pardoning mercy might have an open way to flow to sinners, like the water from the smitten rock ; and the agonies of those slaughtered victims were an imperfect type of the agonies of the soul of Jesus, in the garden and on the cross.

The smiting of a flinty rock, for the purpose of obtaining water, was a scheme of the Divine Mind, whose ways are higher than our ways, and his thoughts than our thoughts. It was certainly the last place to which Moses would have gone for water; and he might have expected the stroke to elicit sparks of fire, rather than cool refreshing streams. What eye had not seen and ear had not heard, either of men or of angels—what had not entered into the heart of any created being to conceive, terrestrial or celestial—was, that the smiting of the Shepherd should save the sheep; that the condemnation of the just should bring the unjust to God; that the making of Messiah a curse should secure infinite blessings to mankind ; that the poverty-of Jesus should enrich us, and his death raise us to life eternal. Consuming flames of Divine indignation might have been expected to flash upon the guilty world from every wound of the thorns, the nails and the spear, in the sacred person of Emmanuel; but, to the astonishment of men and angels, a tide of love and mercy ran freely from every bleeding vein, to wash away the guilt and pollution of human crimes, according to the determinate counsel and immutable promise of our God.

The rock must be smitten by a rod. Had Moses been left to choose his own instrument, he would probably have taken a hammer, or perhaps a lever; but God commands him to take the rod The rock would not have yielded water to any other instrument than the rod that smote the waters of Egypt, and turned them into blood. This rod was an emblem of the sovereignty of God over Israel, and is therefore called "the rod of God, which the Lord gave unto Moses"—as his deputy governor—"to lead Israel, and to work miracles before their eyes." It was also a symbol of the royal law of Heaven; which, prior to the fall, was a rod of life; but afterward became a rod of iron, to break in pieces the offender—an angry serpent, to sting the transgressor with dreadful torments; and finally, when Christ endured the curse, and honored the violated mandate, by his death upon the tree, it was transformed again into a guiding and correcting rod. As the rock would have yielded water under no other stroke than that of "the rod of God," so the sufferings of Christ would have been ineffectual, had they not happened under the law of the Father, and according to the counsel of Infinite Wisdom. When Isaac was about to be offered up on mount Moriah, the wood, the fire, and the knife, must all come from his father's house, and the dreadful deed must be done by his father's hand. So Jesus must die in no ordinary or accidental way. He must not suffer himself to be slain by the sword of Herod, nor cast over the brow of the hill by the people. He must receive the mortal cup from no other hand than that of the Father. He must die the appointed death; at the appointed time; in the appointed place, without the camp; and in the appointed manner, by hanging on a tree. The wreath of thorns, the scarlet robe, the nails, the cross, the spear, and even the vinegar offered him in his agony, were all according to his Father's counsel. He knew the necessity, and said—"Thy will be done!" The Shepherd of Israel would bow under no other stroke than that of the Lord of Hosts. A cradle, a cross, and a grave, all of his Father's appointing, must Jesus have, in order to open a fountain of living water to the world.

The rock must be smitten in a public manner, in the sight of the sun, and before all the elders of Israel, that God might be sanctified in the eyes of his people. This was intended to foreshadow the publicity of the death of Christ, which took place during one of the great public festivals of the Jews, in the presence of nearly the whole nation, and on the hill Calvary; and to denote the proclamation of Christ crucified throughout the world, as the true propitiation and object of faith, to be looked upon by Jews and Gentiles, to the softening of the heart, and the flowing of repentant tears, according to the prophecy—"They shall look on him whom they have pierced, and mourn for him, as one mourneth for an only son." The Spirit of grace directs the eyes of men to the cross, upon which the prophet Isaiah, with transcendant sublimity of language, describes the Saviour as passing from Calvary to the grave, from the grave to the empyrean, and thence back again to earth, crying—"Look unto me, and be ye saved, all ye ends of the earth; for I am God, and beside me there is no Savior!"

The rock must be smitten in the presence of God. "Behold, I will stand before thee there on the rock in Horeb." (Ex. xvii. 6.) He stood upon the rock in Horeb, though invisible, in the glory of his loving-kindness and his power, to guide the hand of his servant Moses, and open a source of timely succour to his perishing people. But when the rod of the law smote the Rock of our salvation, when the curse fell upon the sinner's Substitute and Surety, then God stood forth before the world upon the rock of Calvary, amid the darkened heavens, the trembling earth, and the opening sepulchres, as if all the machinery of nature had been suddenly disordered and dis-organized—stood forth in the plenitude of his power, his wisdom, his justice, his mercy, and his truth, to prosper the work of man's redemption, and open a channel through which the river of life might flow out to a famishing race. On Calvary still he stands, with the cup of salvation in his hand, and streams of living water rolling at his feet, and cries—"Ho, every one that thirsteth, come ye to the waters!"

According to the command of God, the rock was to be smitten but once. Once smitten, it needed only to be spoken to; and, though it was more than thirty years afterward, it would yield forth its water. But Moses, provoked to anger by the murmurings and complainings of the people, transcended the Divine injunction, and though he had once smitten the rock, smote it again; yea, when he should have spoken to it only, smote it twice with his rod. This was his sin, for which God would not permit him to enter the pro-mised land. Christ has been once smitten, and wo to those who smite him again! He has once offered himself a sacrifice, and once entered into the holy place, having finished his work of atone-ment, and made an end of sin, and superseded the sacrifices of the law. Henceforth, ye Jews, relinquish your burnt-offerings, your meat-offerings, your drink-offerings, your peace-offerings; and trust no longer in beasts, and birds, and flour, and oil; but in " the Lamb of God, that taketh away the sin of the world." Crucify him afresh no more, O ye backsliders; for "there remaineth no other sacrifice for sin!" Smite him not again, lest he swear unto you in his wrath, as unto Moses, that ye shall not enter into his rest!

II. Having spoken of the smiting, let us now look at the result, the flowing of the waters; a timely mercy to "the many thousands of Israel," on the point of perishing in the desert; shadowing forth a far greater mercy, the flowing of living waters from the " spiritual rock," which is Christ.

In the death of our Redeemer, we see three infinite depths moved for the relief of human misery; the love of the Father, the merit of the Son, and the energy of the Holy Spirit. These are the depths of wonder whence arise the rivers of salvation.

The waters flowed in the presence of the whole assembly. The agent was invisible, but his work was manifest.

*   *

The water flowed in great abundance, filling the whole camp, and supplying all the people. Notwithstanding the immense number, and the greatness of their thirst, there was enough for each and for all. The streams ran in every direction to meet the sufferers, and their rippling murmur seemed to say—"Open thy mouth, and I will fill it." Look to the cross! See there the gracious fountain opened, and streams of pardoning and purifying mercy flowing down the rock of Calvary, sweeping over the mount of Olives, and cleaving it asunder, to make a channel for the living waters to go out over the whole world, that God may be glorified among the Gentiles, and all the ends of the earth may see his salvation!

The water flowed from the rock, not pumped by human labor, but drawn by the hand of God. It was the same power, that opened the springs of mercy upon the cross. It was the wisdom of God that devised the plan, and the mercy of God that furnished the victim. His was the truth and love that gave the promise by the prophet—" In that day there shall be a fountain opened to the house of David, and to the inhabitants of Jerusalem, for sin and uncleanness." His was the unchanging faithfulness that fulfilled it in his Son—" Not by works of righteousness which we have done, but according to his mercy he saved us, by the washing of regeneration, and renewing of the Holy Ghost, which he shed on us abundantly, through Jesus Christ our Lord." Our salvation is wholly of God; and we have no other agency in the matter, than the mere acceptance of his proffered grace.

The water flowed in twelve different channels; and, according to Dr. Pococke, of Scotland, who visited the place, the deep traces in the rock are visible to this day. But the twelve streams, one for each tribe, all issued from the same fountain, in the same rock. So the great salvation flowed out through the ministry of the twelve apostles of the Lamb, and went abroad over all the earth. But the fountain is one. All the apostles preached the same Savior, and pointed to the same cross. " Neither is there salvation in any other, for there is no other name under heaven, given among men, whereby we must be saved." We must come to this spring, or perish.

The flowing of the waters was irresistible by human power. Who can close the fountain which God hath opened? Can Edom, or Moab, or Sihon, or Og, dam up the current which Jehovah hath drawn from the rock? Can Caiaphas, and all the Jews, aided by the Prince of this world—can all the powers of earth and hell combined—arrest the work of redemption, and dry up the fountain of mercy that Christ is opening on Calvary? As soon might they dry up the Atlantic, and stop the revolutions of the globe. It is written, and must be fulfilled. Christ must suffer, and enter into his glory—must be lifted up, and draw all men unto him—and repentance and remission of sins must be preached in his name among all nations, beginning at Jerusalem.

The water flowing from the rock was like a river of life to the children of Israel. Who can describe the distress throughout the camp; and the appearance of the people, when they were invited to approach a flinty rock, instead of a fountain or a stream, to quench their thirst? What angry countenances were there, what bitter censures, and ungrateful murmurings, as Moses went up to the rock, with nothing in his hand but a rod! "Where is he going," said they, " with that dry stick? What is he going to do on that rock? Does he mean to make fools of us all? Is it not enough that he has brought us into this wilderness to die of thirst? Will he mock us now by pretending to seek water in these sands, or open fountains in the solid granite?" But see! he lifts the rod; he smites the rock; and lo, it bursts into a fountain; and twelve crystal streams roll down before the people! Who can conceive the sudden transport? Hear the shout of joy ringing through the camp, and rolling back in tumultuous echoes from the crags and cliffs of Horeb! "Water! water! A miracle! a miracle! Glory to the God of Israel! Glory to his servant Moses!" It was a resurrection day to Israel, the morning light bursting upon the shadow of death. New life and joy are seen throughout the camp. The maidens are running, with cups and pitchers, to the rock. They fill and drink; then fill again, and haste away to their respective tents, with water for the sick, the aged, and the little ones, joyfully exclaiming—"Drink, father! Drink, mother! Drink, children! Drink, all of you! Drink abundantly! Plenty of water now! Rivers flowing from the rock!" Now the oxen are coming, the asses, the camels, the sheep, and the goats—coming in crowds to quench their thirst, and plunging into the streams before them. And the feathered tribes are coming, the turtle-dove, the pigeon, the swallow, the sparrow, the robin, and the wren; while the croaking raven and the fierce-eyed eagle, scenting the water from afar, mingle with them around the rock.

Brethren, this is but a faint emblem of the joy of the church, in drinking the waters that descend from Calvary, the streams that gladden the city of our God. Go back to the day of Pentecost for an instance. O what a revolution of thought, and feeling, and character! What a change of countenance, and conscience, and heart! Three thousand men, that morning full of ignorance, and corruption, and guilt—idolaters, sensualists, blasphemers, persecutors—before night were perfectly transformed—the lions converted into lambs—the hard heart melted, the dead conscience quickened, and the whole man become a new creature in Christ Jesus! They thirsted, they found the "Spiritual rock," tasted its living waters, and suddenly leaped into new life, like Lazarus from the inanition of the grave!

This is the blessing which follows the church through all her wanderings in the wilderness; accompanies her through the scorching desert of affliction, and the valley of the shadow of death; and when at last she shall come up out of great tribulation, her garments shall be found washed and made white in the blood of the Lamb; and the Lamb who is in the midst of the throne shall lead her to everlasting fountains, and she shall thirst no more!

Sermon 4

FALL AND RECOVERY OF MAN

For if, through the offence of one, many be dead; much more the grace of God, and the gift by grace, which is by one man, Jesus Christ, hath abounded unto many (Romans 5:15).

MAN was created in the image of God. Knowledge and perfect holiness were impressed upon the very nature and faculties of his soul. He had constant access to his Maker, and enjoyed free communion with him, on the ground of his spotless moral rectitude. But alas! the glorious diadem is broken; the crown of righteousness is fallen. Man's purity is gone, and his happiness is forfeited. "There is none righteous; no, not one." "All have sinned, and come short of the glory of God." But the ruin is not hopeless. What was lost in Adam, is restored in Christ. His blood redeems us from bondage, and his gospel gives us back the forfeited inheritance. "For if, through the offence of one, many be dead; much more the grace of God, and the gift by grace, which is by one man, Jesus Christ, hath abounded unto many." Let us consider ;—*First*, The corruption and condemnation of man ; and *Secondly*, His gracious restoration to the favor of his offended God.

I. To find the cause of man's corruption and condemnation, we must go back to Eden. The eating of the "forbidden tree" was "the offence of one," in consequence of which "many are dead." This was the "sin," the act of "disobedience," which "brought death into the world, and all our wo." It was the greatest in-. gratitude to the Divine bounty, and the boldest rebellion against the Divine sovereignty. The royalty of God was contemned; the riches of his goodness slighted ; and his most desperate enemy preferred before him, as if he were a wiser counsellor than Infinite

Wisdom. Thus man joined in league with hell, against Heaven; with demons of the bottomless pit, against the Almighty Maker and Benefactor; robbing God of the obedience due to his command, and the glory due to his name; worshipping the creature, instead of the Creator; and opening the door to pride, unbelief, enmity, and all wicked and abominable passions. How is the "noble vine," which was planted "wholly a right seed," "turned into the degenerate plant of a strange vine!"

Who can look for pure water from such a fountain? "That which is born of the flesh is flesh." All the faculties of the soul are corrupted by sin; the understanding dark; the will perverse; the affections carnal; the conscience full of shame, remorse, confusion, and mortal fear. Man is a hard-hearted and stiff-necked sinner; loving darkness rather than light, because his deeds are evil; eating sin like bread, and drinking iniquity like water; holding fast deceit, and refusing to let it go. His heart is desperately wicked; full of pride, vanity, hypocrisy, covetousness, hatred of truth, and hostility to all that is good.

This depravity is universal. Among the natural children of Adam, there is no exemption from the original taint. "The whole world lieth in wickedness." "We are all as an unclean thing, and all our righteousness is as filthy rags." The corruption may vary in the degrees of development, in different persons; but the elements are in all, and their nature is everywhere the same; the same in the blooming youth, and the withered sire; in the haughty prince, and the humble peasant; in the strongest giant, and the feeblest invalid. The enemy has "come in like a flood." The deluge of sin has swept the world. From the highest to the lowest, there is no health or moral soundness. From the crown of the head to the soles of the feet, there is nothing but wounds, and bruises, and putrifying sores. The laws, and their violation, and the punishments everywhere invented for the suppression of vice, prove the universality of the evil. The bloody sacrifices, and various purifications, of the pagans, show the handwriting of remorse upon their consciences; proclaim their sense of guilt, and their dread of punishment. None of them is free from the fear which hath torment, whatever their efforts to overcome it, and however great their boldness in the service of sin and Satan. "Mene! Tekel!" is written on every human heart. "Wanting!

wanting!" is inscribed on heathen fanes and altars; on the laws, customs, and institutions of every nation; and on the universal consciousness of mankind.

This inward corruption manifests itself in outward actions. "The tree is known by its fruit." As the smoke and sparks of the chimney show that there is fire within; so all the " filthy conversa tion" of men, and all " the unfruitful works of darkness" in which they delight, evidently indicate the pollution of the source whence they proceed. "Out of the abundance of the heart the mouth speaketh." The sinner's speech betrayeth him. "Evil speaking" proceeds from malice and envy. "Foolish talking and jesting," are evidence of impure and trifling thoughts. The mouth full of cursing and bitterness, the throat an open sepulchre, the poison of asps under the tongue, the feet swift to shed blood, destruction and misery in their paths, and the way of peace unknown to them, are the clearest and amplest demonstration that men "have gone out of the way," "have together become unprofitable." We see the bitter fruit of the same corruption in robbery, adultery, gluttony, drunkenness, extortion, intolerance, persecution, apostasy, and every evil work—in all false religions; the Jew, obstinately adhering to the carnal ceremonies of an abrogated law; the Mohammedan, honoring an impostor, and receiving a lie for a revelation from God; the Papist, worshipping images and relics, praying to departed saints, seeking absolution from sinful men, and trusting in the most absurd mummeries for salvation; the Pagan, attributing divinity to the works of his own hands, adoring idols of wood and stone, sacrificing to malignant demons, casting his children into the fire or the flood as an offering to imaginary deities, and changing the glory of the incorruptible God into the likeness of the beast and the worm.

"For these things' sake the wrath of God cometh upon the children of disobedience." They are under the sentence of the broken law; the malediction of Eternal Justice. "By the offence of one, judgment came upon all men unto condemnation." "He that believeth not is condemned already." "The wrath of God abideth on him." "Cursed is every one that continueth not in all things written in the book of the law, to do them." "Wo unto the wicked; it shall be ill with him, for the reward of his hands shall be given him." "They that plow iniquity, and sow wickedness, shall reap the same." "Upon the wicked the Lord shall rain fire, and snares, and a horrible tempest; this shall be the portion of their cup." "God is angry with the wicked every day; if he turn not, he will whet his sword; he hath bent his bow, and made it ready."

Who shall describe the misery of fallen men! His days, though few, are full of evil. Trouble and sorrow press him forward to the tomb. All the world, except Noah and his family, are drowning in the deluge. A storm of fire and brimstone is fallen from heaven upon Sodom and Gomorrah. The earth is opening her mouth to swallow up alive Korah, Dathan, and Abiram. Wrath is coming upon "the Beloved City," even "wrath unto the uttermost." The tender and delicate mother is devouring her darling infant. The sword of man is executing the vengeance of God. The earth is emptying its inhabitants into the bottomless pit. On every hand are "confused noises, and garments rolled in blood." Fire and sword fill the land with consternation and dismay. Amid the universal devastation, wild shrieks and despairing groans fill the air. God of mercy! is thy ear heavy, that thou canst not hear? or thy arm shortened, that thou canst not save? The heavens above are brass, and the earth beneath is iron; for Jehovah is pouring his indignation upon his adversaries, and he will not pity or spare.

Verily, "the misery of man is great upon him!" Behold the wretched fallen creature! The pestilence pursues him. The leprosy cleaves to him. Consumption is wasting him. Inflammation is devouring his vitals. Burning fever has seized upon the very springs of life. The destroying angel has overtaken the sinner in his sins. The hand of God is upon him. The fires of wrath are kindling about him, drying up every well of comfort, and scorching all his hopes to ashes. Conscience is chastising him with scorpions. See how he writhes! Hear how he shrieks for help! Mark what agony and terror are in his soul, and on his brow! Death stares him in the face, and shakes at him his iron spear. He trembles, he turns pale, as a culprit at the bar, as a convict on the scaffold. He is condemned already. Conscience has pronounced the sentence. Anguish has taken hold upon him. Terrors gather in battle-array about him. He looks back, and the storms of Sinai pursue him; forward, and hell is moved to meet him; above, and the heavens are on fire; beneath, and the world is burning. He listens, and the judgment trump is calling; again, and the brazen chariots of vengeance are thundering from afar; yet again, and the sentence penetrates his soul with anguish unspeakable—"Depart! ye accursed! into everlasting fire, prepared for the devil and his angels!"

Thus, "by one man, sin entered into the world, and death by sin; and so death passed upon all men, for that all have sinned." They are "dead in trespasses and sins;" spiritually dead, and legally dead; dead by the mortal power of sin, and dead by the condemnatory sentence of the law; and helpless as sheep to the slaughter, they are driven fiercely on by the ministers of wrath to the all-devouring grave, and the lake of fire!

But is there no mercy? Is there no means of salvation? Hark! amidst all this prelude of wrath and ruin, comes a still small voice, saying: "much more the grace of God, and the gift by grace, which is by one man, Jesus Christ, hath abounded unto many."

II. This brings us to our second topic, man's gracious recovery to the favor of his offended God.

I know not how to represent to you this glorious work, better than by the following figure. Suppose a vast graveyard, surrounded by a lofty wall, with only one entrance, which is by a massive iron gate, and that is fast bolted. Within are thousands and millions of human beings, of all ages and classes, by one epidemic disease bending to the grave. The graves yawn to swallow them, and they must all perish. There is no balm to relieve, no physician there. Such is the condition of man as a sinner. All have sinned; and it is written, "The soul that sinneth shall die." But while the unhappy race lay in that dismal prison, Mercy came and stood at the gate, and wept over the melancholy scene, exclaiming—"O that I might enter! I would bind up their wounds; I would relieve their sorrows; I would save their souls!" An embassy of angels, commissioned from the court of Heaven to some other world, paused at the sight, and Heaven forgave that pause. Seeing Mercy standing there, they cried:—"Mercy! canst thou not enter? Canst thou look upon that scene and not pity? Canst thou pity, and not relieve?" Mercy replied: "I can see!" and in her tears she added, "I can pity, but I cannot relieve!" "Why canst thou not enter?" inquired the heavenly host. "Oh!" said

Mercy, " Justice has barred the gate against me, and I must not—cannot unbar it!" At this moment, Justice himself appeared, as if to watch the gate. The angels asked, " Why wilt thou not suffer Mercy to enter?" He sternly replied: " The law is broken, and it must be honored! Die they or Justice must!" Then appeared a form among the angelic band like unto the Son of God. Addressing himself to Justice, he said: " What are thy demands?" Justice replied: " My demands are rigid; I must have ignominy for their honor, sickness for their health, death for their life. Without the shedding of blood there is no remission!" " Justice," said the Son of God, " I accept thy terms! On me be this wrong! Let Mercy enter, and stay the carnival of death!" " What pledge dost thou give for the performance of these conditions?" " My word; my oath!" " When wilt thou perform them?" " Four thousand years hence, on the hill of Calvary, without the walls of Jerusalem!" The bond was prepared, and signed and sealed in the presence of attendant angels. Justice was satisfied, the gate was opened, and Mercy entered, preaching salvation in the name of Jesus. The bond was committed to patriarchs and prophets. A long series of rites and ceremonies, sacrifices and oblations, was instituted to perpetuate the memory of that solemn deed. At the close of the four-thousandth year, when Daniel's " seventy weeks" were accomplished, Justice and Mercy appeared on the hill of Calvary. " Where," said Justice, " is the Son of God?" " Behold him," answered Mercy, " at the foot of the hill!" And there he came, bearing his own cross, and followed by his weeping church. Mercy retired, and stood aloof from the scene. Jesus ascended the hill, like a lamb for the sacrifice. Justice presented the dreadful bond, saying, " This is the day on which this article must be cancelled." The Redeemer took it. What did he do with it? Tear it in pieces, and scatter it to the winds? No! he nailed it to his cross, crying, " It is finished!" The Victim ascended the altar. Justice called on holy fire to come down and consume the sacrifice. Holy fire replied: " I come! I will consume the sacrifice, and then I will burn up the world!" It fell upon the Son of God, and rapidly consumed his humanity; but when it touched his Deity, it expired. Then was there darkness over the whole land, and an earthquake shook the mountain; but the heavenly host broke forth in rapturous song—" Glory to God in the highest! on earth peace! good will to man!"*

* The substance of this transcendent passage Christmas Evans often repeated in his preaching, and of course with considerable variation on different occasions. There are two other versions of it in English. One of them, translated many years ago, and published under the title of " A Specimen of Welsh Preaching," has been everywhere justly admired, as one of the finest productions of sanctified genius. The other, which we give below, was taken from the lips of the preacher, and rendered into English, by one of his frequent hearers and intimate friends. " All the stores of his energy," says the editor of the English memoir, " and the resources of his voice, which was one of great compass, depth, and sweetness, seemed reserved for the closing portions of the picture, when he delineated the routed and battered hosts of the pit, retreating from the cross, where they had anticipated a triumph, and met a signal and irretrievable overthrow."—EDITOR.

" Methinks I find myself standing upon the summit of one of the highest of the everlasting hills, permitted thence to take a survey of our earth. It shows to me a wide and far-spread burial-ground, over which lie scattered in countless multitudes the wretched and perishing children of Adam. The ground is full of hollows, the yawning caverns of death, while over it broods a thick cloud of fearful darkness. No light from above shines upon it, nor is the ray of the sun or moon, or the beams of a candle seen through all its borders. It is walled around. Its gates, large and massive, ten thousand times stronger than all the gates of brass forged among men, are one and all safely locked. It is the hand of Divine Justice that has locked them, and so firmly secured are the strong bolts which hold those doors, that all the created powers even of the heavenly world, were they to labor to all eternity, could not drive so much as one of them back. How hopeless the wretchedness to which the race are doomed, and into what irrecoverable depths of ruin has the disobedience of their first parent plunged them!

" But behold, in the cool of the day there is seen descending from the eternal hills in the distance, the radiant form of Mercy, seated in the chariot of the divine promise, and clothed with splendor, infinitely brighter than the golden rays of the morning when seen shooting over mountains of pearls. Seated beside Mercy in that chariot is seen another form like unto the Son of man. His mysterious name is the 'Seed of the Woman,' and girt around him shines the girdle of eternity, radiant with the lustre of the heaven of heavens. 'He has descended into the lower parts of the earth.' I see Mercy alight from that chariot, and she is knocking at the huge gate of this vast cemetery. She asks of Justice: 'Is there no entrance into this field of death? May I not visit these caverns of the grave, and seek, if it may be, to raise some names at least of the children of destruction, and bring them again to the light of day? Open, Justice, open; drive back these iron bolts and let me in, that I may proclaim the jubilee of deliverance to the children of the dust.' But I hear the stern reply of Justice from within those walls; it is,—' Mercy, surely thou

Thus grace has abounded, and the free gift has come upon all, and the gospel has gone forth proclaiming redemption to every

lovest Justice too well, to wish to burst these gates by force of arm, and thus obtain entrance by mere lawless violence. And I cannot open the door. I cherish no anger towards the unhappy wretches. I have no delight in their eternal death, or in hearing their cries as they lie upon the burning hearth of the great fire kindled by the wrath of God, in the land that is lower than the grave. But I am bound to vindicate the purity, holiness, and equity of God's laws; for, ' without shedding of blood there is no remission.' ' Be it so,' said Mercy, ' but wilt thou not accept of a surety who may make a sufficient atonement for the crime committed and the offence given ?' ' That will I,' said Justice, ' only let him be duly allied to either party in this sad controversy, a kinsman, near alike to the injured Lawgiver, and to the guilty tenants of the burial-ground.' ' Wilt thou, then,' said Mercy, ' accept of the puissant Michael, prince among the hosts of heaven, who fought bravely in the day when there was war in heaven, and also vanquished Apollyon upon the summit of the everlasting hills ?' ' No,'—said Justice, ' I may not, for his goings forth are not from the beginning, even from everlasting.' ' Wilt thou not then accept of the valiant Gabriel, who compelled Beelzebub to turn and seek safety in flight from the walls of the heavenly city ?' ' No,'—cried Justice, ' for Gabriel is already bound to render his appointed service to the King Almighty; and who may serve in his place while he should be attempting the salvation of Adam's race ? There needs,' continued Justice, ' one who has, of right belonging to him, both omnipotence and eternity, to achieve the enterprise. Let him clothe himself with the nature of these wretches. Let him be born within these gloomy walls, and himself undergo death within this unapproachable place, if he would buy the favor of Heaven for these children of the captivity !'

"But while this dialogue was held, behold, a form fairer than the morning dawn, and full of the glory of heaven, is seen descending from that chariot. Casting, as he passes, a glance of infinite benignity upon the hapless' tenants of that burial-ground, he approaches, and asks of Justice : ' Wilt thou accept of me ?' 'I will,' said Justice, ' for greater art thou than heaven and the whole universe.'

" ' Behold, then,' said the stranger, 'I come : in the volume of the book has it been written of me. I will go down, in the fulness of time, into the sides of the pit of corruption. I will lay hold of this nature, and take upon me the dust of Eden, and, allied to that dust, I will pour into thy balance, Justice, blood of such worth and virtue that the court of heaven shall pronounce its claims satisfied, and bid the children of the great captivity go free.'

"Centuries have rolled by, and the fulness of time is now accomplished; and see, an infant of days is born within the old burial ground of Eden. Behold a Son given to the dwellers of the tomb, and a spotless Lamb, the Lamb of God, is seen within that gloomy enclosure. When the hour came at which the ministers of the Divine Justice must seize upon the victim, I see them hurrying towards Gethsemane. There, in heaviness and sorrow of soul, praying more earnestly, the surety is seen bowed to the earth, and the heavy creature. " By grace ye are saved, through faith; and that not of yourselves; it is the gift of God; not of works, least any man should boast." By grace ye are loved, redeemed and justified. By grace ye are called, converted, reconciled and sanctified. Salvation is wholly of grace. The plan, the process, the consummation, are all of grace.

> " Grace all the work shall crown,
> Through everlasting days;
> It lays in heaven the topmost stone,
> And well deserves the praise!"

" Where sin abounded, grace hath much more abounded." " Through the offence of one, many were dead." And as men mul-

---

burden he had assumed is now weighing him down. Like a lamb, he is led towards Golgotha—the hill of skulls. There are mustered all the hosts of darkness, rejoicing in the hope of their speedy conquest over him. The monsters of the pit, huge, fierce, and relentless, are there. The lions,* as in a great army, were grinding fearfully their teeth, ready to tear him in pieces. The unicorns,* a countless host, were rushing onwards to thrust him through, and trample him beneath their feet. And there were the bulls of Bashan,* roaring terribly; the dragons* of the pit are unfolding themselves, and shooting out their stings, and dogs* many are all around the mountain. 'It is the hour and power of darkness.' I see him passing along through this dense array of foes, an unresisting victim. He is nailed to the cross; and now Beelzebub and all the master-spirits in the hosts of hell have formed, though invisible to man, a ring around the cross. It was about the third hour of the day, or the hour of nine in the morning, that he was bound as a sacrifice, even to the horns of the altar. The fire of divine vengeance has fallen, and the flames of the curse have now caught upon him. The blood of the victim is fast dropping, and the hosts of hell are shouting impatiently: 'The victory will soon be ours.' And the fire went on burning until the ninth hour of the day, or the hour of three in the afternoon, when it touched his Deity,—and then it expired. For the ransom was now paid and the victory won. It was his. His hellish foes, crushed in his fall, the unicorns and the bulls of Bashan retreated from the encounter with shattered horns; the jaws of the lions had been broken and their claws torn off, and the old dragon, with bruised head, dragged himself slowly away from the scene, in deathlike feebleness. 'He triumphed over them openly,' and now is He for ever the Prince and Captain of our salvation, made perfect through sufferings. The graves of the old burial-ground have been thrown open; and from yonder hills gales of life have blown down upon this valley of dry bones, and an exceedingly great army have already been sealed to our God, as among the living in Zion."

* Allusion to the language in which Psalm xxii. predicts the Saviour's sufferings. The Psalm which our Saviour himself quoted upon the Cross, when he cried, "My God, why hast thou for-saken me."

tiplied, the offence abounded. The waters deluged the world, but could not wash away the dreadful stain. The fire fell from heaven, but could not burn out the accursed plague. The earth opened her mouth, but could not swallow up the monster sin. The law thundered forth its threat from the thick darkness on Sinai; but could not restrain, by all its terrors, the children of disobedience. Still the offence abounded, and multiplied as the sands on the sea-shore. It waxed bold, and pitched its tents on Calvary, and nailed the Lawgiver to a tree. But in that conflict sin received its mortal wound. The Victim was the Victor. He fell, but in his fall he crushed the foe. He died unto sin, but sin and death were crucified upon his cross. Where sin abounded to condemn, grace hath much more abounded to justify. Where sin abounded to corrupt, grace hath much more abounded to purify. Where sin abounded to harden, grace hath much more abounded to soften and subdue. Where sin abounded to imprison men, grace hath much more abounded to proclaim liberty to the captives. Where sin abounded to break the law and dishonor the Lawgiver, grace hath much more abounded to repair the breach and efface the stain. Where sin abounded to consume the soul as with unquenchable fire and a gnawing worm, grace hath much more abounded to extinguish the flame and heal the wound. Grace hath abounded! It hath established its throne on the merit of the Redeemer's sufferings. It hath put on the crown, and laid hold of the golden scepter, and spoiled the dominion of the prince of darkness, and the gates of the great cemetery are thrown open, and there is the beating of a new life-pulse throughout its wretched population, and Immortality is walking among the tombs!

This abounding grace is manifested in the gift of Jesus Christ, by whose mediation our reconciliation and salvation are effected. With him, believers are dead unto sin, and alive unto God. Our sins were slain at his cross, and buried in his tomb. His resurrection hath opened our graves, and given us an assurance of immortality. " God commendeth his love toward us, in that, while we were yet sinners, Christ died for us ; much more, then, being now justified by his blood, we shall be saved from wrath through him ; for if, when we were enemies, we were reconciled to God by the death of his Son, much more, being reconciled, we shall be saved by his life."

" The carnal mind is enmity against God ; it is not subject to the
law of God, neither indeed can be." Glory to God, for the death
of his Son, by which this enmity is slain, and reconciliation is
effected between the rebel and the law! This was the unspeakable
gift that saved us from ruin ; that wrestled with the storm, and turned
it away from the devoted head of the sinner. Had all the angels
of God attempted to stand between these two conflicting seas, they
would have been swept to the gulf of destruction. " The blood of
bulls and goats, on Jewish altars slain," could not take away sin,
could not pacify the conscience. But Christ, the gift of Divine
Grace, " Pascal Lamb by God appointed," " a sacrifice of nobler
name and richer blood than they," bore our sins, and carried our
sorrows, and obtained for us the boon of eternal redemption. He
met the fury of the tempest, and the floods went over his head ;
but his offering was an offering of peace, calming the storms and
the waves, magnifying the law, glorifying its Author, and rescuing
its violator from wrath and rain. Justice hath laid down his sword
at the foot of the cross, and amity is restored between heaven and
earth.

Hither, O ye guilty ! come and cast away your weapons of rebellion! Come with your bad principles, and wicked actions ; your
unbelief, and enmity, and pride ; and throw them off at the Redeemer's feet! God is here, waiting to be gracious. He will
receive you ; he will cast all your sins behind his back, into the
depths of the sea ; and they shall be remembered against you no
more for ever. By Heaven's " Unspeakable Gift," by Christ's
invaluable atonement, by the free and infinite grace of the Father
and the Son, we persuade you, we beseech you, we entreat you,
" be ye reconciled to God !"

It is by the work of the Holy Spirit within us, that we obtain a
personal interest in the work wrought on Calvary for us. If our
sins are cancelled, they are also crucified. If we are reconciled in
Christ, we fight against our God no more. This is the fruit of faith
" With the heart man believeth unto righteousness." May the Lord
inspire in every one of us that saving principle!

But those who have been restored to the Divine favor may sometimes be cast down and dejected. They have passed through the
sea, and sung praises on the shore of deliverance ; but there is yet
between them and Canaan " a waste howling wilderness," a long

and weary pilgrimage, hostile nations, fiery serpents, scarcity of food, and the river Jordan. Fears within and fightings without, they may grow discouraged, and yield to temptation, and murmur against God, and desire to return to Egypt. But fear not, thou worm Jacob! Reconciled by the death of Christ; much more, being reconciled, thou shalt be saved by his life. His death was the price of our redemption; his life insures liberty to the believer. If by his death he brought you through the Red Sea in the night, by his life he can lead you through the river Jordan in the day. If by his death he delivered you from the iron furnace in Egypt, by his life he can save you from all the perils of the wilderness. If by his death he conquered Pharaoh, the chief foe, by his life he can subdue Sihon, king of the Amorites, and Og, the king of Bashan. "We shall be saved by his life." "Because he liveth, we shall live also." "Be of good cheer!" The work is finished; the ransom is effected; the kingdom of heaven is opened to all believers. "Lift up your heads and rejoice," "ye prisoners of hope!" There is no debt unpaid, no devil unconquered, no enemy within your own hearts that has not received a mortal wound! "Thanks be unto God, who giveth us the victory, through our Lord Jesus Christ!"

Sermon 5

ONE GOD AND ONE MEDIATOR

For there is one God, and one Mediator between God and man, the man Christ Jesus (1 Timothy 2:5).

THE apostle Paul urges the propriety and importance of praying for all men, in the several conditions and relations of life, from a consideration of God's merciful intentions toward all men, as exhibited in the sufficiency of the gospel provision for their salvation. But if any are saved, it must be through the medium which God has ordained, and in the manner which God has prescribed. Therefore the apostle adds: " For there is one God, and one Mediator between God and man, the man Christ Jesus." " There is one God," to whom sinners have to be reconciled ; " and one Mediator," through whom that reconciliation is to be effected. We have a nearly parallel passage in another epistle : " To us there is but one God, the Father, of whom are all things, and we in him ; and one Lord Jesus Christ, by whom are all things, and we by him." The unity of God, and the mediation of Christ, are the two great topics of the text, to which we solicit your attention.

I. " For there is one God." Two infinite beings cannot co-exist, unless they are one in essence and in operation. The God of Israel pervades the universe of matter, and fills the immensity of space. There is no room for another God, possessing the same ubiquity. " There is one God and Father of all, who is above all, and through all, and in you all." In him alone, all things live, move, and have their being.

This doctrine is stamped on all the works of nature. They all exhibit unity of design, and must have been contrived by the same infinite wisdom, and executed by the same infinite power. The nand which created and arranged them is constantly seen in their preservation. The Maker of all things continues to uphold all things by the word of his power. The great Architect still presides over the immense fabric which he has reared. The universe, from age to age, is governed by the same unvarying laws. All things remain as they were from the beginning. The earth, the air, and the sea, sustain the same mutual relations, and answer the same important ends; and the sun, the moon, and the stars, shine on for ever. The same order and regularity everywhere prevail, as when the chorus of the morning stars welcomed the new creation into being. Nature proclaims aloud: "There is one God."

The same doctrine is impressed upon the Bible. It is not only the book of God, but evidently the book of " one God." It is a series of Divine Revelations, reaching from Eden to Calvary, and from Calvary onward to the end of the world. It is a golden chain, passing through all time, and uniting the two eternities; and all its links are similar, and depend upon each other. Its several parts are perfectly harmonious, proving them to have emanated from the same infinite mind. Everywhere we find the same character of God and of man; the same description of the law and of sin; the same way of pardon, and holiness, and immortal life. The same Eternal Spirit, that inspired the Historian of Creation, speaks in the Apocalypse of St. John, and in all the intervenient books of the Bible. It was the same Sun of Righteousness, that rose in Eden, and set on Calvary; and thence rose again the third day, to set no more for ever.

" The world by wisdom knew not God." The heathen lost the doctrine of the unity of God; not because it was difficult to pre- serve, but because they did not love the character of God, " did not like to retain God in their knowledge." The pride of the carnal mind led them to turn away from the light of heaven, to walk amid sparks of their own kindling. They boasted of their wisdom; they boasted of their philosophy. And what gained they by the exchange? The most absurd and stupid notions of the Great First Cause; almost total ignorance of his attributes. " Pro- fessing themselves to be wise, they became fools; and changed the glory of the incorruptible God into an image made with hands, like unto corruptible man, and to birds, and four-footed beasts, and creeping things." Shame to philosophic Greece and Rome!

No nation, having once lost the doctrine of the unity of God, ever regained it by the light of nature. If the light of nature is sufficient to preserve it in possession, it is not sufficient to restore it lost. It is restored only by the gospel. The gospel has restored it in India, in Otaheite, and other heathen lands. It has done more; it has revealed to the savage the only way of salvation; it has "brought life and immortality to light."

> "Fly abroad, thou mighty gospel!
> Win and conquer! never cease!"

Lift up thy voice with strength, and proclaim to Greece and Rome, and to all the ends of the earth, as well as to the cities of Judah, that the Son of Mary is the God of Israel, "God manifest in the flesh," "God blessed forever!" "The man Christ Jesus" is "the brightness of the Father's glory, and the express image of His person, in whom dwelleth all the fulness of the Godhead bodily;" "in whom also we have redemption through his blood, the forgiveness of sins, according to the riches of his grace."

II. But this leads us to our second topic: "And one Mediator between God and man, the man Christ Jesus." The two doctrines, you perceive, are intimately related to each other. "One God"— "One Mediator." As we have but "one God," we need but "one Mediator." As that Mediator is himself God, the merit of his mediation is sufficient for the salvation of all them that believe.

The office of a Mediator supposes two parties at variance, between whom he interposes to produce a reconciliation. It is thus "between God and man." God gave man a law, "holy, and just, and good;" man revolted, and "there is wrath." Reconciliation is impossible, without the intervention of a mediator. Let us look at the parties engaged in this dreadful controversy.

On one side we see Jehovah, possessed of infinite perfections, and clothed with uncreated excellence and glory. He is self-existent, independent and eternal. Omnipresence, Omniscience, and Almightiness are his. He is great in wisdom, full of goodness, slow to anger, and ready to pardon. His love is ineffable, and "his mercy endureth for ever." He is "glorious in holiness, fearful in praises, doing wonders." These perfections are the pearls and diamonds in his crown. "With him also is terrible majesty." Life and joy are in his smile, but the angel of destruction waits upon his frown. One beam of his love can raise thousands of men

to heaven: one glance of his anger, sink myriads of angels to hell.
" He sitteth upon the circles of the earth, and the inhabitants
thereof are as grasshoppers." " All nations before him are as
nothing; they are counted less than nothing and vanity." " He
doeth according to his will among the children of men, and ruleth
the armies of heaven." " At his wrath the earth shall tremble, and
the nations shall not be able to abide his indignation." O what
majesty and power belong unto the Lord our God!

With this imperfect view, contrast the impotence and insignifi-
cance of sinful man. What is he? A being of yesterday, " whose
breath is in his nostrils," and " whose foundation is in the dust."
A frail, helpless, perishing thing; dependent upon God, the Creator,
for all his comforts, for life itself. What is man? A fool; an alien
from all good; an imbodiment of all evil. His understanding is
dark; his will perverse; his affections carnal. His " throat is an
open sepulchre;" swallowing up " whatsoever things are true, pure,
lovely, or of good report;" emitting a pestilential vapor, which
withers every green herb, and sweet flower, and delicious fruit, of
honor to God, and happiness to man. " The poison of asps is
under his tongue;" an inflaming poison, affecting all the members,
and " setting on fire the whole course of nature, and it is set on fire
of hell." " His heart is fully set in him to do evil;" " deceitful
above all things, and desperately wicked." He is an enemy to his
Maker; a rebel against Jehovah; a blank—nay, worse—a blot in
God's creation; dead to every virtue, dead to every thing but sin;
lost to every gracious purpose of his being; a withered branch, fit
only to be plucked off, and cast into the fire; stubble, ready for
the burning. " Let him alone!" said Reason. " Cut him down!"
cried Justice. " I hate the workers of iniquity!" added Holiness.
" He or I must perish!" exclaimed Truth. " Spare him! Spare
him! Spare him!" pleaded weeping Mercy. And Wisdom came
forth, leading the Son of God, and said: "I have found a ransom!
Behold the Mediator!" And all the attributes met and embraced
at the manger, and kissed each other at the cross!

It was man's place, as the offender, to seek a reconciliation
God was under no obligation. But, alas! man had neither the
means nor the inclination. What could be done? Hear, O ye
heavens! and be astonished! Listen, O earth! and wonder and
adore! While man was far from God, an enemy in his heart by

wicked works, rushing on in determined hostility to his Maker's government, and there was no sacrifice found for his sin, and no disposition in him to seek a sacrifice, God sought within himself the adequate and only means of pardon and peace. He found in his own bosom the Lamb for the altar; exhibited him to Israel in the predictions and promises of the Old Testament; and in the fulness of time, sent him forth to expiate sin, by the offering of himself, once for all. "For the Word was made flesh, and dwelt among us; and we beheld his glory, the glory as of the Only Begotten of the Father, full of grace and truth." "And being found in fashion as a man, he humbled himself, and became obedient unto death, even the death of the Cross."

God provided a Mediator. Why? Did he fear that the deserved ruin of the human race would dethrone eternal Justice? No. Eternal Justice would have been honored as much in their destruction as in their salvation. The law would have been as fully vindicated in the infliction of its penalty upon the transgressor, as in the reparation of its breach by a vicarious atonement. The glory of the Divine government would have been untarnished, as when the rebel angels were cast down from heaven, and locked up in everlasting darkness. This wondrous provision was not the result of necessity, but the prompting of Infinite Love. Divine Mercy sought to remove the barrier interposed by Divine Justice. The sinner cannot be pardoned, till his Great Substitute has met the demands of the law. There must be a full satisfaction and settlement of its claims, as the only ground on which the rebel can be acquitted.

Love is the "Alpha and Omega" of redemption, the love of God to man. Read it in the journey of the Mediator from heaven to earth! Read it in his pilgrimage through the land of sorrow! Behold him "nailed to the shameful tree!" See the blood and water gushing from his side! Hear the sound of the water-spouts, as the floods of wrath roll over him! Then ask the reason. The answer is: "God is love." "He is not willing that any should perish." It seemed good in his sight to save his rebel children, whatever it might cost him. "God so loved the world, that he gave his only begotten son, that whosoever believeth in him should not perish, but have eternal life." "Herein is love, not that we loved God"—no; we hated him; we were his sworn, inveterate foes; "but that he loved us"—loved us while we were yet enemies—loved us with an ineffable love; "and sent his Son to be the propitiation for our sins."

Wonderful must be the qualifications of such a Mediator. He fills with his own merit the gap between two worlds. He bows the heavens, and lifts up the earth to meet them. He takes hold of God and man, and brings them together in himself. He reconciles the rebel and the law, glorifies the Father by humbling himself, and his cross becomes our life, and his tomb the birthplace of our immortality.

England and Wales could not be united till the son of the king of England was born in Wales, and became Prince of Wales. The English regarded him as heir to the throne of England; while the Welsh claimed him as their brother, a native of their own country, born in the castle of Caernarvon. Behold "the well beloved"— "the only begotten of the Father," "heir of all things," "Lord of lords, and King of kings," born "in Bethlehem of Judea;" "the Son of God—the Son of man;" partaking of both natures, and representing both parties in the great controversy. He is "the Mighty God, and the Everlasting Father;" yet he is our near kinsman—bone of our bone, and flesh of our flesh. In his person, heaven and earth are joined; by his blood, God and man are reconciled. Heaven is his throne, for God is his father; earth is his principality, for it is the land of his nativity. In him angels recognise their King, and men behold their brother.

I gaze on the cross, and methinks I hear the victim say: "Look unto me, and be ye saved, all ye ends of the earth; for I am God, and beside me there is none else. I opened a way for my people of old, by dividing the waters, to the Canaan of Promise; I am now preparing a path for believers, through the red sea of my blood, to the inheritance in heaven. I gave the law amid fire and smoke on Sinai, and thundered forth my curse upon its violater; I am here on Calvary, to honor that violated law, and remove that curse from its violater by taking it upon myself. Behold my hands, my feet, my side! This blood, O men! is your sacrifice. I will expiate your sin by my sufferings. I will magnify the law, and make it honorable. And though in your nature I hang on this tree to-day, I will revive, and live for ever, to make intercession for the transgressors, and save to the uttermost all that come unto God by me!"

The mediatorial office of "the man Christ Jesus" consists of two parts, sacrifice and intercession. They are equally important, and mutually dependent. Without sacrifice, there is no ground of intercession; without intercession, there is no benefit in sacrifice. The former renders the latter influential with God; the latter renders the former available to man. The one removes the obstacles to reconciliation, the other brings the adverse parties together.

The first part of the mediatorial office is sacrifice. In order to understand this aright, we must have correct views of God, of man, and of sin. We must consider God as the lawgiver and governor of the universe, eternally hostile to all iniquity, and determined to sustain his just administration. We must consider man as a guilty and polluted creature, a rebel in arms against his Maker, a prisoner under sentence and deserving punishment. We must consider sin as an inexcusable omission of duty, and a flagrant transgression of the law, under circumstances of peculiar aggravation. The debt must be paid, or the sinner must perish. An atonement must be made, of merit equal to the turpitude of our crimes. The stain which we have cast upon the law, must be washed out by blood of infinite preciousness. This is the work of our Mediator. He "gave himself a ransom for all." He made a perfect satisfaction for our sins. "He was wounded for our transgressions, and bruised for our iniquities; the chastisement of our peace was upon him, and with his stripes we are healed." It is not by blood of bulls and goats, slain on Jewish altars, but by a nobler and costlier sacrifice—the paschal "Lamb of God," that heaven and earth are reconciled—God and man united.

The second part of the mediatorial office is intercession. It was through the High-priest, the typical mediator, that God communicated with Israel, and Israel communicated with God; it is through "the man Christ Jesus," the real Mediator, that God speaks to the world, and receives the prayers of his people. Having "borne the sins of many," he "maketh intercession for the transgressors." "He hath entered into heaven himself, there to appear in the presence of God for us." He has gone into the holy of holies, with "the blood of sprinkling, which speaketh better things than the blood of Abel." "If any man sin, we have an advocate with the Father, Jesus Christ the righteous." "Through him we both"—that is, both Jews and Gentiles—"have access by one Spirit unto the

Father." He holds in his hand the golden censer, and offers much incense before the throne. It is this that perfumes our prayers, and renders them acceptable to God. He pleaded for his murderers when he hung upon the cross, and now he pleads in heaven for those who crucify him afresh. And what is the ground of his plea? Not the merit of our works, but the merit of his own sufferings. Not the infinitude of the Father's mercy, but the sufficiency of his own sacrifice. This is the sure foundation of a sinner's hope. If Satan suggests that his crimes are too great to be forgiven, he may reply: " The man Christ Jesus" is my advocate, the advocate of " the chief of sinners ;

> And should I die with mercy sought,
>   When I his grace have tried,
> I sure should die—delightful thought !—
>   Where sinner never died !"

" One Mediator." There is no choice. You must accept of him, or remain unreconciled, and be cast into hell. Israel found but one path through the Red Sea ; the church shall never find more than one way to the heavenly Canaan. It is only by faith in the " One Mediator," that you can obtain the favor of the " One God." He is the elect and beloved of the Father, the appointed medium of man's approach, the designated channel of God's communication. " Neither is there salvation in any other." No other has been provided. No other is suited to our necessities. O sinner ! come through this " new and living way !" Christ invites your confidence.

> " Venture on him; venture freely;
>   Let no other trust intrude !
> None but Jesus, none but Jesus,
>   Can do helpless sinners good."

These glorious truths, we cannot read too often, or meditate too much. They represent to us the great evil of sin, the infinite mercy of God, the inflexible character of the law, and the incalculable preciousness of the gospel. Such is the Father's estimate of the Mediator, that he will be reconciled to sinners only through his blood. He is well pleased with his Son, and well pleased with all who seek him through his Son, and nothing is more offensive to him than the rejection of his Son. May these remarks preserve you from despair under a sense of your guilt and wretchedness ; drive you from all false refuges to the cross, with a penitent and grateful heart; induce you to trust, not in your own strength, or wisdom, or righteousness, but in the adorable name of Jesus; to live a life of faith in him, of love towards him, and of patient waiting for his mercy unto eternal salvation!

If you are already partakers of these blessings, how transcendent is your privilege! "Ye are come unto mount Zion, the city of the living God, the heavenly Jerusalem; and to an innumerable company of angels; and to the spirits of just men made perfect; and to the general assembly and church of the first-born, which are written in heaven; and to God, the judge of all; and to Jesus, the Mediator of the new covenant; and to the blood of sprinkling, that speaketh better things than that of Abel." Follow the Captain of your salvation. Cleave to him in the fire and the flood. Turn not aside to the lying vanities of the world, lest you drink the cup of its eternal sorrows. Remember that those who suffer with the crucified shall reign with the glorified; that such as are faithful unto death shall receive the crown of life. Be careful to "keep the unity of the spirit in the bond of peace." Endure unto the end, and ye shall be saved.

"Now the God of peace, that brought again from the dead our Lord Jesus, that Great Shepherd of the sheep, through the blood of the everlasting covenant, make you perfect in every good work, to do his will, working in you that which is well pleasing in his sight, through Jesus Christ our Lord, to whom be glory for ever and ever." Amen.

THE LIVING REDEEMER

Oh that my words were now written! Oh that they were printed in a book!
that they were graven with an iron pen and lead in the rock forever! For
I know that my Redeemer liveth, and that he shall stand at the latter day
upon the earth: and though after my skin worms destroy this body, yet in
my flesh shall I see God: whom I shall see for myself, and mine eyes shall
behold, and not another; though my reins be consumed within me (Job
19:23-27).

IT is the common opinion of learned divines, that Job was an
ancient prince in some part of Arabia, known in his day by the
name of Uz. His three friends also—"Eliphaz the Temanite,
Bildad the Shuhite, and Zophar the Naamathite"—were neighboring princes. In their visit of condolence, they were accompanied
by Elihu, who seems to have been a young man of extraordinary
intelligence and virtue. The occasion of this visit was the apparent judgments of God upon the patriarch. They held a long
controversy with him, in which they insisted that his unparalleled
calamities and sufferings proved him the chief of hypocrites. Job
as strenuously maintained his innocence and integrity, and argued
that his providential afflictions were intended only for the proof
and the improvement of his piety; and that when this purpose
should be accomplished, he would come forth as gold purified from
the furnace. God, answering out of the whirlwind, settled the dispute, deciding in favor of his servant Job; his three friends were
required to offer sacrifice for their faults, and Job must pray for
their forgiveness. Then the wheel of fortune turned in his favor,
and he was restored to his former prosperity.

Job and his friends evidently had a clear understanding of the
evil of sin, the wickedness of hypocrisy, the importance of the fear
of God, and the doctrine of an allwise superintending providence;

and knew how to approach Jehovah through sacrifice, in anticipa
tion of the promised Messiah.

We shall offer a few general remarks on Job's faith in a living
Redeemer, as expressed in our text.

I. Our minds are struck with wonder and pleasure, in beholding
the patriarchs and prophets of ancient times, moved by the Spirit
of God, searching diligently for the person and grace of the Messiah ; like miners, opening an entrance to a precious treasure, which
is to redeem them and their brethren from bondage.

Job has no reference here to any temporal deliverer, nor to any
other than the Messiah himself. He evidently saw what he needed,
when he was speaking of the Daysman, the Umpire, one that might
argue and settle the case between him and his Maker, one that
might lay his hand alike on God and man. With the eye of faith,
he saw the Messiah, setting one foot on the continent of eternity,
and the other on the sea of human misery, and lifting up his hand
and saying—" Time and eternity are mine ! I am God, and beside
me there is no Saviour !" Elihu also speaks of the same person,
under the name of " a messenger," " an interpreter," " one of a
thousand," that might commune with both God and man, concerning atonement, and justifying righteousness, and deliverance from
the pit of eternal destruction.

The promise of a Redeemer descended from Eden like a precious
ark, containing, for all mankind, the bread of life, and the unsearchable riches of Divine grace. It was conveyed from the house of
Adam to the house of Seth, from the house of Seth to the house of
Noah, from the house of Noah to the house of Abraham, and thence
down through successive generations to the time of Messiah's
advent. The patriarchs, before their departure, received from this
ark invaluable spiritual blessings, and a passport to the everlasting
city ; but the ark itself they left behind for the benefit of their posterity, who found therein the balm of life, and died in the faith of a
Saviour to come, according to the promise.

Job's living Redeemer is none other than the promised " Seed,"
that should " bruise the serpent's head"—Jacob's " Lion," "stoop-
ing down" to the " new tomb hewn out of a rock," aiming at the
King of Terrors, and on the third morning leaping and " rushing
upon the prey," and becoming the plague of death, and the destruction of the grave—the " Jehovah-jireh" of Abraham—the " I

Am," who appeared to Moses in the burning bush—the "Won-derful," the "Councillor," the "Child-born," and "the Ever-lasting Father," predicted by Isaiah—Jeremiah's "Jehovah our Righteousness"—the "Branch" and "Fountain" of Zachariah—the "Shepherd and Stone of Israel"—the "Shiloh," to whom should be "the gathering of the people"—the "Governor," who should "come out of Bethlehem"—Malachi's "Sun of Righteous-ness"—Paul's "Captain of our Salvation," "bringing many sons to glory;" opening a tunnel under the river of his own sufferings, and the seas of human guilt and wo, through which his redeemed might go home to their Father's house—Peter's "Prince of Life," "slain and hung on a tree"—John's "Word," that "was in the begin-ning with God, and was God;" but "was made flesh, and dwelt among us, full of grace and truth."

II. The word here rendered Redeemer, is Goel in the original; and in the book of Ruth, is translated kinsman, one who has a right to redeem. The Redeemer is our near kinsman; for "he that sanctifieth, and they that are sanctified, are all of one; for which cause he is not ashamed to call them brethren."

An individual in this country returned from India so rich that he conferred upon all his relatives an independent fortune. To us also a brother was born against the day of adversity, who is able to enrich us all with eternal riches. You know not what hardships your brother endured in the East, while gathering the wealth you now enjoy; but we know that our brother, "though he was rich, for our sakes became poor, that we through his poverty might be rich."

When Naomi returned from the land of Moab, Elimelech, her husband, was dead, and the inheritance greatly involved in debt. According to the law of the tribes, the nearest kinsman of the deceased debtor was obliged to marry the widow, and redeem the inheritance, so as to retain it in the same tribe. The purchaser was sought in the land of Bethlehem. One was found, sufficiently rich, but unwilling. He preferred to take off his own shoes, before the elders, at the gate of the city, rather than stand in the shoes of his deceased brother. It was done, however, by another, of the name of Boaz. But who will stand in the place of sinners, who have forfeited all claim to the heavenly inheritance, and deserve eternal damnation? Let heaven and earth meet in council, and see who is able and willing to "redeem his brother, or give to God a ransom

for him." Earth replies—"There is no such person here." AL
the angels around the throne answer—"There is none in the celestial city." Search the streets of Jerusalem; go to the garden of
Gethsemane; inquire on the hill of Calvary. Who is willing to die
for sinners to-day? There is the tree. There is the executioner,
with hammer and nails. Who will offer himself a sacrifice there,
for the redemption of man? None but Jesus. None but Jesus was
able; none but Jesus was willing. "Here am I," said he; "if
ye seek me, let these go their way." And without the gates of
Jerusalem, he honored the law, spoiled principalities, and redeemed
his people. He suffered the curse in the sinner's stead, and swallowed up all its plagues in himself. As your representative, he
endured all the agony and ignominy you justly deserved.* And
when you by faith lay hold of his atonement, you shall be made the
righteousness of God in him—shall be dealt with, not according to
your deserts, but according to his merit and his mercy. He was
humbled that you might be exalted, impoverished that you might
be enriched, bound that you might be released, punished that you
might be sᵱared, condemned that you might be acquitted, wounded
that you might be healed, cursed that you might be blessed, and
slain that you might live for ever.

III. Job's faith anticipated a Living Redeemer. "I know that
my Redeemer liveth"—is the Living One—he that has life, underived and independent, in himself—the agent and source of all
life in the universe, who will at last quicken the dead.

The first woman was called Eve—that is, Life—because she was
the mother of all living—the mother of him who is the life of the
world. This was fulfilled four thousand years afterward in one of
her daughters, a virgin, who brought forth a son, whose name is
Jesus, Emmanuel, the Living God, the true God, and eternal Life.
He is the Lord of life, and the life of all that believe. "Because
I live, ye shall live also." With the flame of one candle you may
light many others, and the light of all is the same. Christ is the
source whence all his people derive their light, the great central
luminary of his church. "In him was life, and the life was the
light of men."

---

* Was it the amount of suffering, or the dignity of the sufferer, that gave
merit to the sacrifice sufficient for the world's redemption? Eᴅ.

When the prophet stood in the valley of dry bones and prophesied, there was a wonderful agitation, and the bones came together, and formed themselves into skeletons, and sinews and flesh covered them, and each form was enclosed with a skin ; but they were still dead, and it was not till the breath of God blew upon them, and kindled the flame of life within them, that they " stood up an exceeding great army." So Christ is the resurrection and life alike of the soul and of the body. " He that believeth on him, though he were dead, yet shall he live." He is the bread and the water of life. " He that cometh unto him, shall never hunger ; and he that believeth on him, shall never thirst." " He that hath the Son, hath life ; and he that hath not the Son, hath not life." " We are dead ; and our life is hid with Christ in God ; when Christ who is our life shall appear, then shall we also appear with him in glory."

IV. The Living Redeemer of Job was to appear in this world. " He shall stand at the latter day upon the earth."

A woman who is travelling, and has no money to bear her expenses, obtains credit on her husband's account, who afterward passes that way, and discharges the obligation. So ancient saints went home to glory on credit : and in the fulness of time, Christ came and paid their debt ; not by instalments, but all at once ; and the virtue of his own offering went up to the gate of Eden, and down to the end of the world. As on both sides of the altar of burnt-offering, were pipes, conveying the blood into the basins, till they were full ; so the great altar on Calvary communicates with past generations, and generations yet to come ; and the saving merit of the one sacrifice runs back to Abel and to Adam, and forward to the last believer.

Whom do I see in the garden yonder, in such agony of soul, prostrate in prayer, and sweating great drops of blood ? Job's Living Redeemer. Why is his heart thus wrung with anguish ? Is there a dark register of sins in his conscience, like the fiery handwriting of God upon the wall ? No, he has not a single crime to confess. He has done no iniquity, neither is guile found in his mouth. Why then does he suffer ? He is bearing our griefs, carrying our sorrows, and receiving the chastisement of our peace. Behold him on the mountain, " wounded for our transgressions, and bruised for our iniquities." " All we like sheep have gone astray we have turned every one to his own way; and the Lord hath laid on him the iniquity of us all." "He is brought as a lamb to the slaughter; and as a sheep before her shearers is dumb, so he openeth not his mouth." "Who shall declare his generation?" Who shall give us his pedigree, his history, his character? Will none of the angels of heaven make the air of Calvary ring with the sufferer's name? Behold! the darkened sun and quaking earth proclaim him God! Hark! he speaks—"I am the true God, and eternal life. I was set up from everlasting, from the beginning of the Creator's way, or ever the earth was. When there was no depths, nor fountains of water; before the mountains were settled, before the hills was I brought forth; while as yet he had not made the earth, nor the fields, nor the highest part of the dust of the world. When he prepared the heavens, I was there; when he set a compass upon the deep; when he established the clouds above; when he strengthened the foundations of the deep; when he gave the sea his decree, that the waters should not pass his command-ment; when he established the foundations of the earth; then I was by him, as one brought up with him; and I was daily his delight, rejoicing always before him; rejoicing in the habitable parts of his earth, and my delights were with the sons of men; and therefore I am here, hanging on the cross to-day!"

V. Job's Living Redeemer was to deliver him from the power of death.

Job anticipated the coming of "the last enemy," who should give his flesh to be food for worms. The Sabeans had taken away the oxen and the asses, and slain the servants with the edge of the sword. The fire had fallen from heaven, and burnt up the sheep and the shepherds. The Chaldeans had robbed him of his camels, and murdered his domestics. The whirlwind had killed his sons and his daughters in the house of their feasting. His body was covered with putrid ulcers, from head to foot. His best friends turned against him, and even his wife tempted him to "curse God and die." But amid all his calamities, he saw another enemy, ready to assail his body, and drag it away to the tomb, and reduce it to dust and ashes. At the same time, his faith beheld the Messiah swallowing up death in victory. He saw the Son of Mary in the house of Jairus, where the lion had just slain his victim; and on the street of Nain, where he was taking the prey to his den; and at the grave in Bethany, where he was banquetting with worms in the joy of victory. Death could not stand before the Prince of Life. The spoiler yielded up his spoil. Christ sailed on the open channel like a man of war, delivering the hapless captives of the great pirate Death, to the astonishment and joy of the people, from Samaria to the borders of Tyre and Sidon. But on a certain day, ever to be remembered, as he drew near the ramparts of Sinai, all its batteries were opened upon him. He stood in the fire all night, and fought till he sweat great drops of blood. He threw himself between his friends and the fort, and sustained the shock of its heaviest artillery, which played upon him without intermission, especially the old cannon of Eden—"Dying thou shalt die"— until three o'clock in the afternoon of the next day, when he received a shot in the heart, and, crying, "It is finished!" gave up the ghost. The whole creation trembled when he fell, and was swallowed up in the horrible abyss. But on the morning of the third day, the earth was seized with new spasms, and he that was dead came forth to be the life of his people; and the cable of faith, the anchor of hope, and the sails of love, ascended with him from the deep, never to go down again. He is alive for evermore, and has the keys of hell and of death.

VI. Job speaks of the period of Messiah's advent, under the term of "the latter day." This may refer, either to the end of the Jewish dispensation, or to the end of the world.

Christ has already once appeared on earth, fulfilled the types and shadows, made an end of sins, and brought in everlasting righteousness; "and to them that look for him, he shall appear the second time, without a sin-offering, unto salvation." "When the Son of man shall come in his glory, then shall he sit upon the throne of his glory, and before him shall be gathered all nations, and he shall separate them as the shepherd divideth the sheep from the goats." Then shall God have finished his work in mount Zion, and the trumpets of the gospel shall cease to sound, and the great net shall be taken up from the sea, and the laborers in the vineyard shall receive their wages, and the tares shall be cast into the unquenchable fire.

Wonderful shall be the glory and the terror of that day; "when the Lord Jesus shall be revealed from heaven, with his mighty angels, in flaming fire; taking vengeance on them that know not

God, and obey not the gospel; who shall be punished with ever-lasting destruction from the presence of the Lord, and from the glory of his power; when he shall come to be glorified in his saints, and admired in all them that believe." What a glorious army shall attend him down the sky—myriads of his saints, and all the celestial powers and principalities! "Fire shall devour before him, and it shall be very tempestuous round about him. He shall call to the heavens above, and to the earth, that he may judge his people." His throne shall be "like a fiery flame, and his wheels like a burning furnace." He "shall descend with a shout, and the voice of the archangel, and the trump of God." The sound of the trumpet on Sinai was long and loud, and "exceeding terrible;" but how much more powerful shall be the voice of "the last trumpet," penetrating the cold ear of death, and awaking into immortality the dust of the grave! Then the Messiah shall not appear "as a root out of dry ground;" but shall stand forth before heaven and earth "in the glory of the Father, and of his holy angels;" in addition to the glory of his own person as God-man, and the glory of his work as Mediator. Before him, "the heavens shall pass away with a great noise, and the elements shall melt with fervent heat; the earth also, and the works that are therein, shall be burned up;" and death and hell shall deliver up their dead; and all men shall stand and receive their sentence from him who was an infant in Bethlehem—"a man of sorrows, and acquainted with grief"—condemned by Pilate, mocked by the multitude, and nailed upon the cross. This is Job's living Redeemer, the resurrection and life of all who believe.

VII. Our text contains Job's confession of faith. It is brief, but very comprehensive, and may be called an epitome of the gospel. Here we have the Divinity and the humanity of Christ, his work of redemption, his victory over death and hell, his second advent, and the resurrection of the dead.

The Athenians mocked when they heard of the resurrection of the dead; and the Sadducees greatly erred on this subject, "not knowing the scriptures, nor the power of God;" and many of the Corinthians imbibed the same poison of unbelief. But the patriarch of Uz thought it not "a thing incredible that God should raise the dead." He firmly believed the doctrine, and gave it a prominent place in his confession. He knew that God is able to watch and preserve the dust of his saints; has his eye upon every particle, throughout all the periods of time ; and through the Divine Mediator, " will raise it up at the last day." This doctrine was to him a great consolation in his unparalleled afflictions. " Though my skin," says he, " is a tissue of disease and corruption—yea, though my body sink into the earth, and be eaten up of the worms, and my very reins be consumed within me—yet in my flesh, in this same body, reorganized, reanimated, and made immortal from the tomb, I shall see God—shall see him for myself, with these self-same eyes."

Yes, brethren ; the souls and bodies of all the human race shall be reunited ; and with our own eyes, we shall see the judge of quick and dead, with his fan in his hand, thoroughly purging his floor, gathering the wheat into his garner, and burning up the chaff with unquenchable fire. In that day, the tares and the wheat shall be for ever separated, and there shall be no more foolish virgins among the wise. " For we must all appear before the judgment-seat of Christ, that we may receive the things done in the body, according to that we have done, whether it be good or evil."

How vast the difference between Messiah's first and second advents ! When he " tabernacled and dwelt among us," he appeared " in the form of a servant ;" but when he shall come again, he shall come as a judge, and " sit upon the throne of his glory ;" and " all that are in their graves shall hear his voice, and come forth ; they that have done good, unto the resurrection of life ; and they that have done evil, unto the resurrection of damnation." " For the Son of man shall send forth his angels ; and they shall gather out of his kingdom all things that offend, and them that do iniquity ; and shall cast them into a furnace of fire ; there shall be weeping and gnashing of teeth ; then shall the righteous shine forth as the Sun in the kingdom of their Father."

VIII. I call your attention to one other topic suggested by the text—the confidence with which Job speaks of his interest in the living Redeemer. " For I know that my Redeemer liveth." It was not a mere conjecture. There was no doubt in the case. The patriarch had reached the assurance of faith ; and so perfectly satisfied was he of the fact, that he expressed an intense desire that his words might be recorded on the most durable materials, that they might be read by generations to come.

How may we acquire the same confidence ? What is the evidence of our interest in Job's living Redeemer? The nature and effects of the change which has taken place in our hearts. You that " were sometime darkness, are now light in the Lord ;" have been " called out of darkness into his marvellous light ;" and can say—" One thing I know, that whereas I was once blind, now I see." " The carnal mind is enmity against God ;" but those that are born of the Spirit love God ; and love and hatred are not so much alike, that you cannot tell by which principle you are governed. While the strong man armed kept the palace, his goods were in peace ; but when a stronger than he came and cast him out, there was a warfare commenced between the old man and the new. You were formerly dead in trespasses and sins ; but are now alive to God, through our Lord Jesus Christ. You were once destitute of faith in the Redeemer ; but now you believe in him, and rely upon his righteousness alone, as the ground of your acceptance and salvation. How can you experience such a transformation, and know nothing of the matter? As well might the sick, when Christ healed them—as well might the blind, when Christ opened their eyes—as well might the dead, when Christ raised them to second life from the bed, the bier, or the grave—have been ignorant of the mighty change.

In the word of God, we have the testimony of many who had obtained the assurance of faith. " I know that my Redeemer liveth, and that he shall stand upon the earth at the latter day"— was the testimony of Job. " The Lord is my rock, and my fortress, and my deliverer, and the horn of my salvation, in whom I will•trust"—was the testimony of David. " I will greatly rejoice in the Lord ; my soul shall be joyful in God ; for he hath clothed me with the garments of salvation ; he hath covered me with the robe of righteousness"—was the testimony of Isaiah. " I know in whom I have believed, and am persuaded that he is able to keep that which I have committed unto him against that day"—was the testimony of the apostle Paul. " We know that we are of God ; we know that we have passed from death unto life ; we know that when he shall appear, we shall be like him, for we shall see him as he is"—was the testimony of John, " the beloved disciple."

" These things," saith the apostle, " have I written unto you that believe in the name of the Son of God, that ye might know that ye have eternal life." This is the design of God, in revealing his will to the church. We may—we should know that we have eternal life. " He that believeth on the Son of God hath the witness in himself." But this assurance of faith is not a mere imagination of the brain. It is not founded on a vague notion of your being one of the elect, without any other evidence. It is not founded on a voice from heaven, bidding you be of good cheer, and go in peace, because your sins are forgiven you. It is founded on the fruits of the Spirit, and the testimony of Divine Revelation. True believers are "created anew in Christ Jesus, unto good works;" evincing the reality of their love to God by keeping his commandments.

Let us, therefore, give all diligence to make our calling and election sure. Let us examine ourselves, whether we are in the faith. Let us compare our religion with the precepts of the Bible, and the example of ancient saints. But as our hearts are so wicked and deceitful, let us not trust them, but pray to God for the aid of his Holy Spirit, in this important work of self-examination. Behold " the Sweet Singer of Israel," praying—" Search me, O God, and try me; prove me, and know my heart." The Holy Spirit has given you a rule by which you are to examine yourselves; and he works in you a conformity to that rule, and bears witness with your spirits that you are the children of God. In proportion to his operation upon the heart, will be the assurance of faith; and in proportion to the assurance of faith, will be your spiritual comfort and joy. The Lord grant us that " faith which worketh by love, and purifieth the heart!"

Are you stript of property, bereft of children, afflicted in body, forsaken of friends, persecuted and insulted by relatives? Think of Job, and of Job's living Redeemer! Imitate the patriarch's patience and confidence amid all the troubles and conflicts of life! Go your way until the end; for ye shall rest, and stand in your several lots at last!

Sermon 7

MESSIAH'S KINGDOM

And in the days of these kings shall the God of heaven set up a kingdom, which shall never be destroyed; and the kingdom shall not be left to other people, but it shall break in pieces and consume all these kingdoms, and it shall stand for ever. Forasmuch as thou sawest that the stone was cut out of the mountain without hands, and that it brake in pieces the iron, the brass, the clay, the silver, and the gold; the great God hath made known to the king what shall come to pass hereafter: and the dream is certain, and the interpretation thereof sure (Daniel 2:44, 45).

In these words we have a prophetic description of the kingdom of Christ, as the fifth empire that should arise after the date of this prophecy. The wonderful image which so troubled the king of Babylon in his dream, and occasioned him so much solicitude when he awoke, denoted four of the great empires of the world. The head of gold represented the Babylonian empire; the breasts and arms of silver, the Medo-Persian empire; the belly and thighs of brass, the Grecian empire, under Alexander the Great; the legs and feet of iron, the Roman empire in its strength and glory; and the ten toes of mingled iron and clay, the same empire in its divided and enfeebled state. The last circumstance was intended to denote the same thing as the ten horns on the head of the Beast in the book of Revelation. As iron is firm and strong, and able to bruise and break all materials of a softer quality; so the Roman empire once crushed beneath its power all other kingdoms, and dictated laws to the world. As the beast with iron teeth trampled and rent to pieces all that came in its way; so the Roman tyrant, like a lion among the lambs of the flock, tore and devoured the followers of the meek and lowly Jesus.

The kingdom of Christ is represented under the figure of " a stone cut out of the mountain without hands:" that is, without human agency—without any wisdom or power of man, but by the Spirit of God ; smiting the feet of the image, and shattering it into fragments ; then becoming a great mountain, and filling the whole earth. In the history of Christianity we have the counterpart of the emblem. Messiah appeared in the form of a servant ; born of a poor virgin, in the despised town of Bethlehem ; lived a life of poverty, persecution, and various sorrow, from the manger to the tree ; died the most painful and ignominious of deaths, even the accursed death of the cross ; but rose from the dead on the predicted morning, the morning of the third day ; commissioned his apostles, the fishermen of Galilee, to " go into all the world, and preach the gospel to every creature ;" ascended on high, and sent down the Holy Spirit, the promised Comforter, to give energy and efficacy to the word, to prove its divinity, and convince and save mankind. The apostles immediately commenced their work ; persevered in the divine employment ; were prospered by the power of God ; and the stone, rolling forth from Mount Zion, and raising a dust which darkened the very heavens, smote the feet and legs of the image, until it shook, and the earth trembled around it ; and that stone is still rolling on, and shall crush and demolish the image, and grind it to powder, and scatter it to the winds of heaven ; and shall increase, till it becomes a great mountain, and fills the whole earth for ever.

In speaking of the accomplishment of this prophecy, we will notice—its certainty, its attendant glory, and the nearness of its approach.

I. The certainty of the accomplishment of this prophecy is founded, *first*, on the Father's promise to the Son, made on the express condition of his pouring out his soul unto death. " I the Lord have called thee in righteousness, and will hold thy hand, and will keep thee, and give thee for a covenant of the people, for a light of the Gentiles, to open the blind eyes, to bring forth the prisoners from the prison, and them that sit in darkness out of the prison-house." Christ's universal dominion is the promised reward of his sufferings, and the Father speaks as if he intended to raise his wages. " Thus saith the Lord ; It is a light thing that thou shouldst be my servant, to raise up the tribes of Jacob, and restore the preserved of Israel ; I will also give thee for a light of the gentiles, that thou mayest be my salvation unto the ends of the earth." "Ask of me, and I shall give thee the heathen for thine inheritance, and the uttermost parts of the earth for thy possession." Such is the promise. All nations shall come and worship before him. All that the Father hath given shall come unto him, and the gates of hell shall not prevail against them.

The certainty of Messiah's universal dominion is founded, *secondly*, on his perfect qualification to accomplish the work which the Father hath given him to do. "No one knoweth the Father," in all the perfection of his nature, all the wisdom of his counsels, and all the immutability of his purposes, "but the Son; and no one knoweth the Son, but the Father," as he alone is of the same essence, and exhibits the same attributes. Christ is "God manifest in the flesh;" "the brightness of the Father's glory, and the express image of his person." None but a divine person could give, and none but a divine person could receive, such a privilege as is here promised. None but a divine person could be competent to the eternal redemption of countless millions of the human race. Christ "is the true God, and Eternal Life"—"the Faithful Witness, the First Begotten from the dead, and the Prince of the kings of the earth"—"the Alpha and Omega, the Beginning and the Ending, the First and the Last"—"the Root and the Offspring of David, and the Bright and Morning Star"—"Over all, God, blessed for ever." These are Messiah's titles, which evince his equality to the work which he has undertaken—the salvation of the world, and the subjugation of all things unto himself. He is able, not only to set up his kingdom, but also to establish it for ever. It shall never be destroyed, nor left to other people; but shall break in pieces and destroy all other kingdoms, and the kingdoms of this world shall become the kingdom of our God and of his Christ.

Take courage, ye fearful saints! Your king is the Almighty God. He shall conquer all your enemies. The victory of Calvary is the pledge and earnest of his universal dominion. You shall soon be more than conquerors, through him that hath loved you, and given himself for you. He is able to protect you against the combined powers of earth and hell. Omniscient, he is well acquainted with all the plots of his enemies; Almighty, he can at any moment frustrate them. The prince of darkness, with all his hosts, cannot impede the progress of his kingdom. In all their councils, he is present, hearing their deliberations and discovering their malice He overturns their schemes, or employs them for the accomplish ment of his own gracious purposes. "His counsel shall stand, and he will do all his pleasure." Too wise to err, and too powerful to be overcome, he marches in the van of battle, and will never forsake his soldiers. The very sight of his helmet and his plume is victory to his followers, and death to his foes.

Courage, ye friends of Zion! "Lift up your hearts and rejoice, for your redemption draweth nigh." Take the whole armor of God; quit you like men; be strong; for the decisive conflict is at hand. Behold your General, clothed with a garment white as snow, girt about the loins with a golden girdle, his feet as fine brass burning in a furnace, his countenance as the sun shining in his strength, his eyes as a flame of fire, his voice as the sound of many waters, a sharp two-edged sword proceeding out of his mouth, seven stars in his right hand, and at his girdle the keys of death and hell. This is the Captain of your salvation, of whom the Evangelical Prophet inquires—"Who is this that cometh from Edom, with dyed garments from Bozrah? this that is glorious in his apparel, travelling in the greatness of his strength?" This is Emmanuel; mighty to conquer, and mighty to save. Who can stand before the glory of his power? Who can hinder the universal triumph of his cause? The government shall be upon his shoulder, and he shall reign for ever and ever.

What has been said is deemed sufficient to show the certainty of Messiah's universal empire. The promises of the Father to the Son are so many drafts of immense amount, upon the bank of heaven, which will be paid without discount at the appointed time; and the character of Christ is a sufficient guarantee that he will carry forward to its completion the work which he has begun. Having secured a title to the kingdom by his sufferings, he shall certainly come, and take possession, and reign for ever. The gospel is a lever, whose fulcrum is the Rock of Ages, and it shall yet lift our fallen world to heaven. Balaam knew that his curses could not injure Israel, whom Jehovah had blessed. The kingdom of Messiah is mightier than Moab. The people beloved of the Lord shall prosper in spite of their enemies—as gardens by the rivers, and willows by the water-courses. "There shall be a handful of corn," not a sackful, only so much as the sower may hold in his nand—not on the bank of the Nile, nor in the valley of the Jordan, but " on the top of the mountain"—the wild, high, rocky, unculti- vated mountain ; " the fruit thereof shall shake like Lebanon," and the wind shall carry the seed to the uttermost parts of the earth, and young Lebanons shall grow up everywhere, and even the barren rocks and sands of Arabia shall become as the garden of God. It was but a handful of the seed of the kingdom, which Peter cast abroad on the day of Pentecost ; it was but a handful he sowed in the house of Cornelius, the captain of the Italian band ; but it soon spread throughout Judea, and even to the isles of the sea, so that nothing was more manifest or more abundant than its fruit. But the prevalence of Christ's millennial kingdom shall be still more rapid and glorious; and " from the rising to the setting of the sun, his name shall be great among the Gentiles."

Already the church is singing—" Gird thy sword upon thy thigh, O thou Most Mighty; and in thy majesty, ride prosperously, because of truth, and meekness, and righteousness. Thine arrows are sharp in the hearts of the king's enemies, whereby the people fall under thee." The song has reached the ear of the Prince of Darkness, and he " hath come in great wrath" to the battle, " for he knoweth that he hath but a short time." He knows that " the Desire of nations" is come ; and that his kingdom, already begun, shall be established for ever, and extend from sea to sea, till the knowledge of his glory and the victories of his grace shall cover the earth. He sees the Stone rolling against the idols of India, and Africa, and the islands of the sea, and feels his kingdom shake beneath its progress. He sees the Bramins, the Karens, the worshippers of Juggernaut and the Ganges, plucked as brands out of the burning. He trembles to anticipate the announcement—" The kingdoms of this world are become the kingdom of our Lord and of his Christ !" He beholds the mighty angel, with the keys of the bottomless pit, and a great chain in his hand, descending from heaven, to bind him in his prison. He hates the church, with her various benevo- lent enterprises ; for he sees in them the artillery of Heaven, playing upon his fortresses of infidelity, and idolatry, and vice—the enginery of God, setting up a kingdom which shall consume all others, and stand for ever. " The dream is certain, and the interpretation thereof is sure."

II. We call your attention to the glory of Messiah's universa reign. It includes three things ; the victory obtained, the blessings bestowed, and the duration of the kingdom. Let us consider them distinctly.

First. The victory obtained. Here we behold the "stone cut out of the mountain," rolling down the steep, rushing and leaping toward the great image, and smiting and breaking its feet of iron and clay, so that it falls like Dagon before the ark. And still the Stone, instinct with the power of God, and increasing in size and velocity, keeps rolling to and fro, bounding and rebounding, till it grinds the fallen image to powder, and scatters it as the dust of the summer thrashing-floor. It is endued with perpetual motion ; keeping up a constant action and reaction, crushing whatever opposes its progress, and growing to such a magnitude as shall shortly fill the whole earth. This is the salt of Galilee, seasoning the nations —the leaven of Jerusalem, spreading through the world. This is the victorious reign of Christ, from the Tiber to the Thames, from the Euphrates to the Ganges, from Britain to Japan, from sea to sea, and from pole to pole. This glorious conquest is to be obtained by "the sword of the Spirit, which is the word of God ;" in connection with the vast machinery of Divine Providence, all the wheels of which are under the direction of Jesus the Christ. It is a victory over Satan, by bruising his head ; a victory over sin, by destroying its power ; a victory over death, by swallowing it up for ever. Emmanuel has already successfully engaged all these foes; and having routed them on Calvary eighteen hundred years ago, he still pursues their flight; and shall not turn again, till he has trampled "the last enemy" under his feet.

Satan is the prince and the god of this world. In the management of his affairs, he employs a policy similar to that of the Sultan of Constantinople, who sets up many pashas or governors under him, as the Pasha of Egypt, the Pasha of Aleppo, the Pasha of Damascus, all possessing the same despotic spirit, and carrying out the same tyrannical measures. The devil has established a great number of pashas throughout his dominion. Three of them are described by the Revelator, as unclean spirits, like frogs ; one of them issuing from the mouth of Satan himself, representing undisguised Paganism; another from the mouth of the Beast, representing a persecuting civil power ; the third from the mouth of the False Prophet, representing abominable and damnable heresies.

But these shall all be conquered; these, and every other enemy of Messiah upon earth. Jewish impenitence and unbelief, which, for a period of eighteen centuries, has ruled with an absolute sceptre the lineal descendants of Abraham, shall be overcome. Mohammedism, the "king of fierce countenance, understanding dark sentences," that has reigned over so large a portion of the world, practising and prospering, deceiving millions of souls, and destroying the holy people, shall be broken without hand, and his kingdom shall come to naught. The drunken harlot of Rome, riding on her scarlet beast, that is, a cruel and persecuting civil government, and making all nations drink of the wine of her fornication, shall be obliged to drink the wine of the wrath of Almighty God; and all the saints shall clap their hands at her overthrow, and shout hallelujah to the Captain of their salvation. And all those Protestant pashas of Satan, who would undermine the gospel by denying its peculiar and fundamental doctrines—such as the Divinity of Christ, the merit of his sacrifice, the excellency of his offices, the personality and work of the Holy Spirit—and even the existence of his own infernal majesty, shall be destroyed by the brightness of Emmanuel's coming, when he shall appear in the glory of his millennial kingdom. Then shall the song of the heavenly host break once more upon the ear of Zion—"Arise, shine, for thy light is come, and the glory of the Lord is risen upon thee!" And "the Gentiles shall come to her light, and kings to the brightness of her rising." "Her sons shall come from far, and her daughters shall be nursed at her side." "The glory of the Lord shall be displayed, and all flesh shall see it together."

Secondly. The blessings bestowed. Christ "hath ascended on high, and received gifts for men; yea for the rebellious also, that God may dwell among them." The celestial reservoir is full; and the golden pipes are laid, for conveying the waters of life to every soul of man; and the time shall yet come, when all shall know the Lord, from the least to the greatest. The gospel salvation shall be an ocean, spreading over the whole earth; and there shall be no more ebbing and flowing of the waters, but a continual full tide from shore to shore. The Chinese, the Hottentot, and the American Indian, shall be as thoroughly instructed in Divine things as the Welshman; and the Welshman shall be seven times more intelligent than now. And this universally prevalent knowledge of

Christ shall be, not merely nominal and theoretical, but experimental and practical. It shall be a "faith unfeigned," "of the operation of God," "working by love, and purifying the heart." The light of the gospel shall be "as the sun shining in his strength," scattering all clouds from the face of the world, and the moon and the stars shall be lost in its effulgence. Living waters shall flow out from the spiritual Jerusalem in summer and winter; neither frozen by the cold, nor evaporated by the heat. Like the deluge of Noah, they shall cover the mountains; but they shall save, and not destroy, all whom they shall overwhelm. "In that day, there shall be one Lord, and his name shall be one;" and he "shall be king over all the earth." The cause of Christ shall be pre-eminent in the estimation of mankind. The duties and interests of Christianity shall constitute no secondary concern. "The mountain of the Lord's house shall be established in the tops of the mountains, and exalted above the hills, and all nations shall flow unto it."

Among the blessings of this happy period, shall be that of a universal and everlasting peace. There shall be no more contention and bloodshed upon earth. "Nation shall no more lift up sword against nation, neither shall they learn war any more." The arsenals shall empty their contents into the founderies and black-smith-shops, and the weapons of war shall be converted into scythes and plowshares. O, glorious day! when heaven shall be seen upon earth, and earth itself shall seem like heaven! Behold the ferocious wolf dwelling with the gentle lamb; the furious leopard lying down with the innocent kid; the cow and the bear feeding in the same pasture; the infant leading the lion by the mane, and playing upon the den of the adder and the asp; and no disposition to hurt or destroy. These are the scriptural emblems of that blessed peace. Holiness and happiness, more united than David and Jonathan, more inseparable than Ruth and Naomi, hand in hand, two heavenly twins, shall go singing over the world. All envy and jealousy and hostility, whether of nations, of churches, or of individuals, shall perish before Messiah's kingdom, as perished the image in the vision before that wondrous stone.

Thirdly. The duration of the kingdom. This is the crowning circumstance of its glory. It "shall not be destroyed, nor left to other people." Its enemies, however numerous and mighty, cannot overthrow it; and it "shall stand for ever." Where now are the

illustrious empires of Babylon, and Persia, and Greece, and Rome?
Where are the Pharaohs, the Ptolemies, the Alexanders, the Cæsars,
the Napoleons, whose voice terrified nations, and whose tread
shook the world? Where—with all their power and splendor,
their iron sceptres and golden crowns? Gone; mouldering in the
dust; and their magnificence nourishes the worm. They are
utterly demolished, and shall rise no more. But the King of Zion
liveth through all time, and is himself "the Father of Eternity,"
"the Alpha and Omega, the Beginning and the Ending, the First
and the Last." "His kingdom is an everlasting kingdom, and of
his dominion there shall be no end."

III. Let us consider the nearness of its approach. The language of prophecy, viewed in connection with the signs of the times,
will lead us to the conclusion that it is nigh at hand, even at the
door.

Many learned divines are of opinion that Popery and Mohammedism, the Antichrists of the east and the west, must fall about the year
1866. This notion is founded on the following words : "From the
time that the daily sacrifice shall be taken away, and the abomination that maketh desolate set up, there shall be a thousand two
hundred and threescore days—Blessed is he that waiteth, and
cometh to the thousand three hundred and five and thirty days."*
Different writers on the prophecies, however, differ in opinion concerning the times of their fulfilment. All these speculations are very
uncertain, if not utterly unprofitable. What matters it, if our watches
do not exactly agree? We all know that the night is far spent, and
the day is at hand, and the magnitude and importance of our duty
requires prompt and earnest attention.

Five men were determined to rise early in the morning, to engage
in a great work, upon which depended their future fortunes. The
first was up before the morning star; and though uncertain as to
the hour, immediately prepared for business. The second, when
he rose, saw the star just above the horizon, and hastened to his
work with animation and joy. The third slept a little too long,
and awoke in great confusion and alarm; but hurrying through the
day as well as he could, though with a heavy heart and many a
blunder, he made out partially to redeem his delinquency. The

---

* Dan. xii. 11, 12.

fourth heard the cock crowing, but thought there was no need of being in a hurry, and composed himself to sleep again ; and when his neighbors called him, turned in his bed, and answered—" A little more slumber ;" and awaking about nine of the clock, found the day too far advanced, and abandoned his purpose in despair. The fifth, disturbed by the bustle of the others before daylight, got up and looked out of the window ; and finding it as dark as it was at midnight, was very angry, called his neighbors a set of fools, and declared he would have nothing to do with the enterprise ; and while all the others made themselves rich, he lived and died in deserved poverty ; and some pitied him for his misfortune, and others ridiculed him for his folly.   Mark the wise man, and follow his example.

The kingdom of Antichrist has of late been greatly weakened in many parts of the world.   Providence is pouring the vials of wrath upon the Beast and the False Prophet.   The idols and altars of Paganism fall before the advancing ark of God.   The church, with its train of benevolent institutions—like the bride, with her attendant virgins, going forth to meet the royal bridegroom—proclaims the coming of the Prince of Peace.   The Bible, Missionary, Sabbath-school, and Tract societies, are four heralds, running before Messiah's chariot ; rather, the four wheels of that chariot in which he rides victoriously.

The rise and progress of the British and Foreign Bible Society remind me of the stream in Ezekiel's vision.   This great river had its source in one of the mountains of Wales.   In the year 1802, the Rev. Mr. Charles of Bala, an ordained minister of the established church, officiating in connection with the Calvinistic Methodists, deeply impressed with the preciousness of the Bible, and aware of the scarcity of copies throughout the principality, felt that some measures ought to be adopted to furnish it at a reduced price, and circulate it gratuitously among the poor.   He wrote concerning it to his countryman, the Rev. Mr. Owen, an Episcopal clergyman in London.   The subject was subsequently introduced to a circle of Christian gentlemen, who had met to transact other business.   It elicited much conversation, and excited a lively interest.   The Rev. Joseph Hughes, a Welshman, and Baptist minister at Battersea, near London, suggested that Wales was not the only part of the world that felt a want of the Bread of Life ; and that it was desirable to awaken, if possible, a more extensive interest on the subject among Christians of every name ; and stir them up to the adoption of some measure, which might lead to a general circulation of the Scriptures. The suggestion was heartily entertained, and warmly supported by the rest of the company; and its discussion led to those incipient efforts, which, in 1804, issued in the organization of the British and Foreign Bible Society. The little spring of Bala soon became a stream large enough for a man to swim in; and now it widens and deepens into a great river, on which float the merchandise of Zion, and the navies of God.

Welshmen! it is your privilege and honor, as well as your duty, to sustain this excellent institution. It is a native of Wales, born in your northern mountains. It is your own child, and you are bound to protect and support it to the extent of your ability. I call upon you as Welshmen, to aid an institution originating in Welsh philanthropy. I call upon you as Welsh Baptists, to help forward an enterprise which sprang from the heart of a Welsh Baptist minister. I appeal to you in the language of another :—

" The cause in which we are engaged is the cause of God, and must succeed. Divine goodness has inspired, divine wisdom and power will sustain it. The Bible will be carried throughout the habitable globe. Nor deserts—nor oceans—nor Alpine solitudes —nor Himalayan heights, will obstruct its progress. It will go through polar ice and equatorial fire, wherever a soul may possibly be saved. It will go on victorious, like the sword of the Lord and of Gideon, carrying every thing before it. Error and delusion must vanish as the mists of the morning before the rising splendor of the sun. The powers of darkness must recede like spectres before the bursting of the day-spring from on high. False gods and their altars must fall together in the dust. The followers of Confucius and Zoroaster will take up their cross and follow Christ. The wandering Arab will sit and sing at Messiah's feet ; and the deluded disciples of Mohammed, instead of going in painful pilgrimage to Mecca, will turn their penitent eyes to Calvary. The dark places of the earth will be enlightened, and the habitations of cruelty will become the abodes of love. Rivers will no longer roll with human blood, nor sacrificial fires be fed with human victims. Mothers will no longer destroy their innocent children, nor aged parents be immolated by their inhuman offspring. Marriage will be instituted in places where it is now unknown, and savage practices be supplanted by the virtuous institutions of the gospel. The Cannibal of New Zealand will be humanized, and the Caffre and the Hottentot clothed and in their right minds. The descendants of Abraham must be gathered from the four quarters of the earth; Jerusalem arise and shine ; and the dejected Jordan roll his streams with joy. Barren climes will teem with life—dreary deserts blossom as the rose. Rivers of salvation will run down the hills, and fertilize the plains. The Saviour will ride forth in the chariot of the everlasting gospel, conquering and to conquer. Nations will fall down before him, and mountains melt at his approach. And thus nation after nation will be converted, and empire upon empire will be conquered; and Christianity will spread from clime to clime, and from pole to pole ; until the final arrival of the blessed day, when the knowledge of the Lord shall literally cover the earth as the waters cover the deep—when there shall be but one people and one God —when the millennial day shall burst upon the earth, like a flood of glory from on high—when the trump of Jubilee shall sound, and countless millions of the redeemed shall sing, Hallelujah! the Lord God omnipotent reigneth!"

Such, brethren, is the approaching triumph of Emmanuel. The mighty angel, having found an old copy of the everlasting gospel, which the Pope had kept locked up in his bureau for many centuries, is flying in the midst of heaven, in sight of all the world. His progress is rapid as the wings of the wind, and his sweet strong voice is publishing the glad tidings to all people. But we look for greater things than these. Following, comes another mighty angel, casting a great millstone into the sea, and saying— " Thus shall Babylon, that great city, be thrown down, and found no more at all." Another follows, crying with a loud voice— " Babylon is fallen, is fallen!" Another descends with the key and the chain, and binds the dragon in the bottomless pit. Then appears one " like unto the Son of Man," sitting upon a white cloud, and wearing a golden crown. He thrusts in his sharp sickle, and reaps the harvest of the earth, and gathers the wheat into his garner, the church. Again the sickle falls, and the vintage of wickedness is gathered, and cast into the wine-press of the wrath of Almighty God. Then comes the voice of a great multitude, as of many waters and mighty thunderings—the blended minstrelsy of earth and heaven—ascribing salvation and dominion and glory to him that sitteth upon the throne, and to the Lamb for ever and ever.

The Prince of Darkness, with all his infernal hosts, and all his allies upon earth, is fearfully agitated, as he witnesses the preparation for the great decisive battle. " Why so much benevolence? Why so many societies? Why such extraordinary schemes and efforts?" Nothing disturbs them so much as the sight of Emmanuel's troops, with their faces toward the field of Armageddon, led on by the Captain of their Salvation, on his white horse, with his vesture dipped in blood. They know that this is the Lion of the tribe of Judah; and the redness of his apparel, reminding them of their defeat when he bruised their heads on Calvary, shoots consternation and anguish through all their ranks; and the gates of hell tremble at the shaking of the iron rod in his hand, which shall dash them in pieces as a potter's vessel. But the saints are rejoicing in his train; for they know that not one of the faithful shall perish—that not one of them shall be wounded—that each shall be more than conqueror, and all shall appear with songs of everlasting joy at the marriage supper of the Lamb.

And now, my brethren, children of my heavenly Father, of every name and order, loved with the same love, redeemed with the same blood, called by the same Spirit, clothed with the same garment, fed on the same manna, engaged in the same cause—the great Missionary enterprise—as you love the Savior as you appreciate his salvation, as you desire the introduction of his millennial kingdom, we beseech you to give us a liberal contribution!

We are now ready to receive your money for Missionary purposes; and while you are casting it into the treasury, let me remind you that your gold and your silver are beautiful birds plumed for flight, that Christian liberality is the scissors with which you may clip their wings, and a short winged bird is better than none. May we all act to-day as stewards of the Lord, in the immediate presence of our Master, before whom we must soon appear to account for the use made of our talents; and when the time of reckoning shall come, may each receive the gracious plaudit— " Well done, good and faithful servant! thou hast been faithful over a few things, I will make thee ruler over many! Enter thou into the joy of thy Lord!" Amen.

Sermon **8**

THE SUFFERINGS OF CHRIST

Who his own self bore our sins in his own body on the tree; that we, being dead to sins, should live unto righteousness; by whose stripes ye were healed (1 Peter 2:24).

WHAT great encouragement to patience and fortitude is afforded the followers of Jesus, by the apostle's contrast of the light and transient afflictions of the present time, with the eternal weignt of glory reserved for them in heaven! How forcible the argument which he draws from the approaching scenes of another world, to urge Christians in this to a life of holiness and self-denial! How vivid and terrible his picture of the dissolution of nature by the great conflagration! Imagine the heavens wrapped in dissolving flames, and the elements melting to the centre of the globe. The victorious and inextinguishable fire towers to the empyrean; the magnificent palace of creation is lost in the smoke of its own burning; and the ear is stunned, and the soul is horrified, by the crash of its final fall. " Seeing then, that all these things must be dissolved, what manner of persons ought ye to be in all holy conversation and godliness; looking for, and hasting unto the coming of the day of God;" " using all diligence to make your calling and election sure;" "that ye may be found of him in peace, without spot, and blameless;" that " so an abundant entrance may be ministered unto you, into the everlasting kingdom of our Lord and Saviour Jesus Christ!"

Such, substantially, is the argument. But the apostle employs another; the Christian's obligation to imitate Christ, suffering for him as he suffered for us, with the same fortitude and resignation, though not to the same extent, nor for the same purpose. It is in this connection he uses the language of the text :- " Servants, be subject to your masters with all fear; not only to the good and gentle, but also to the froward. For this is thankworthy, if a man for conscience toward God endure grief, suffering wrongfully. For what glory is it, if, when ye be buffeted for your faults, ye shall take it patiently? but if, when ye do well, and suffer for it, ye take it patiently, this is acceptable with God. For even hereunto were ye called: because Christ also suffered for us, leaving us an example, that ye should follow his steps: who did no sin, neither was guile found in his mouth: who, when he was reviled, reviled not again; when he suffered, he threatened not; but committed himself to him that judgeth righteously: who his own self bare our sins in his own body on the tree, that we, being dead to sins, should live unto righteousness: by whose stripes ye were healed." We are to suffer for Christ as his disciples and confessors; he suffered for us as our substitute, our atoning sacrifice and Saviour. Let us attend, first, to this description of his sufferings; and then to the end for which he endured them.

I. The text describes Christ in his vicarious sufferings, as *bearing our sins;* bearing our sins, *his own self;* bearing our sins, his own self, *in his own body;* and bearing our sins, his own self, in his own body, *on the tree.*

1. *He bore our sins.* To get a correct understanding of this expression, we must turn to the record of the ordinance to which it alludes, which is as follows:—" And when he hath made an end of reconciling the holy place, and the tabernacle of the congregation, and the altar, he shall bring the live goat, and Aaron shall lay both his hands upon the live goat, and confess over him all the iniquities of the children of Israel, and all their transgressions, in all their sins, putting them on the head of the goat; and shall send him away, by the hand of a fit man, into the wilderness; and the goat shall bear upon him all their iniquities into a land not inhabited; and he shall let go the goat in the wilderness." But this part of the ceremony was preceded by another, of very solemn import. A goat was selected for a sin-offering. He was brought before the Lord, and Aaron put his hands upon him, and devoted him to death. He was slain, and his blood was sprinkled upon the altar and the mercy-seat. Then the sins of the children of Israel were laid upon the head of the other goat, and he was led forth, and

sent away into the wilderness, to return no more. Both these goats represented Christ; who, as our Savior, answers to both; at once, suffering for our sins, and bearing them away into the land of forgetfulness.

Three things were found continually in the temple; fire, and blood, and sweet incense. The fire denoted the wrath of God against sin; the blood prefigured the sacrificial sufferings of Christ; and the sweet incense typified his intercession at the right hand of the Father, on the ground of his vicarious death upon the cross. The goat of the sin-offering was bound and slain; and then burnt up, with the fat thereof, upon the altar. So Christ was crucified for us without the gates of Jerusalem; and his humanity was consumed by the fire of God's holy indignation against sin, on the altar of his Divinity; while from that altar ascended a column of the sweetest incense to the heaven of heavens—" Father, forgive them!" In hell also there is fire, where sinners suffer upon the altars of eternal justice. Every sacrifice is salted with fire, and the smoke of their torment ascendeth up for ever and ever. But the black and sulphurous smoke of the bottomless pit is not a sweet smelling savor unto God, like the fumes of the sacrifice once offered on Calvary—a sacrifice which satisfied the claim of Heaven, and expiated the offence of earth.

The form of expression used in our text is one which frequently occurs in the Old Testament, and signifies the enduring of punishment. Of the impenitent sinner it is said, " He shall bear his iniquity"—that is, he shall endure the just punishment of his sins. He shall carry the burden alone, and for ever sink beneath the load, and mercy shall never come to his relief. Christ's bearing our sins, then, signifies his enduring the punishment in our stead. Glory to God, that every poor trembling sinner may cast his burden upon one who is able to sustain it, who has already sustained it in his stead! The law passed the guilty, and arrested the guiltless. Jesus willingly gave himself up as the victim, saying—" I am he; if ye seek me, let these go their way." His sufferings constitute the sea, in which are buried for ever the sins of his people; sins of the greatest magnitude; sins of the deepest dye. The Father, who turned his back upon the sufferings of his Son, hath said—" I will cast all thy sins behind my back, into the depth of the sea." This is the abyss, in which they are swallowed up, and seen no more.

2. He bore our sins, *his own self.* God and man were parties at variance. There was but one who could stand between them as mediator, and he gave himself a substitute and sacrifice for the sinner. Uniting in his person the two natures, human and Divine, he was fully qualified for his work; and by once offering himself, he satisfied the demands of the insulted law, and "became the author of eternal salvation to all them that obey him." He offered up himself, without the aid of another; and it was his own blessed person that he threw between you and the destroying angel, between you and the mortal plague of sin, between you and the unquenchable fires of hell.

None but Moses, the mediator, could penetrate the thick darkness in which, as in a pavilion, God dwelt, upon the mount of terror; and none but Aaron, the high-priest, dared enter the holy of holies, and he only once a year, on the great day of atonement, with trembling steps, and sacrificial blood. So Jesus, the mediator of a better covenant, and high-priest of the true sanctuary, the sum and substance of all the types and shadows of the old dispensation, when, in the garden of Gethsemane, he approached the black and terrible cloud, where God revealed the terrors of his justice, and the fierceness of his wrath, said to his disciples :—" Tarry ye here, while I go yonder. Ye cannot go; the place is too dreadful. I will go alone." Alone he went; and as he drew near the furnace, his countenance was marvellously altered, his heart melted in the midst of his bowels, and the very substance of his life pressed through the pores of his skin. All the visible fire which flamed on the summit of Sinai, now breaks forth anew on Calvary; and though unseen by man, envelopes in its burning the soul and the body of our glorious Substitute. Behold him rushing between you and the flames, shielding you, and quenching the flames in his blood!

3. He bore our sins, his own self, *in his own body.* Atonement was made for the sins of Israel by the blood of slaughtered beasts. But " the blood of bulls and goats, and the ashes of an heifer, sprinkling the unclean, sanctified only to the purifying of the flesh.' The blood of Christ alone has power to "purge the conscience from dead works, to serve the living God." It was his own body, that our blessed Redeemer offered as a sacrifice for our sins, a sacrifice of a sweet savor unto God. The Divine person bore the

punishment of sins in human nature. "It was not possible that the blood of bulls and goats should take away sins." We hear the Son saying to the Father:—"Sacrifice and offering thou wouldest not, but a body hast thou prepared for me. I see that the services of the altar are of no avail, and are passing away. In burnt-offerings and sacrifices for sin thou hast no pleasure. At this moment, the great cause of difference between heaven and earth remains untaken away. The bills are all uncancelled. The handwriting in the book of the law, and in the book of conscience, continues in full force unto this day. But lo, I come to do thy will, O my God. Yea, thy law is within my heart. I delight to honor its claims, while I save its violaters. I will obey, even unto the death of the cross, and expiate human transgression by my meritorious sufferings. Then, as first begotten from the dead, will I declare the decree which thou didst read to me before the foundation of the world— 'Thou art my Son; this day have I begotten thee. Because I have bruised thee, and put thee to grief, thou shalt see thy seed, and prolong thy days; and the pleasure of the Lord shall prosper in thy hand. Because thou hast borne the sins of many, thou shall justify many. Because thou hast been numbered with the transgressors, and made intercession for them, thou shalt see of the travail of thy soul, and be satisfied. Because thou hast made thy soul an offering for sin, pouring it out unto death, I will divide thee a portion with the great, and thou shalt divide the spoil with the strong. I will make thee king in Zion, and thou shalt reign for ever and ever!'"

The sufferings of the Son are accomplished, and the promise of the Father is receiving its fulfilment. The law of the Spirit of Life hath gone forth; and sinners, with songs of salvation, are crowding to the cross!

4. He bore our sins, his own self, in his own body, *on the tree.* In Deut. xxi. 22, 23, we find that death by hanging on a tree was .eemed an accursed death. Paul refers to this passage in the third chapter of his epistle to the Galatians :—"As it is written ; cursed is every one that hangeth on a tree." By consenting to crucifixion, Christ was "made a curse for us." What shame and ignominy did he endure in our behalf! See him arrayed in royal purple, the reed of scorn in his hand, the crown of thorns upon his head, and the cross of infamy upon his back. He grows faint beneath his

burden. His murderers, fearing lest his woes should pass endurance before their cruel thirst for his blood could be satiated, compel Simon of Cyrene to carry one end of the cross. Thus they move on to the summit of Calvary. They lay the tree upon the ground, and stretch the Son of God upon it, and nail his hands and his feet to the wood. It is reared on high, with its bleeding victim; and there he hangs, before the gazing world, and the wondering heavens; suffering the most excruciating death ever invented, the most shameful in the sight of man, the most accursed in the sight of God. All the springs of consolation are sealed to the glorious sufferer; and he finds not a single drop of comfort in his great extremity. True, the fountains of the deep are broken up, and the windows of heaven are opened; but not to supply him with drink who saith—"I thirst!" From below burst forth upon him the streams of hellish rage, a fiery deluge from the mouth of the dragon; while from above Divine Justice pours down a cataract of wrath, overwhelming his soul with agony, and baptizing his body with blood. This is the baptism which he anticipated in talking with his disciples:—"I have a baptism to be baptized with, and how am I straitened till it be accomplished!" Let us pause a moment to contemplate this baptism. It was the anguish of his soul, wringing the blood from his person, till the crimson dew stood thick upon his brow, and rolled down in great drops to the ground. The sufferings of his soul constituted the soul of his sufferings. "My soul is exceeding sorrowful, even unto death." It was not the taunt of the rabble, the derision of the governors, nor the cruelly lacerating scourge, that Jesus dreaded in the garden, and deprecated in that mysterious agony. Nor was it the thorns, the nails, the tree, or the spear. It was the burden, O man! of thy guilt; the flaming curse of the law; the felt displeasure of the Father against sin. When the martyrs suffered death for Jesus' sake, they rejoiced in the midst of the fire, for the Son of man was there to sustain them; but when Christ suffered, the Just for the unjust, he felt the hidings of his Father's face, and cried after him through the blackening heavens— "My God! my God! why hast thou forsaken me!"

In the Bible we read of two very remarkable trees; "the tree of the knowledge of good and evil in the midst of the garden," and the tree of redemption high planted on "the place of skulls." Milton

has made the former the theme of his majestic song, which he
opens with the following strain :—

> "Of man's first disobedience, and the fruit
> Of that forbidden tree, whose mortal taste
> Brought death into the world, and all our wo,
> With loss of Eden,   *   *   *   *   *
> *   *   *   *   * sing, Heavenly Muse!"

But let me extol that mysterious tree of life on Golgotha, by
which,—

> ————"One Greater Man
> Restores us, and regains the blissful seat!"

"Sing, Heavenly Muse," of Jesus and his cross! Sing of the
wormwood and the gall, of the strife and the triumph of Calvary!
Let us compare these two trees. By the former, "the first Adam"
transgressed, and entailed ruin upon his posterity; by the latter,
"the second Adam" "became obedient unto death," and "brought
life and immortality to light." By a forbidden approach to the one,
the chain of the covenant was broken, Paradise forfeited, God's image
and favor lost, the league with hell signed, and sealed, and ratified,
and the whole earth converted into a province of the Prince of
Darkness, and delivered up to the despotism of Sin and Death;
but four thousand years afterward, the Son of God took his stand
on the other, wrestled gloriously with the tyrant usurpers, dethroned
Satan, condemned and abolished Sin, swallowed up Death in
victory, disannulled the league of earth with hell, restored to
believers the favor and image of God, reopened the gates of the
forfeited Eden to the exiles, and established a new and everlasting
covenant of grace. The blood of Jesus cancelled the debt of man,
and quenched the wrath of God; and from all them that obey him,
it will ultimately wash away all the stains of sin, and all the dust
of death. This is the newly consecrated way into the holy of
holies; this is eternal life! "Sing, Heavenly Muse," once more!

> "We too with him are dead,
> And shall with him arise:
> The cross on which he bows his head
> Shall lift us to the skies!"

Thus, the Son of God, "his own self, bore our sins, in his own
body, on the tree." The burden beneath which he fainted was
our burden, and would have sunk us to perdition. It was for us

he suffered and died. Though our iniquities were laid on him, they were yet our iniquities. He endured the punishment in our stead. He stood between us and the uplifted arm of Justice; and the sword which would have cleft our souls asunder, was sheathed in Emmanuel's heart. His righteousness, imputed to us, and appropriated by faith, is " the righteousness of God, which is unto all and upon all them that believe," covering their sins, and rendering them " accepted in the Beloved."

Can we pass by mount Calvary, and gaze upon that wondrous sight, and still remain unmoved? Have we no tears of gratitude and love? Pause we not to wonder and adore? O the depth of the riches! the riches of his wisdom! the riches of his grace!

II. Having thus spoken of Christ's vicarious sufferings, let us notice a little more particularly the end for which he endured them. " That we, being dead to sins, should live unto righteousness; by whose stripes ye were healed."

This death unto sin, and this new life unto righteousness, denote the sanctification of the soul " by the renewing of the Holy Spirit." The " spiritually minded" man is made, through the grace of God, a " partaker of the Divine nature." He has received a new principle, whereby his lusts and corruptions are mortified, crucified, and slain. The right hand that offended is cut off; the right eye that offended is plucked out. He delights in the law of God; he feels a strong desire, and makes strenuous efforts, to conform himself, in heart and life, to its holy requirements. Made free from the dominion and condemning power of sin, he still needs, however, the aid of the Holy Spirit, to crucify the old man; to live soberly, righteously, and godly, in this present evil world; to die to sins, and live unto righteousness. In the court of heaven, he is justified by the righteousness of Christ; but before men, he is justified by his own righteousness. " Let your light so shine before men, that they may see your good works, and glorify your Father who is in heaven." Be as a candle, not under a bushel, but on a candlestick, enlightening all around you. Paul to the Ephesians says, that Christ loved the Church, and gave himself for it, that he might sanctify and cleanse it with the washing of water by the word; that he might present it to himself a glorious church, not having spot or wrinkle, or any such thing, but that it should be holy and without blemish. God hath not called us unto uncleanness but unto holiness. Let us, therefore cleanse ourselves from all filthiness—from all manner of pollution—of the flesh and spirit, perfecting holiness in the fear of God. For it is written, Be ye holy, for I am holy; holy in all manner of conversation; holy in all stations, relations, and conditions of life—as husbands and wives, parents and children, masters and servants; and this always, and in all places—at home and abroad, in private and in public, in prosperity and adversity. Our conversation should be such as becometh the nature and requirements of the gospel of Christ. Forgetting the things that are behind, we should be ever pressing forward towards those things that are before—not as though we had already attained, either were already perfect; but making perfection our mark; for we know not yet what we shall be, but one thing we do know—that when he shall appear, we shall be like him! Then, and not till then, shall we be satisfied, when we awake in his likeness. We must be conformed to the image of God's Son in this world, otherwise we cannot have the enjoyment of him in the world to come. We must have the spirit of Christ, to love righteousness, and to hate iniquity. We must imitate his example in zeal and activity, doing our Father's work while the day lasts. Die to sin, we must. "For if ye live after the flesh, ye shall die, but if ye through the spirit do mortify the deeds of the body, ye shall live." Mortify therefore your members which are upon the earth. Put off the old man with all his deceitful lusts, and put on the new man, which, after God, is created in righteousness and true holiness. Abstain from those fleshy lusts that war against the soul; always keeping in mind, that they that are Christ's have crucified the flesh, with the affections and lusts. To die to sin, implies a perfect hatred of it, deep sorrow and contrition on account of it, and a constant desire and effort to forsake it. We should conscientiously use all the means of grace, and depend entirely upon the grace of God, as that by which alone we can obtain a victory—final and complete,—over all our enemies, the flesh, the world, and the devil. Be sober, be vigilant, because your adversary, the devil, as a roaring lion goeth about, seeking whom he may devour. Good reason have you to pray without ceasing, that you may be made strong in the Lord, and in the power of his might. You must put on the whole armor of God, that you may be able to stand against the wiles of the devil Your loins must be girt about with truth. The breast-plate of righteousness you must wear. Your heart must be protected by the shield of faith, and your feet shod with the preparation of the gospel of peace. Forget not the helmet of salvation, nor the sword of the Spirit, nor to write often to the King—directing to the care of Jesus, that your petitions may not fail—"Praying always with all prayer and supplication in the spirit, and watching thereunto with all perseverance and supplication for all saints." As ye formerly yielded your members servants to uncleanness, even so now yield your members servants of righteousness unto holiness. Live unto righteousness. Yield yourselves up unto God, as those that are alive from the dead, and your members as instruments of righteousness unto God. Conform to his revealed will, and keep an eye single to his glory in the performance of every duty.

To produce in his people this happy change, was the end of Messiah's sufferings. But this was not all, for the apostle adds,— "By whose stripes ye were healed." Divine philosophy! supernatural science! transcending all original conception of men and angels! Who could ever have dreamed of healing by his stripes, soundness by his wounds, pleasure by his pains, and life eternal by his death! We are afflicted by the old inveterate plague of sin, but there is balm in Gilead, and a Physician there. His blood alone can cure the malady, and that is infallible. All the way from Bethlehem to Calvary, he was employed in preparing his materia medica. The Gospel is the great store-house of this precious preparation. It is always full; it is always free; and the sign over its entrance is—"Able to save to the uttermost." The Holy Spirit is continually making the application, and all who come are cured.

It is a matter of all others the most momentous, that we know our personal interest in these things. If we be not dead to sins, and alive unto righteousness—if we be not healed by the stripes of Jesus—his sufferings upon the cross, and our theoretical faith in their vicarious character and saving power, will profit us nothing. "If any man have not the spirit of Christ, he is none of his." There is a vast difference between sanctification and morality. A man may perform many excellent deeds, while the principle that actuates him is averse to true godliness. Happy are they, whose sins are pardoned, whose persons are justified, and whose bodies are become temples of the Holy Ghost. The Lord is their God and Father. They have passed from death unto life, and shall not come into condemnation. "There is now no condemnation to them that are in Christ Jesus, who walk not after the flesh, but after the Spirit; for the law of the Spirit of life, in Christ Jesus, hath made me free from the law of sin and death."

Sermon 9

THE PURIFICATION OF CONSCIENCE

How much more shall the blood of Christ, who through the eternal Spirit offered himself without spot to God, purge your conscience from dead works to serve the living God? (Hebrews 9:14).

THE Hebrew Christians, to whom the apostle wrote, were well acquainted with the laws of ceremonial purification by the blood of beasts and birds, for by blood almost every thing was purified in the service of the temple. But it is only the blood of Christ that can purge the human conscience. In speaking of this purification, as presented in our text, let us notice—*the object, the means*, and *the end*.

I. The object of this purification is the conscience; which all the sacrificial blood shed, from the gate of Eden, down to the extinction of the fire on the Jewish altar, was not sufficient to purge.

What is the conscience? An inferior judge, the representative of Jehovah, holding his court in the human soul; according to whose decision we feel either confidence and joy in God, or condemnation and tormenting fear. His judicial power is graduated by the degree of moral and evangelical light which has been shed upon his palace. His knowledge of the will and the character of God is the law by which he justifies or condemns. His intelligence is the measure of nis authority; and the perfection of knowledge would be the infallibility of conscience.

This faithful recorder and deputy judge is with us through all the journey of life, and will accompany us with his register over the river Jordan, whether to Abraham's bosom or the society of the rich man in hell. While conscience keeps a record on earth, Jehovah keeps a record in heaven; and when both books shall be opened in the final judgment, there shall be found a perfect correspondence. When temptations are presented, the understanding opposes them, but the carnal mind indulges them, and there is a contest between the judgment and the will, and we hesitate which to obey, till the warning bell of conscience rings through the soul, and gives distinct notice of his awful recognition; and when we turn away recklessly from his faithful admonitions, we hear low mutterings of wrath stealing along the avenues, and the quick sound of writing-pens in the recording office, causing every denizen of the mental palace to tremble.

There is *a good conscience, and an evil conscience.* The work of both, however, is the same; consisting in keeping a true record of the actions of men, and passing sentence upon them according to their deserts. Conscience is called good or evil only with reference to the character of its record and its sentence. If the record is one of virtues, and the sentence one of approval, the conscience is good; if the record is one of vices, and the sentence one of condemnation, the conscience is evil.

Some have a *guilty conscience;* that is, a conscience that holds up to their view a black catalogue of crimes, and rings in their ears the sentence of condemnation. If you have such a conscience, you are invited to Jesus, that you may find peace to your souls. He is ever in his office, receiving all who come, and blotting out with his own blood the handwriting which is against them.

But some have a *despairing conscience.* They think that their crimes are too great to be forgiven. The registry of guilt, and the decree of death, hide from their eyes the mercy of God, and the merit of Christ. Their sins rise like mountains between them and heaven. But let them look away to Calvary.. If their sins are a thousand times more numerous than their tears, the blood of Jesus is ten thousand times more powerful than their sins. "He is able to save to the uttermost all that come unto God by him, seeing he ever liveth to make intercession for them."

And others have a *dark and hardened conscience.* They are so deceived, that they "cry peace and safety, when destruction is at the door." They are "past feeling, having the conscience seared as with a hot iron." They have sold themselves to work evil; to eat sin like bread, and drink iniquity like water. They have bribed or gagged the recorder and accuser within them. They will betray the just cause of the righteous, and slay the messengers of salvation, and think that they are doing God service. John the Baptist is beheaded, that Herod may keep his oath of honor. A dead fish cannot swim against the stream; but if the king's conscience had been alive and faithful, he would have said:—" Girl, I promised to give thee thy request, even to the half of my kingdom; but thou hast requested too much; for the head of Messiah's herald is more valuable than my whole kingdom, and all the kingdoms of the world!" But he had not the fear of God before his eyes, and the proud fool sent and beheaded the prophet in his cell.

A *good conscience* is a faithful conscience, a lively conscience, a peaceful conscience, a conscience void of offence toward God and man, resting in the shadow of the cross, and assured of an interest in its infinite merit. It is the victory of faith unfeigned, working by love, and purifying the heart. It is always found in the neighborhood and society of its brethren; " a broken heart, and a contrite spirit;" an intense hatred of sin, and an ardent love of holiness; a spirit of fervent prayer and supplication, and a life of scrupulous integrity and charity; and above all, an humble confidence in the mercy of God, through the mediation of Christ. These constitute the brotherhood of Christianity; and wherever they abound, a good conscience is never lacking. They are its very element and life; its food, its sunshine, and its vital air.

Conscience was a faithful recorder and judge under the law; and notwithstanding the revolution which has taken place, introducing a new constitution, and a new administration, Conscience still retains his office; and when "purged from dead works to serve the living God," is appropriately called a *good conscience*.

II. The means of this purification is "the blood of Christ, who through the Eternal Spirit offered himself without spot to God."

Could we take in, at a single view, all the bearings of "the blood of Christ," as exhibited in the gospel, what an astonishing light would it cast upon the condition of man; the character of God; the nature and requirements of his law; the dreadful consequences of sin; the wondrous expiation of the cross; the reconciliation of Heaven and earth; the blessed union of the believer with God in Christ, as a just God and a Savior; and the whole scheme of our justification, sanctification, and redemption, through free, sovereign, infinite, and unspeakable grace!

There is no knowledge like the knowledge of Christ, for the excellency of which the apostle counted all things but loss. Christ is the Sun of Righteousness, in whose light we see the tops of the mountains of immortality, towering above the dense clouds which overhang the valley of death. All the wisdom which philosophers have learned from nature and providence, compared with that which is afforded by the Christian Revelation, is like the ignis fatuus compared with the sun. The knowledge of Plato, and Socrates, and all the renowned sages of antiquity, was nothing to the knowledge of the feeblest believer in " the blood of Christ."

" The blood of Christ" is of infinite value. There is none like it flowing in human veins. It was the blood of a man, but of a man who knew no iniquity; the blood of a sinless humanity, in which dwelt all the fullness of the Godhead bodily; the blood of the second Adam, who is the Lord from heaven, and a quickening spirit upon earth. It pressed through every pore of his body in the garden; and gushed from his head, his hands, his feet, and his side, upon the cross. I approach with fear and trembling, yet with humble confidence and joy. I take off my shoes, like Moses, as he draws near the burning bush; for I hear a voice coming forth from the altar, saying—" I and my Father are one ; I am the true God, and eternal life."

The expression, " the blood of Christ," includes the whole of his obedience to the moral law, by the imputation of which we are justified ; and all the sufferings of his soul and his body as our Mediator, by which an atonement is made for our sins, and a fountain opened to wash them all away. This is the spring whence rise the rivers of forgiving and sanctifying grace.

In the representation which the text gives us of this redeeming blood, are several points worthy of our special consideration :—

1. It is *the blood of Christ ;* the appointed Substitute and Saviour of men; "the Lamb of God, that taketh away the sins of the world."

2. It is the blood of Christ, *who offered himself.* His humanity was the only sacrifice which would answer the demands of justice, and atone for the transgressions of mankind. Therefore " he made his soul an offering for sin."

3. It is the blood of Christ, who offered himself *to God*. It was the eternal Father, whose broken law must be repaired, whose dishonored government must be vindicated, and whose flaming indignation must be turned away. The well beloved Son must meet the Father's frown, and bear the Father's curse for us. All the Divine attributes called for the offering; and without it, could not be reconciled to the sinner.

4. It is the blood of Christ, who offered himself to God, *without spot*. This was a perfect sacrifice. The victim was without blemish or defect; the altar was complete in all its appurtenances; and the high-priest possessed every conceivable qualification for his work. Christ was at once victim, altar, and high-priest; "holy, harmless, and undefiled;" "God manifest in the flesh." Being himself perfect God, and perfect man, and perfect Mediator between God and man, he perfects for ever all them that believe.

5. It is the blood of Christ, who offered himself to God, without spot, *through the eternal Spirit*. By the eternal Spirit here, we are to understand, not the third person of the Godhead, but the second; Christ's own Divine nature, which was co-eternal with the Father before the world was; and which, in the fulness of time, seized on humanity, sinless and immaculate humanity, and offered it body and soul, as a sacrifice for human sins. The eternal Spirit was at once the priest that offered the victim, and the altar that sanctified the offering. Without this agency, there could have been no atonement. The offering of mere humanity, however spotless, aside from the merit derived from its connection with Divinity, could not have been a sacrifice of sweet-smelling savor unto God.

6. It is the blood of Christ, who offered himself to God, without spot, through the eternal Spirit, *that he might purge your conscience*. As the typical sacrifices under the law purified men from ceremonial defilement, so the real sacrifice of the Gospel saves the believer from moral pollution. Blood was the life of all the services of the tabernacle made with hands, and gave significance and utility to all the rites of the former dispensation. By blood the covenant between God and his people was sealed. By blood the officers and vessels of the sanctuary were consecrated. By blood the children of Israel were preserved in Egypt from the destroying angel. So the blood of Christ is our justification, sanctification, and redemption. All the blessings of the gospel flow to us through the blood

of the Lamb. Mercy, when she writes our pardon, and when she registers our names in "the Book of Life," dips her pen in the blood of the Lamb. And the vast company that John saw before the throne had come out of great tribulation, having "washed their robes and made them white in the blood of the Lamb."

The children of Israel were delivered from Egypt, on the very night that the paschal lamb was slain, and its blood sprinkled upon the doorposts, as if their liberty and life were procured by its death. This typified the necessity and power of the atonement, which is the very heart of the gospel, and the spiritual life of the believer. In Egypt, however, there was a lamb slain for every family; but under the new covenant God has but one family, and one Lamb is sufficient for their salvation.

In the cleansing of the leper, several things were necessary; as running water, cedar wood, scarlet and hyssop, and the finger of the priest; but it was the blood that gave efficacy to the whole. So it is in the purification of the conscience. Without the shedding of blood, the leper could not be cleansed; without the shedding of blood, the conscience cannot be purged. "The blood of Christ" seals every precept, every promise, every warning, of the New Testament. "The blood of Christ" renders the Scriptures "profitable for doctrine, for reproof, for correction, for instruction in righteousness." "The blood of Christ" gives efficiency to the pulpit; and when "Jesus Christ and him crucified" is shut out, the virtue is wanting which heals and restores the soul. It is only through the crucifixion of Christ, that "the old man" is crucified in the believer. It is only through his obedience unto death, even the death of the cross, that our dead souls are quickened, to serve God in newness of life.

Here rest our hopes. "The foundation of God standeth sure." The bill of redemption being presented by Christ, was read by the prophets, and passed unanimously in both houses of parliament. It had its final reading in the lower house, when Messiah hung on Calvary; and passed three days afterward, when he rose from the dead. It was introduced to the upper house by the Son of God himself, who appeared before the throne "as a lamb newly slain," and was carried by acclamation of the heavenly hosts. Then it became a law of the kingdom of heaven, and the Holy Ghost was sent down to establish it in the hearts of men. It is "the perfect law of liberty," by which God is reconciling the world unto himself It is " the law of the Spirit of Life," by which he is "purging our conscience from dead works to serve the living God."

III. The end of this purification is twofold :—that we may cease from dead works, and serve the living God.

1. The works of unrenewed souls are all " dead works," can be no other than " dead works," because the agents are " dead in trespasses and sins." They proceed from "the carnal mind," which " is enmity against God," which " is not subject to the law of God, neither indeed can be." How can a corrupt tree bring forth good fruit, or a corrupt fountain send forth pure water?

But " the blood of Christ is intended to " purge the conscience from dead works." The apostle says—" Ye are not redeemed with corruptible things, as silver and gold, from your vain conversation, received by tradition from your fathers ; but with the precious blood of Christ, as of a lamb without blemish, and without spot." The Jews were in a state of bondage to the ceremonial law, toiling at the " dead works," the vain and empty forms, which could never take away sin ; and unjustified and unregenerate men are still captives of Satan, slaves of sin and death, tyrannized over by various evil habits and propensities, which are invincible to all things but " the blood of Christ." He died to redeem, both from the burdens of the Mosaic ritual, and from the despotism of moral evil—to purge the conscience of both Jew and Gentile " from dead works, to serve the living God."

2. We cannot " serve the living God," without this preparatory purification of conscience. If our guilt is uncancelled—if the love of sin is not dethroned—the service of the knee and the lip is nothing but hypocrisy. " If we regard iniquity in our hearts, the Lord will not hear us." Cherishing what he hates, all our offerings are an abomination to him ; and we can no more stand in his holy presence than the dry stubble can stand before a flaming fire. He who has an evil conscience, flees from the face of God, as did Adam in the garden. Nothing but " the blood of Christ," applied by the Holy Spirit, can remove the sinner's guilty fear, and enable him to draw nigh to God in the humble confidence of acceptance through the Beloved.

The service of the living God must flow from a new principle of life in the soul. The Divine word must be the rule of our actions.

The Divine will must be consulted and obeyed. We must remember that God is holy, and jealous of his honor. The consideration that he is everywhere, and sees every thing, and will bring every work into judgment, must fill us with reverence and godly fear. An ardent love for his law and his character must supplant the love of sin, and prompt to a cheerful and impartial obedience.

And let us remember that he is " the *living* God." Pharaoh is dead, Herod is dead, Nero is dead; but Jehovah is " the living God," and it is a fearful thing to have him for an enemy. Death cannot deliver from his hand. Time, and even eternity, cannot limit his holy anger. He has manifested, in a thousand instances, his hatred of sin; in the destruction of the old world, the burning of Sodom and Gomorrah, the drowning of Pharaoh and his host in the sea; and I tell thee, sinner, except thou repent, thou shalt likewise perish! O, think what punishment " the living God" can inflict upon his adversaries—the loss of all good—the endurance of all evil—the undying worm—the unquenchable fire—the blackness of darkness for ever!

The gods of the heathen have no life in them, and they who worship them are like unto them. But our God is " the living God," and " the God of the living." If you are united to him by faith in " the blood of Christ," your souls are " quickened together with him," and " the power which raised him from the dead shall also quicken your mortal body."

May the Lord awaken those who are dead in trespasses and sins, and revive his work in the midst of the years, and strengthen the feeble graces of his people, and bless abundantly the labors of his servants, so that many consciences may be purged from dead works to serve the living God!

> " There is a fountain filled with blood,
>   Drawn from Emmanuel's veins,
> And sinners, plunged beneath that flood,
>   Lose all their guilty stains.
>
> " The dying thief rejoiced to see
>   That fountain in his day;
> And there may I, as vile as he,
>   Wash all my sins away.
>
> " Dear dying Lamb! thy precious blood
>   Shall never lose its power,
> Till all the ransomed sons of God
>   Are saved to sin no more!"

Sermon 10

THE CEDAR OF GOD

Thus saith the Lord God: I will also take of the highest branch of the high cedar, and will set it; I will crop off from the top of his young twigs a tender one, and plant it upon a high mountain and eminent; in the mountain of the height of Israel will I plant it: and it shall bring forth boughs, and bear fruit, and be a goodly cedar; and under it shall dwell all fowl of every wing; in the shadow of the branches thereof shall they dwell; and all the trees of the field shall know that I, the Lord, have brought down the high tree, have exalted the low tree, have dried up the green tree, and have made the dry tree to flourish. I, the Lord, have spoken and have done it (Ezekiel 17:22-24).

You perceive that our text abounds in the beautiful language of allegory. In the context is portrayed the captivity of the children of Israel, and especially the carrying away of the royal family, by the king of Babylon. Here God promises to restore them to their own land, in greater prosperity than ever; and to raise up Messiah, the Branch, out of the house of David, to be their king. All this is presented in a glowing figurative style, dressed out in all the wealth of poetic imagery, so peculiar to the orientals. Nebuchadnezzar, the great eagle—the long-winged, full-feathered, embroidered eagle—is represented as coming to Lebanon, and taking the highest branch of the tallest cedar, bearing it off as the crow bears the acorn in its beak, and planting it in the land of traffic. The Lord God, in his turn, takes the highest branch of the same cedar, and plants it on the high mountain of Israel, where it flourishes and bears fruit, and the fowls of the air dwell under the shadow of its branches.

We will make a few general remarks on the character of the promise, and then pass to a more particular consideration of its import.

I. This is an *evangelical* promise. It relates to the coming and kingdom of Messiah. Not one of the kings of Judah since the captivity, as Boothroyd well observes, answers to the description here given. Not one of them was a cedar whose branches could afford shadow and shelter for all the fowls of heaven. But the prophecy receives its fulfilment in Christ, the desire of all nations, to whom the ends of the earth shall come for salvation.

This prophecy bears a striking resemblance in several particulars, to the parable of the mustard-seed, delivered by our Lord. The mustard-seed, said Jesus, " is the least of all seeds ; but when it is grown, it is the greatest among herbs, and becometh a tree, so that the birds of the air come and lodge in the branches thereof." So the delicate twig of the young and tender branch becomes a goodly cedar, and under its shadow dwell all fowl of every wing. The prophecy and the parable are alike intended to represent the growth and prosperity of Messiah's kingdom, and the gracious protection and spiritual refreshment afforded to its subjects. Christ is the mustard plant, and cedar of God ; and to him shall the gathering of the people be ; and multitudes of pardoned sinners shall sit under his shadow with great delight, and his fruit shall be sweet to their taste.

This prophecy is a promise of the true, and faithful, and immutable God. It begins with—" Thus saith the Lord God, I will do thus and so ;" and concludes with—" I, the Lord, have spoken, and I have done it." There is no peradventure with God. His word is for ever settled in heaven, and cannot fail of its fulfilment. When he says—" I promise to pay," there is no failure, whatever the sum. The bank of heaven cannot break. It is the oldest and best in the universe. Its capital is infinite ; its credit is infallible. The mighty God, the everlasting Father, the Prince of Peace, is able to fulfil to the utmost all his engagements. He can do any thing that does not imply a contradiction, or a moral absurdity. He could take upon himself the form of a servant, and become obedient unto death, even the death of the cross ; but he can never forget or disregard his promise, any more than he can cease to exist. His nature renders both impossible. Heaven and earth shall pass away, but his word shall not pass away. Every jot and tittle shall be fulfilled. This is the consolation of the church. Here rested the patriarchs and the prophets. Here reposes the faith of the saints to the end of time. God abideth faithful ; he cannot deny himself. Our text is already partially verified in the advent of Christ, and the establishment of his church; the continuous growth of the gospel kingdom indicates its progressive fulfil- ment; and we anticipate the time, as not far distant, when the whole earth shall be overshadowed by the branches of the cedar of God.

II. We proceed to consider, with a little more particularity, the import of this evangelical prophecy. It describes the character and mediatorial kingdom of Christ, and the blessings which he confers upon his people.

1. His character and mediatorial kingdom. "I will take of the highest branch of the high cedar, and will set it; I will crop off from the top of his young twigs a tender one, and plant it upon a high mountain and eminent; in the mountain of the height of Israel will I plant it."

Christ, as concerning the flesh, is of the seed of Abraham—a rod issuing from the stem of Jesse, and a branch growing out of his root. "As the new vine is found in the cluster, and one saith, destroy it not, for a blessing is in it;" so the children of Israel were spared, notwithstanding their perverseness and their back- slidings, because they were the cluster from which should be expressed in due time the new wine of the kingdom—because from them was to come forth the blessing, the promised seed in whom all the families of the earth shall be blessed. The Word that was in the beginning with God, one with God in essence and in attri- butes, in the fulness of time assumed our nature, and tabernacled and dwelt among us. Here is the union of God and man. Here is the great mystery of godliness—God manifest in the flesh. But I have only time now to take off my shoes, and draw near the burning bush, and gaze a moment upon this great sight.

The Father is represented as preparing a body for his Son. He goes to the quarry to seek a stone, a foundation stone for Zion. The angel said to Mary:—"The Holy Ghost shall come upon thee, and the power of the Highest shall overshadow thee; there- fore that Holy Thing which shall be born of thee shall be called the Son of God." The eternal lays hold on that nature which is hastening downward, on the flood of sin, to the gulf of death and destruction, and binds it to himself. Though made in the likeness of sinful flesh, he was holy, harmless, and undefiled. He did no iniquity, neither was guile found in his mouth. The rod out of the stem of Jesse is also Jehovah our righteousness. The child born in Bethlehem is the mighty God. The Son given to Israel is the everlasting Father. He is of the seed of Abraham, according to the flesh; but he is also the true God and eternal life. Two natures and three offices meet mysteriously in his person. He is at once the bleeding sacrifice, the sanctifying altar, the officiating priest, the prophet of Israel, and the Prince of Peace. All this was necessary, that he might become " the author of eternal salvation to all them that obey him."

Hear Jehovah speaking of Messiah and his kingdom :—" Why do the heathen rage, and the people imagine a vain thing? The kings of the earth set themselves, and the rulers take counsel together against the Lord, and against his anointed. Yet have I set my king upon my holy hill of Zion. I will declare the decree by which he is to rule his redeemed empire." That decree, long kept secret, was gradually announced by the prophets; but at the new tomb of Joseph of Arimathea, Jehovah himself proclaimed it aloud, to the astonishment of earth, the terror of hell, and the joy of heaven :—" Thou art my Son ; this day have I begotten thee. Come forth from the womb of the grave, thou whose goings forth have been from of old, even from everlasting. Ask of me, and I shall give thee the heathen for thine inheritance, and the uttermost parts of the earth for thy possession. I will exalt thee to the throne of the universe, and thou shalt be chief in the chariot of the gospel. Thou shalt ride through the dark places of the earth, with the lamps of eternal life suspended to thy chariot, enlightening the world. Be wise now, therefore, O ye kings ; be instructed ye judges of the earth. Serve the Lord with fear, and rejoice with trembling. Kiss the Son, lest he be angry, and ye perish from the way when his wrath is kindled but a little. Let no man withstand him. Let no man seek to stay his progress. Herod, Pilate, Caiaphas, stand off! clear the way! lest ye be crushed beneath the wheels of his chariot! for that which is a savor of life to some, is to others a savor of death ; and if this stone shall fall upon you, it shall grind you to powder !"

Behold, here is wisdom ! All other mysteries are toys in comparison with the mystery of the everlasting gospel—the union of three persons in the Godhead—the union of two natures in the

Mediator—the union of believers to Christ, as the branches to the vine—the union of all the saints together in him, who is the head of the body, and the chief stone of the corner—the mighty God transfixed to the cross—the son of Mary ruling in the heaven of heavens—the rod of Jesse becoming the sceptre of universal dominion—the Branch growing out of his root, the little delicate branch which a lamb might crop for its food, terrifying and taming the serpent, the lion, the leopard, the tiger, and the wolf, and transforming into gentleness and love the wild and savage nature of all the beasts of prey upon the mountain! "And such," old Corinthian sinners, "were some of you; but ye are washed, ye are sanctified, ye are justified, in the name of the Lord Jesus, and by the spirit of our God." And such, my brethren, were some of you; but ye have been made a new creation in Christ Jesus; old things are passed away, and all things are become new. Ye are dead, and your life is hid with Christ in God. He is one with the Father, and ye are one in him; united and interwoven, like the roots of the trees in the forest of Lebanon; so that none can injure the least disciple of Christ, without touching the apple of his eye, and grieving all his members.

2. The blessings which he confers upon his people. "It shall bring forth boughs, and bear fruit, and be a goodly cedar, and under it shall dwell all fowl of every wing; in the shadow of the branches thereof shall they dwell; and all the trees of the field shall know that I, the Lord, have brought down the high tree, and have exalted the low tree—have dried up the green tree, and have made the dry tree to flourish."

Christ is a fruitful tree. "The tree is known by his fruit. Men do not gather grapes of thorns, nor figs of thistles. Every good tree bringeth forth good fruit, and every evil tree bringeth forth evil fruit." This is a singular, supernatural tree. Though its top reaches to the heaven of heavens, its branches fill the universe, and bend down to the earth, laden with the precious fruits of pardon, and holiness, and eternal life. On the day of Pentecost, we see them hang so low over Jerusalem, that the very murderers of the Son of God reach and pluck and eat, and three thousand sinners feast on more than angels' food. That was the feast of first-fruits. Never before was there such a harvest and such a festival. Angels know nothing of the delicious fruits of the tree of redemption

They know nothing of the joy of pardon, and the spirit of adoption. The bride of the Lamb alone can say :—" As the apple tree among the trees of the forest, so is my beloved among the sons. I sat down under his shadow with great delight, and his fruit was sweet to my taste. He brought me also to his banqueting house, and his banner over me was love."

These blessings are the precious effects of Christ's mediatorial work; flowing down to all believers, like streams of living water. Come, ye famishing souls, and take, without money and without price. All things are now ready. " The mandrakes give a smell, and at our gates are all manner of pleasant fruits, both new and old." Here is no scarcity. Our Elder Brother keeps a rich table in our Father's house. Hear him proclaiming in the streets of the city, in the chief places of concourse :—" Come to the festival. There is bread enough, and to spare. My oxen and my fatlings are killed. My board is spread with the most exquisite delicacies – wine on the lees well refined, and fruits such as angels never tasted."

Christ is a tree of protection to his people. This cedar not only beautifies the forest, but also affords shade and shelter for the fowls of the air. We have the same idea in the parable of the mustard seed :—" the birds of the air came and lodged in the branches thereof." This is the fulfilment of the promise concerning the Shiloh :—" to him shall the gathering of the people be." It is the drawing of sinners to Christ ; and the union of believers with God.

" All fowl of every wing." Sinners of every age and every degree—sinners of all languages, colors, and climes—sinners of all principles, customs, and habits—sinners whose crimes are of the blackest hue—sinners carrying about them the savor of the brimstone of hell—sinners deserving eternal damnation—sinners perish ing for lack of knowledge—sinners pierced by the arrows of conviction—sinners ready to sink under the burden of sin—sinners overwhelmed with terror and despair—are seen flying to Christ as a cloud, and as doves to their windows—moving to the ark of mercy before the door is shut—seeking rest in the shadow of this goodly cedar !

Christ is the sure defence of his church. A thousand times has she been assailed by her enemies. The princes of the earth have set themselves in array against her, and hell has opened upon her all its batteries. But the Rock of Ages has ever been her strong fortress and high tower. He will never refuse to shelter her from her adversaries. In the time of trouble, he shall hide her in his pavilion; in the secret of his tabernacle shall he hide her. When the heavens are dark and angry, she flies, like the affrighted dove, to the thick branches of the "Goodly Cedar." There she is safe from the windy storm and tempest. There she may rest in confidence, till these calamities be overpast. The tree of her protection can never be riven by the lightning, nor broken by the blast.

Christ is the source of life and beauty to all the trees in the garden of God. Jehovah determined to teach "the trees of the forest" a new lesson. Let the princes of this world hear it, and the proud philosophers of Greece and Rome. "I have brought down the high tree, and exalted the low tree—have dried up the green tree, and made the dry tree to flourish." Many things have occurred, in the providence of God, which might illustrate these metaphors; such as the bringing of Pharaoh down to the bottom of the sea, that Israel might be exalted to sing the song of Moses; and the drying up of the pride and pomp of Haman, that Mordecai might flourish in honor and esteem. But for the most transcendant accomplishment of the prophecy, we must go to Calvary. There is the high tree brought down to the dust of death, that the low tree might be exalted to life eternal; the green tree dried up by the fires of Divine wrath, that the dry tree might flourish in the favor of God for ever.

To this, particularly, our blessed Redeemer seems to refer, in his address to the daughters of Jerusalem, as they follow him, weeping, to the place of crucifixion. "Weep not for me," saith he. "There is a mystery in all this, which you cannot now comprehend. Like Joseph, I have been sold by my brethren; but like Joseph, I will be a blessing to all my Father's house. I am carrying this cross to Calvary that I may be crucified upon it between two thieves; but when the lid of the mystical ark shall be lifted, then shall ye see that it is to save sinners I give my back to the smiters, and my life for a sacrifice. Weep not for me, but for yourselves and your children; for if they do these things in the green tree, what shall be done in the dry? I am the green tree to-day; and behold, I am consumed that you may flourish. I am the high tree, and am prostrated that you may be exalted."

The fire-brands of Jerusalem had wellnigh kindled to a flame of themselves, amid the tumult of the people, when they cried out— " Away with him! Crucify him! His blood be on us, and on our children !" O wonder of mercy! that they were not seized and consumed at once by fire from heaven! But he whom they crucify prays for them, and they are spared. Hear his intercession :— "Father, forgive them! Save these sinners, ready for the fire. On me, on me alone, be the fierceness of thy indignation. I am ready to drink the cup which thou hast mingled. I am willing to fall beneath the stroke of thy angry justice. I come to suffer for the guilty. Bind me in their stead, lay me upon the altar, and send down fire to consume the sacrifice !"

It was done. I heard a great voice from heaven :—" Awake, O sword, against my shepherd! Kindle the flame! Let off the artillery !" Night suddenly enveloped the earth. Nature trembled around me. I heard the rending of the rocks. I looked, and lo ! the stroke had fallen upon the high tree, and the green tree was all on fire! While I gazed, I heard a voice, mournful, but strangely sweet :—" My God! my God! why hast thou forsaken me? My heart is like wax; it is melted in the midst of my bowels. My strength is dried up like a potsherd, and my tongue cleaveth to my jaws. One may tell all my bones. Dogs have compassed me about; strong bulls of Bashan have beset me. They stare at me ; they gape upon me with their mouths; they pierce my hands and my feet. Deliver my soul from the lions; my darling from the power of the dogs !"

" It is finished !" O with what majestic sweetness fell that voice upon my soul! Instantly the clouds were scattered. I looked, and saw, with unspeakable wonder, millions of the low trees shooting up, and millions of the dry trees putting forth leaves and fruit. Then I took my harp, and sang this song :—" Worthy is the Lamb! for he was humbled that we might be exalted; he was wounded that we might be healed ; he was robbed that we might be enriched; he was slain that we might live !"

Then I saw the beam of a great scale ; one end descending to the abyss, borne down by the power of the atonement; the other ascending to the heaven of heavens, and lifting up the prisoners of the tomb. Wonderful scheme! Christ condemned for our justifi cation; forsaken of his Father, that we might enjoy his fellowship·

passing under the curse of the law, to bear it away from the believer for ever! This is the great scale of redemption. As one end of the beam falls under the load of our sins, which were laid on Christ; the other rises, bearing the basket of mercy, full of pardons, and blessings, and hopes. "He who knew no sin was made sin for us"—that is his end of the beam; "that we might be made the righteousness of God in him"—this is ours. "Though he was rich, yet for our sakes he became poor"—there goes his end down; "that we, through his poverty, might be rich"—here comes ours up.

O sinners! ye withered and fallen trees, fuel for the everlasting burning, ready to ignite at the first spark of vengeance! O ye faithless souls! self-ruined and self-condemned! enemies in your hearts by wicked works! we pray you in Christ's stead, be ye reconciled to God! He has found out a plan for your salvation—to raise up the low tree by humbling the high, and save the dry tree from the fire by burning up the green. He is able to put, at the same time, a crown of glory on the head of the law, and a crown of mercy on the head of the sinner. One of those hands which were nailed to the cross blotted out the fiery handwriting of Sinai, while the other opened the prison-doors of the captives. From the mysterious depths of Messiah's sufferings flows the river of the water of life. Eternal light rises from the gloom of Gethsemane. Satan planted the tree of death on the grave of the first Adam, and sought to plant it also on the grave of the second; but how terrible was his disappointment and despair, when he found that the wrong seed had been deposited there, and was springing up unto everlasting life! Come! fly to the shelter of this tree, and dwell in the shadow of its branches, and eat of its fruit, and live!

To conclude:—Is not the conversion of sinners an object dear to the hearts of the saints? God alone can do the work. He can say to the north, give up; and to the south, keep not back. He can bring his sons from afar, and his daughters from the ends of the earth. Our Shiloh has an attractive power, and to him shall the gathering of the people be. Pray, my brethren, pray earnestly, that the God of all grace may find them out, and gather them from the forest, and fish them up from the sea, and bring them home as the shepherd brings the stray lambs to the fold. God alone can catch these "fowl of every wing." They fly away from us. To our grief, they often fly far away, when we think them almost in our hands; and then the most talented and holy ministers cannot overtake them. But the Lord is swifter than they. His arrows will reach them and bring them from their lofty flight to the earth. Then he will heal their wounds, and tame their wild nature, and give them rest beneath the branches of the "Goodly Cedar."

Sermon 11
THE PRINCE OF SALVATION

For it became him, for whom are all things, and by whom are all things, in bringing many sons to glory, to make the captain of their salvation perfect through sufferings (Hebrews 2:10).

And being made perfect, he became the author of eternal salvation unto all them that obey him (Hebrews 5:9).

I HAVE put these passages together because of their similarity. In discussing the doctrine which they contain—the doctrine of salvation through the mediatorial work of Christ, I purpose to consider—*First*, His relation to believers, as the author, captain, or prince of their salvation; *Secondly*, His perfect qualification, through meritorious sufferings, to sustain that relation; and *Thirdly*, The character of those who are interested in him as a Saviour.

I. Christ is the prince of our salvation. He is the great antetype of Moses, Joshua, Samson, and David. Their deeds of pious valor faintly foreshadowed the glorious achievements of the Captain of our salvation.

He is a prince in our nature. The Lord from heaven became the second Adam, the seed of the woman, the offspring of David. Divinity and humanity were mysteriously united in his person. The Word that was in the beginning was made flesh, and tabernacled among us. God is now nearer to his people than ever. The Lamb's bride is bone of his bone and flesh of his flesh. As the children were partakers of flesh and blood, he himself took part of the same. By taking human nature into union with himself, he has imparted to believers a new and divine life.

Our Prince has conquered our adversaries. His name is Michael, the power of God. He is the mighty prince that stood up on behalf of his people, and bruised Satan under their feet. He has cast out the strong man, and his goods. He has demolished the kingdom of darkness, spoiled principalities and powers, and made a show of them openly. He has proved to earth and heaven that the devil is a usurper, and has no claim whatever to the title, "God of this world," and "Prince of this world." When Christ was crucified, hell quaked to its centre. Then he obtained liberty for the captives, and the opening of the prisons to them that are bound. His victory is our manumission from the slavery of sin and death ; and if the Son make us free, we are free indeed.

Three offices meet in the Author of our salvation ; the prophetic, the priestly, and the regal. He wears three crowns upon his head ; a crown of gold, a crown of silver, and a crown of precious stones. He " shall bear the glory, and shall sit and rule upon his throne, and shall be a priest upon his throne, and the covenant of peace shall be between them both." This prophecy is fulfilled in Messiah's mediatorial relations. The house was purified, the altar was consecrated, on the morning of his resurrection. This is the Prince of life, who was dead, and is alive for evermore, and hath the keys of hell and of death. That he might sanctify the people with his own blood, he suffered without the gate ; and by suffering, he opened a way for believers into the holiest of all ; and lo ! his people are standing before the mercy-seat within the vail, and worshipping in open sight of the glory of God that dwelleth between the cherubim. If God smelled " a savor of rest" in the sacrifice of Noah, much more in the sacrifice of his beloved Son, in whom he is ever well pleased. His sinless soul and body were offered once for all upon the cross. " He bore the sins of many, and made intercession for the transgressors." The Father proclaims the demands of his law fully answered, and invites sinners to come and rest in the Beloved. This is he of whom it was said—"A man shall be as a hiding-place from the wind, and a covert from the tempest ; as rivers of water in a dry place ; as the shadow of a great rock in a weary land." This is the Author and Captain of our salvation.

II. Let us consider how he is qualified for that relation—made perfect through sufferings.

His sufferings were necessary to constitute him a complete Saviour. "Without the shedding of blood is no remission;" the blood of Jesus is "a fountain opened for sin and uncleanness." It was threatened—"In the day thou eatest thereof thou shalt surely die;" but Christ, by dying in our stead, delivered us from the sentence.

In order that he might bear our sins, it was necessary for him to assume our nature. The Priest must have somewhat to offer as a sacrifice. Divinity could not suffer and die. "A body hast thou prepared for me." The Son of God took that body as his own, and offered it to the Father upon the cross. The blood which he shed was his own blood; the life which he laid down was his own life; the soul which he poured out unto death was his own soul. Moses saw an emblem of this mystery in Mount Horeb—a bush burning with fire, yet unconsumed. "Our God is a consuming fire," dwelling in a tabernacle of clay. The human nature, though slain, is not consumed. On the third day the bush is found still flourishing and fruitful.

It was necessary that the precept of the law should be obeyed, and the penalty of the law endured, in the very nature of its violater. Christ answered the demands of both tables on behalf of his people, in the purity of his life, and the merit of his obedience unto death. He displayed all the fruits of holiness. He loved righteousness and hated iniquity. He paid our debt, a debt which he never contracted; he endured our curse, a curse which he never deserved. He took the cup of the wine of wrath out of our hand, and drained its very dregs upon the cross. In hell, every one drinks his own cup, and can never exhaust its contents; but behold, on Calvary, one man drains the cup of millions, and cries—"It is finished!" Not a drop is left, not a particle of any of its ingredients, for his people. God hath condemned and punished sin in the human nature of Christ, and all who believe are justified freely by his blood.

But the author of our salvation is God as well as man. The Divinity often shone out through the humanity, controlling the elements, quickening the tenants of the tomb, and compelling the very devils to obey him. Had he been less than "God manifest in the flesh," he must have been incompetent to the work of redemption. The Divine nature was necessary to sustain the human nature under its immense burden of sufferings, and render those sufferings sufficiently meritorious to atone for the transgressions of mankind. Christ endured more of the Divine displeasure "from the sixth to the ninth hour," than all the vessels of wrath could endure to all eternity ;* and but for the union of the two natures in his person, he could not have borne his unparalleled woes. But while the man suffered, the God sustained. While the God-man offered up his humanity, his Divinity was the altar that sanctified the gift, and rendered it a sacrifice of sweet smelling savor to the Father. It was man that died upon the cross, but it was man in mysterious union with God, so that the two natures constituted but one person, and the dignity of the Godhead gave infinite value to the tears and sweat and blood of the manhood. No wonder that the cross of Christ is the admiration of men and angels ; and—" worthy is the Lamb that was slain !" the ultimate theme of earth and heaven !

"And being made perfect." In the twentieth chapter of Exodus, we read of "the ram of consecration"—the ram of perfection in the original, or full ram, as the word full signifies complete, mature, perfect. The two rams mentioned in that chapter represent the atonement and intercession of Christ. He is our full, complete, or perfect sacrifice. "In him dwelleth the fulness of the God-head ;" and he has the hand of a man to bestow blessings upon his brethren. "Of his fulness have all we received, and grace upon grace." Our wisdom, righteousness, sanctification, and redemption are all in the Son of man. Aaron never entered the holy place with empty hands, and our great High-priest hath gone into the celestial sanctuary, bearing with him his own most precious blood, wherewith to sprinkle the mercy-seat, and make it approachable to man. Thus suffering on earth, and pleading the merit of his suffering in heaven, "he becomes the author of eternal salvation to all them that obey him."

III. This leads us to our third topic. The character of those who are interested in him as a Saviour—" all them that obey him."

To obey is to submit to authority—to do what is commanded. What is the command of God the Father? That ye should believe on the name of his Son. What is the command of Christ, the Captain of our salvation? "Ye believe in God; believe also in

---

* This sentiment, in different forms, occurs very frequently in these sermons. It is questionable theology.—Ed.

me." It is said that he is precious to them that believe, but unbe-
lievers are disobedient. They are all a disaffected and rebellious
army, who will not obey their Captain. They have made God a
liar, and are condemned for their unbelief. The Father saith—
"Kiss the Son, lest he be angry!" but they reply—"Away with
him! away with him! we will not have him to reign over us!"

Is this your character? You are commanded to "behold the
Lamb of God, that taketh away the sin of the world." Have you
obeyed? What are you doing? Are you determined to rebel?
Will you risk the consequences of disobedience? O, you are reading the book of election, are you? You are looking for your names
in the book of election; but lo! you find them written in the book
of damnation, under the article—"He that believeth not shall not
see life, but the wrath of God abideth on him!" What shall be
done in such a case? Obey the Captain of your salvation. Do ye
not hear him, as he rides along the ranks, proclaiming—"To-day,
if ye will hear my voice, harden not your hearts, as in the provoca-
tion! Incline your ear, and come unto me; hear, and your soul
shall live!" Obey, obey this gracious exhortation. Come, with
your petitions for pardon. Believe on the Lord Jesus Christ, and
you shall be saved. Behold a door of hope opening for you in the
blood of atonement. There is forgiveness and sanctification for all
that believe. Does your sense of guilt overwhelm you with gloomy
fears, and plunge you in despair? Do you tremble at the thought
of the multitude and enormity of your crimes? Cry aloud, with all
your hearts—"God be merciful to me a sinner!" Remember that
your Prince "is able to save unto the uttermost all that come unto
God by him." Hear him calling you—"Come unto me, all ye
that labor and are heavy laden, and I will give you rest! Take
my yoke upon you, and learn of me; for I am meek and lowly in
heart; and ye shall find rest to your souls; for my yoke is easy,
and my burden is light!" Who, then, would not obey thee,
blessed Jesus?

> "Had I, dear Lord, a thousand hearts,
>   I'd give them all to thee;
>   A thousand tongues, they all should join
>   The grateful harmony!"

We have a remarkable instance of faith and obedience in Abraham. There was no natural probability, there was no apparent

possibility of the fulfilment of the promise ; but Abraham believed, rested on the naked word of God, and went to mount Moriah to offer up his only son. Here was the triumph of faith, and it is recorded for our encouragement. Did the patriarch firmly believe the promise—" In Isaac shall thy seed be called?" Yes verily, and it was accounted to him for righteousness. Did the patriarch believe, on the strength of that promise, that God would not permit him to offer up his only son ? No, verily ; but he was determined to obey God, and leave the event with him, well assured that God would fulfil his word, though it should require the miracle of Isaac's resurrection. Thus your faith must soar above nature, and lay hold on the righteousness of Christ, which justifieth the ungodly. When you believe with all your heart, God will smile upon you, and calm your troubled soul, and hush the raging storms of a guilty conscience, for the sake of the satisfaction which he received in the obedience of Christ, as the substitute and surety of his people. This is the Urim and Thummim—light and perfection—of the gospel, beaming upon us through the twelve stars—the apostles of the Lamb, pacifying the conscience, and answering the important question—" What shall I do to be saved ?" I feel within me a sea of corruption, but I know that the blood of Jesus Christ cleanseth from all sin.

Faith and obedience are inseparable, and the former is dead without the latter. They wrought together in Abel, and therefore he offered a more excellent sacrifice than Cain. They wrought together in Noah, and led him to prepare an ark to the saving of his house. Abraham not only believed that God would give him and his seed the land of Canaan ; but he set forth at the Divine command, not knowing whither he went. Moses not only believed that God would deliver Israel out of Egypt ; but, in obedience to his command, he " refused to be called the son of Pharaoh's daughter ; choosing rather to suffer affliction with the people of God, than to enjoy the pleasures of sin for a season." Thus, true faith always leads to obedience. It is a living principle, by which the soul is quickened from the death of sin to a new life of holiness. It is the means through which, by the Holy Ghost, we are created anew in Christ Jesus unto good works. It works by love, and love is always the great motive to obedience. It gives us large and clear views of the love of God in Christ ; then " we love him because he first loved us ;" and " this is the love of God, that we keep his commandments." Thus, by faith, " the love of God is shed abroad in our hearts," leading us to a holy life. Such is the connection between faith and obedience, and the necessity of one to the other.

And now, brethren, let us trust in the Captain of our salvation. In the ages before his advent, many sons were brought to glory through faith in his future sufferings. In the fulness of time, he visited our world ; assumed our nature ; atoned for our transgressions ; and, ascending to the right hand of the Father, as our representative and intercessor, " became the author of eternal salvation to all them that obey him."

> " O Captain of salvation ! make
> Thy power and glory known,
> Till clouds of willing captives come,
> And worship at thy throne !"

Sermon 12
FINISHED REDEMPTION

It is finished (John 19:30).

THIS exclamation derives all its importance from the magnitude of the work alluded to, and the glorious character of the agent. The work is the redemption of the world; the agent is God manifest in the flesh. He who finished the creation of the heavens and the earth in six days, is laying the foundation of a new creation on Calvary. Four thousand years he has been giving notice of his intention to mankind; more than thirty years he has been personally upon earth, preparing the material; and now he lays the chief corner stone in Zion, exclaiming—" It is finished."

We will first consider the special import of the exclamation, and then offer a few remarks of a more general character.

I. "It is finished." This saying of the Son of God is a very striking one; and, uttered, as it was, while he hung in dying agonies upon the cross, cannot fail to make a strong impression upon the mind. It is natural for us to inquire—" What does it mean? To what does the glorious victim refer?" A complete answer to the question would develope the whole scheme of redemption. We can only glance at a few leading ideas.

The sufferings of Christ are ended. Never again shall he be persecuted from city to city, as an impostor and servant of Satan. Never again shall he say—" My soul is exceeding sorrowful, even unto death." Never again shall he agonize in Gethsemane, and sweat great drops of blood. Never again shall he be derided by the rabble, and insulted by men in power. Never again shall he be crowned with thorns, lacerated by the scourge, and nailed to the accursed tree. Never again shall he cry out, in the anguish of his soul, and the baptism of blood—"My God! my God! why hast thou forsaken me!"

The predictions of his death are fulfilled. The prophets had spoken of his crucifixion many hundred years before his birth. They foresaw the Governor who was to come forth from Bethlehem. They knew the babe in the manger, as he whose goings forth are of old, even from everlasting. They drew an accurate chart of his travels, from the manger to the cross, and from the cross to the throne. All these things must be fulfilled. Jesus knew the necessity, and seemed anxious that every jot and tittle should receive an exact accomplishment. His whole life was a fulfilment of prophecy. On every path he walked, on every house he entered, on every city he visited, and especially on the mysterious phenomena which accompanied his crucifixion, it was written—"that the Scriptures might be fulfilled."

The great sacrifice for sin is accomplished. For this purpose Christ came into the world. He is our appointed high-priest, the elect of the Father, and the desire of nations. He alone who was in the bosom of the Father, could offer a sacrifice of sufficient merit to atone for human transgression. But it was necessary also that he should have somewhat to offer. Therefore a body was prepared for him. He assumed the seed of Abraham, and suffered in the flesh. This was a sacrifice of infinite value, being sanctified by the altar of Divinity on which it was offered. All the ceremonial sacrifices could not obtain the bond from the hand of the creditor. They were only acknowledgments of the debt. But Jesus, by one offering, paid the whole, took up the bond—the handwriting that was against us, and nailed it to his cross; and when driving the last nail, he cried—"It is finished!"

The satisfaction of Divine justice is completed. The violated law must be vindicated; the deserved penalty must be endured; if not by the sinner himself, yet by the sinner's substitute. This was the great undertaking of the Son of God. He "bore our sins"—that is, the punishment of our sins—"in his own body on the tree." He was "made a curse for us, that we might be made the righteousness of God in him." There was no other way by which the honor of God and the dignity of his law could be sustained, and therefore "the Lord laid upon him the iniquities of us all." He "died unto sin once;" not merely for sin, enduring its punishment in our stead; but also

" unto sin," abolishing its power, and putting it away. Therefore it is said, he " made an end of sin"—destroyed its condemning and tormenting power on behalf of all them that believe. His sufferings were equal to the claims of justice ; and his dying cry was the voice of Justice himself proclaiming the satisfaction. Here, then, may the dying thief, and the persecutor of the holy, lay down their load of guilt and wo at the foot of the cross.

The new and living way to God is consecrated. A vail has hitherto concealed the holy of holies. None but the high-priest has seen the ark of the covenant, and the glory of God resting upon the mercy-seat between the cherubim. He alone might enter, and he but once a year, and then with fear and trembling, and the sprinkling of atoning blood, after the most careful purification, and sacrifice for himself and the people. But our great High-priest has made an end of sacrifice by the one offering of himself. He has filled his hands with his own blood, and entered into heaven itself, there to appear in the presence of God for us. The sweet incense which he offers fills the temple, and the merit of his sacrifice remains the same through all time, superseding all other offering for ever. Therefore we are exhorted to come boldly to the throne of grace. The tunnel under the Thames could not be completed on account of an accident which greatly damaged the work, without a new subscription for raising money ; but Jesus found infinite riches in himself, sufficient for the completion of a new way to the Father—a living way through the valley of the shadow of death to " the city of the Great King."

The conquest of the powers of darkness is achieved. When their hour was come, the Prince and his hosts were on the alert to accomplish the destruction of the Son of God. They assailed him with peculiar temptations, and leveled against him their heaviest artillery. They instigated one disciple to betray him and another to deny him. They fired the rage of the multitude against him, so that the same tongues that lately sung—" Hosanna to the Son of David !" now shouted—" Crucify him ! Crucify him !" They filled the priests and scribes with envy, that they might accuse him without a cause ; and inspired Pilate with an accursed ambition, that he might condemn him without a fault. They seared the conscience of the false witnesses, that they might charge the Just One with the most flagrant crimes ; and cauterized the hearts of the

Roman soldiers, that they might mock him in his sufferings, and nail him to the cross. Having succeeded so far in their hellish plot, they doubtless deemed their victory certain. I see them crowding around the cross, waiting impatiently to witness his last breath, ready to shout with infernal triumph to the depths of hell, till the brazen walls should send back their echoes to the gates of the heavenly city. But hark! the dying Saviour exclaims—"It is finished!" and the great dragon and his host retreat, howling, from the cross. The Prince of our salvation turned back all their artillery upon themselves, and their own stratagems become their ruin. The old serpent seized Messiah's heel, but Messiah stamped upon the serpent's head. The dying cry of Jesus shook the dominions of death, so that the bodies of many that slept arose; and rang through all the depths of hell, the knell of its departed power. Thus the Prince of this world was foiled in his schemes, and disappointed in his hopes; like the men of Gaza, when they locked up Samson at night, thinking to kill him in the morning; but awoke to find that he was gone, with the gates of the city upon his shoulders. When the Philistines caught Samson, and brought him to their temple, to make sport for them, they never dreamed of the disaster in which it would result—never dreamed that their triumph over the poor blind captive would be the occasion of their destruction. Suffer me, said he, to lean on the two pillars. Then he bowed himself, and died with his enemies. So Christ on Calvary, while the powers of darkness exulted over their victim, seized the main pillars of sin and death, and brought down the temple of Satan upon its occupants; but on the morning of the third day, he left them all in the ruins, where they shall remain for ever, and commenced his journey home to his Father's house.

II. So much concerning the import of our Saviour's exclamation. Such was the work which he finished upon the cross. We add a few remarks of a more general character.

The sufferings of Christ were vicarious. He died, not for his own sins, but for ours. He humbled himself, that we might be exalted. He became poor, that we might be made rich. He was wounded, that we might be healed. He drained the cup of wrath, that we might drink the waters of salvation. He died the shameful and excruciating death of the cross, that we might live and reign with him for ever.

" Ought not Christ to have suffered these things, and to have entered into his glory ?" This " ought" is the ought of mercy and of covenant engagement. He must discharge the obligation which he had voluntarily assumed. He must finish the work which he had graciously begun. There was no other Saviour—no other being in the universe willing to undertake the work ; or, if any willing to undertake, none able to accomplish it. The salvation of one human soul would have been too mighty an achievement for Gabriel—for all the angels in heaven. Had not " the Only Begotten of the Father" become our surety, we must have lain for ever under the wrath of God, amid " weeping, and wailing, and gnashing of teeth." None but the Lion of the tribe of Judah could break the seals of that mysterious book. None but " God manifest in the flesh" could deliver us from the second death.

The dying cry of Jesus indicates the dignity of his nature, and the power of life that was in him to the last. All men die of weakness—of inability to resist death—die because they can live no longer. But this was not the case with the Son of God. He speaks of laying down his life as his own voluntary act ;—" No man taketh it from me, but I lay it down of myself. I have power to lay it down, and I have power to take it again." He " poured out his soul unto death"—did not wait for it to be torn from him— did not hang languishing upon the cross, till life " ebbed out by slow degrees ;" but poured it out freely, suddenly, and unexpectedly. As soon as the work was done for which he came into the world, he cried—" It is finished !" " bowed his head, and gave up the ghost." Then the sun was darkened, the earth quaked, the rocks rent, the graves opened, and the centurion said—" Truly, this man was the Son of God !" He cried with a loud voice, to show that he was still unconquered by pain, mighty even upon the cross. He bowed his head that death might seize him. He was naturally far above the reach of death, his Divine nature being self-existent and eternal, and his human nature entitled to immortality by its immaculate holiness ; yet " he humbled himself, and became obedient unto death, even the death of the cross"—" He bowed his head, and gave up the ghost."

We may regard his last exclamation, also, as an expression of his joy, at having accomplished the great " travail of his soul," in the work of our redemption. It was the work which the Father had given him, and which he had covenanted to do. It lay heavy upon his heart; and O, how was he straitened till it was accomplished! His "soul was exceeding sorrowful, even unto death;" "and his sweat as it were great drops of blood, falling down to the ground." But upon the cross, he saw of the travail of his soul, and was satisfied. He saw that his sacrifice was accepted, and the object of his agony secured—that death would not be able to detain him in the grave, nor hell to defeat the purposes of his grace—that the gates of the eternal city would soon open to receive him as a conqueror, and myriads of exultant angels shout him to his throne; whither he would be followed by his redeemed, with songs of everlasting joy. He saw, and he was satisfied; and, not waiting for the morning of the third day, but already confident of victory, he uttered this note of triumph, and died.

And if we may suppose them to have understood its import, what a source of consolation must it have been to his sorrowing disciples! The sword had pierced through Mary's heart, according to the prediction of old Simeon over the infant Jesus. Her affections had bled at the agony of her supernatural Son, and her wounded faith had wellnigh perished at his cross. And how must all his followers have felt, standing afar off, and beholding their supposed Redeemer suffering as a malefactor! How must all their hopes have died within them, as they gazed on the accursed tree! The tragedy was mysterious, and they deemed their enemies victorious. Jesus is treading the winepress in Bozrah, and the earth is shaking, and the rocks are rending, and the luminaries of heaven are expiring, and all the powers of nature are fainting, in sympathy with his mighty agony. Now he is lost in the fire and smoke of battle, and the dread artillery of justice is heard thundering through the thick darkness, and shouts of victory rise from the troops of hell, and who shall foretell the issue of the combat, or the fate of the Champion? But lo! he cometh forth from the cloud of battle, with blood upon his garments! He is wounded, but he hath the tread and the aspect of a conqueror. He waves his crimsoned sword, and cries —"It is finished!" Courage, ye weepers at the cross! Courage, ye tremblers standing afar off! The Prince of your salvation is victor, and this bulletin of the war shall cheer myriads of believers in the house of their pilgrimage, and the achievement which it announces shall constitute an everlasting theme of praise!

"It is finished!" The word smote on the walls of the celestial city, and thrilled the hosts of heaven with ecstasy unspeakable. How must "the spirits of just men made perfect" have leaped with joy, to hear that the Captain of their salvation was victorious over all his enemies, and that the work he had engaged to do for them and their brethren was completed! and with what wonder and delight must the holy angels have witnessed the triumph of him, whom they were commanded to worship, over the powers of darkness! It was the commencement of a new era in heaven, and never before had its happy denizens seen so much of God.

"It is finished!" Go, ye heralds of salvation, into all the world, and proclaim the joyful tidings! Cry aloud, and spare not; lift up your voice like a trumpet, and publish to all men, that the work of the cross is finished—that the great Mediator, "made perfect through sufferings," has become "the author of eternal salvation to all them that obey him"—"is of God made unto us, wisdom, and righteousness, and sanctification, and redemption!" Go, teach the degraded Pagan, the deluded Mohammedan, and the superstitious Papist, that the finished work of Jesus is the only way of acceptance with God! Go, tell the polished scholar, the profound philosopher, and the vaunting moralist, that the doctrine of Christ crucified is the only knowledge that can save the soul! Go, say to the proud skeptic, the bold blasphemer, and the polluted libertine, "Behold the Lamb of God that taketh away the sin of the world!" Preach it to the gasping sinner upon his death-bed, and the sullen murderer in his cell! Let it ring in every human ear, and thrill in every human heart, till the gladness of earth shall be the counterpart of heaven!

THE RESURRECTION OF
CHRIST

*He is not here; for he is risen, as he said. Come, see the place where the
Lord lay* (Matthew 28:6).

THE celebrated Jonathan Edwards of America begins his History
of Redemption with an account of the Lord's visit to Adam and
Eve at the cool of the day in Eden. All the wonderful works of
God toward the children of men, since the seed of the woman was
promised to bruise the serpent's head, are to be considered as so
many parts of the same great machinery of providence, whose
wheels, like those of Ezekiel's vision, all move in majestic harmony,
though their thousand revolutions may seem to us discordant and
confused. The chief design of all the Divine manifestations recorded in the Old Testament was to prepare the way for the Redeemer's appearance upon earth. Jehovah often suffered his people
to be in great distress and perplexity ; he lengthened the chain of
Satan and his angels, allowed a partial success of their infernal
schemes, and permitted them to prevail for a season against his
people, and pride themselves in their power and their skill, in order
to make their defeat the more signal, and gather more glory to himself from their final overthrow. During the engagement, the victory
often seemed to be on the side of the enemy ; but when the smoke
of battle cleared away, the pillar of God was seen upon the camp
of Israel. If his people are besieged between Pi-hahiroth and Baal-
zephon, he raises the siege by dividing the sea, and making a highway through the deep, while the waters rise up in a solid wall on
the right and the left, and roll back in ruin on the pursuing foe.
If an army comes to arrest Elisha on Carmel, the mountain is

covered with celestial warriors, and the surrounding heavens teem with horsemen and chariots of fire, and the enemy are smitten with blindness, and taken captive by the prophet. If Goliath of Gath confronts the camp of Israel with his challenge, roaring like a lion, till the valley resounds with his voice, a little shepherd-boy goes forth with his sling, and the vaunting blasphemer is smitten to the ground, and slain with his own sword. If the worshippers of the true God are cast into the fiery furnace, or the den of lions, to show the power and gratify the pride of an infamous tyrant, there is one among them " like unto the Son of Man," and the violence of the fire is quenched, and the mouths of the lions are stopped.

But when Messiah was slain and buried, the enemies of God boasted more than ever in their crafty and malicious schemes. This was the great decisive engagement between Heaven and hell. The enemy imagined " the Captain of our salvation" vanquished and destroyed. But his fall was no defeat. He yielded to the powers of darkness apparently, that he might triumph over them openly. He suffered himself to be taken prisoner by death, that he might seize the tyrant on his throne, demolish his empire, and deliver his captives. And if none of his friends on earth had courage to proclaim his resurrection, a preacher descended from heaven to announce the joyful fact:—" He is not here ; for he is risen, as he said. Come, see the place where the Lord lay."

Wonderful message, and wonderful messenger! On the morning of the third day after his crucifixion, Jesus revived in his tomb, and the sound of the earthquake reached the heaven of heavens, and a mighty angel, swifter than the light, descended straight to the new grave in Joseph's garden, calling on no one for the key, instantly rolled away the stone from the door, and sat upon it, and made it his pulpit, from which he preached to the women the doctrine of our Lord's resurrection.

Let us consider, *first*, the testimony by which this fact is sustained, and *secondly*, the fact itself, as the sure basis of Christianity.

I. It appears from the record of the evangelist Luke, that the women were much perplexed at finding the stone rolled away from the mouth of the sepulchre, and the body of Jesus gone. Then they were saluted by two angels in shining apparel, who said ;— " Why seek ye the living among the dead ? He is not here, but is risen. Remember how he spake unto you while he was yet in Galilee, saying--The Son of Man must be delivered into the hands of sinful men, and be crucified, and the third day rise again. And they remembered his words."

Here is the testimony of two credible witnesses, a sufficient number to attest the truth of our Lord's resurrection ; who testified to nothing but what they had personally witnessed, and knew to be fact ; and delivered their testimony in simple and unambiguous language, that could not well be misunderstood.

While the women went to inform the disciples of what they had seen and heard, " behold, some of the watch came into the city, and showed unto the chief priests all the things that were done." And what was done ? What can be the testimony of these enemies of Christ concerning his resurrection ? That " an angel, whose countenance was like lightning, and his garments white as snow, descended from heaven, and rolled away the stone from the door, and sat upon it ;" which so terrified them that they " became as dead men."

To confirm these testimonies, our blessed Lord himself " appeared unto many after his resurrection, who were witnesses of all things which he did, both in the land of the Jews, and at Jerusalem ; and how he was slain, and hanged on a tree ; and how God raised him up the third day, and showed him openly ; not to all the people, but to witnesses chosen before of God ; even to the disciples, who did eat and drink with him after he rose from the dead ; whom he commanded to preach unto the people, and to testify that it is he who is ordained of God to be the judge of quick and dead"—" to whom he showed himself alive after his passion by many infallible proofs ; being seen of them forty days, and speaking of the things pertaining to the kingdom of God."

Here we may observe, that he appeared to those who knew him best, and gave them satisfactory and incontestible evidence of his resurrection. And he appeared, not only to the apostles, but to more than five hundred brethren at once. We have an account of his appearing at ten or eleven different times. On these occasions, he conversed with his disciples, reminded them of what he had said to them before his crucifixion, showed them his hands and his feet, and besought them to touch and examine his person, and satisfy themselves as to his identity. So that they had ample opportunity, and every facility that could be desired, for ascertaining whether he was indeed Jesus of Nazareth, their master, who was lately crucified before their eyes.

It was therefore with great power that the apostles bore witness of the resurrection of the Lord Jesus. And the Holy Spirit corroborated their testimony. Our faith in this distinctive doctrine of Christianity rests on a Divine foundation. " If we receive the witness of men, the witness of God is greater." " And the apostles went forth, and preached everywhere, the Lord also working with them, and confirming the word with signs following." In a few weeks after the resurrection of their Master, their testimony concerning it was received and firmly believed by many thousands, not in some distant and desert part of the world, but in Jerusalem, where he had been crucified.

How nobly the apostle Peter reasoned on this subject when he said :—" Ye men of Israel, hear these words. Jesus of Nazareth, a man approved of God among you, by miracles, and wonders, and signs, which God did by him in the midst of you, as ye yourselves also know; him, being delivered by the determinate counsel and foreknowledge of God, ye have taken, and by wicked hands have crucified and slain ; whom God hath raised up, having loosed the pains of death, because it was not possible that he should be holden of it."

Such was the evidence of our Lord's resurrection, that among those who were living at the time, and even those of them who so strenuously opposed the gospel, it appears to have been scarcely doubted. Pilate, in a letter to Tiberius, the Roman emperor, said, that Jesus, being raised from the dead, was believed by many to be God; whereupon the Roman Senate expressed no doubt of his resurrection, but debated the question of receiving him as one of the gods of Rome ; which, however, was overruled by Divine Providence, for the honor of Christianity ; for he who is higher than heaven, and the heaven of heavens, was not to be ranked with dumb idols upon earth.

II. Let us now consider the fact of our Lord's resurrection, and its bearing upon the great truths of our holy religion.

This most transcendent of miracles is sometimes attributed to the agency of the Father; who, as the Lawgiver, had arrested and imprisoned in the grave the sinner's Surety, manifesting at once his benevolence and his holiness; but by liberating the prisoner, proclaimed that the debt was cancelled, and the claims of the law satisfied. It is sometimes attributed to the Son himself; who had power both to lay down his life, and to take it again; and the merit of whose sacrifice entitled him to the honor of thus asserting his dominion over death, on behalf of his people. And sometimes it is attributed to the Holy Spirit, as in the following words of the apostle:—" He was declared to be the Son of God with power, according to the Spirit of Holiness, by the resurrection from the dead."

The resurrection of Christ is clear and incontestible proof of his Divinity.

He had declared himself equal with God the Father, and one with him in nature and in glory. He had told the people that he would prove the truth of this declaration, by rising from the grave three days after his death. And when the morning of the third day began to dawn upon the sepulchre, lo! there was an earthquake, and the dead body arose, triumphant over the power of corruption.

This was the most stupendous miracle ever exhibited on earth, and its language is:—" Behold, ye persecuting Jews and murdering Romans, the proof of my Godhead! Behold, Caiaphas, Herod, Pilate, the power and glory of your victim! I am he that liveth, and was dead; and lo! I am alive for evermore! I am the root and the offspring of David, and the bright and morning star! Look unto me, and be ye saved, all ye ends of the earth; for I am God, and besides me there is none else!"

Our Lord's resurrection affords incontrovertible evidence of the truth of Christianity.

Pilate wrote the title of Christ in three languages on the cross; and many have written excellent and unanswerable things, on the truth of the Christian Scriptures, and the reality of the Christian religion; but the best argument that has ever been written on the subject, was written by the invisible hand of the Eternal Power, in the rocks of our Saviour's sepulchre. This confounds the skeptic, settles the controversy, and affords an ample and sure foundation for all them that believe.

If any one asks whether Christianity is from heaven or of men, we point him to the "tomb hewn out of the rock," and say— " There is your answer! Jesus was crucified, and laid in that cave; but on the morning of the third day, it was found empty; our Master had risen and gone forth from the grave victorious."

This is the pillar that supports the whole fabric of our religion; and he who attempts to pull it down, like Samson, pulls down ruin upon himself. " If Christ is not risen, then is our preaching vain, and your faith is also vain, ye are yet in your sins;" but if the fact is clearly proved, then Christianity is unquestionably true, and its disciples are safe.

This is the ground on which the apostle stood, and asserted the divinity of his faith :—" Moreover, I testify unto you the gospel, which I preached unto you; which also ye have received, and wherein ye stand; by which also ye are saved, if ye keep in memory what I preached unto you, unless ye have believed in vain ; for I delivered unto you first of all that which I also received, how that Christ died for our sins according to the Scriptures, and that he was buried, and that he rose again the third day, according to the Scriptures."

The resurrection of Jesus is the most stupendous manifestation of the power of God, and the pledge of eternal life to his people.

The apostle calls it " the exceeding greatness of his power to us ward who believe, according to the working of his mighty power, which he wrought in Christ when he raised him from the dead." This is a river overflowing its banks—an idea too large for language. Let us look at it a moment.

Where do we find " the exceeding greatness of his power?" In the creation of the world? in the Seven Stars and Orion? in the strength of Behemoth and Leviathan? No! In the deluge? in the fiery destruction of Sodom? in the overthrow of Pharaoh and his host? in hurling Nebuchadnezzar like Lucifer from the political firmament? No! It is the power which he wrought in Christ. When? When he healed the sick? when he raised the dead? when he cast out devils? when he blasted the fruitless fig-tree? when he walked upon the waters of the Galilee? No! It was " when he raised him from the dead." Then the Father placed the sceptre in the hand of the Son, " and set him above all principality, and power, and might, and dominion, and every name that is named, not only in this world, but also in that which is to come ; and put all things under his feet, and gave him to be head over all things to the church."

This is the source of our spiritual life. The same power that raised the dead body of our Lord from the grave, quickens the soul of the believer from the death in trespasses and sins. His riven tomb is a fountain of living waters; whereof if a man drink, he shall never die. His raised and glorified body is the sun, whence streams eternal light upon our spirits; the light of life, that never can be quenched.

Nor here does the influence of his resurrection end. He who raised up Jesus from the dead shall also quicken our mortal bodies. His resurrection is the pledge and the pattern of ours. "Because he liveth we shall live also." "He shall change our vile body, that it may be fashioned like unto his glorious body." We hear him speaking in the prophet:—"Thy dead men shall live; together with my dead body shall they arise. Awake and sing, ye that dwell in the dust; for thy dew is as the dew of herbs, and the earth shall cast out her dead."

How divinely does the apostle speak of the resurrection-body of the saints! " It is sown in corruption, it is raised in incorruption; it is sown in dishonor, it is raised in glory; it is sown in weakness, it is raised in power; it is sown a natural body, it is raised a spiritual body. For this corruptible must put on incorruption, and this mortal must put on immortality. Then shall be brought to pass the saying that is written—Death is swallowed up in victory! O death, where is thy sting? O grave, where is thy victory? Thanks be unto God, that giveth us the victory, through our Lord Jesus Christ."

Ever since the fall in Eden, man is born to die. He lives to die. He eats and drinks, sleeps and wakes, to die. Death, like a dark steel-clad warrior, stands ever before us; and his gigantic shadow comes continually between us and happiness. But Christ hath " abolished death, and brought life and immortality to light through the gospel." He was born in Bethlehem, that he might die on Calvary. He was made under the law, that he might bear the direst penalty of the law. He lived thirty-three years, sinless among sinners, that he might offer himself a sin-offering for sinners upon the cross. Thus he " became obedient unto death," that he might destroy the power of death; and on the third morning, a mighty angel, rolling away the stone from the mouth of the sepulchre, makes the very door of Death's castle the throne whence he proclaims " the resurrection and the life."

The Hero of our salvation travelled into Death's dominion, took possession of the whole territory on our behalf, and returning laden with spoils, ascended to the heaven of heavens. He went to the palace, seized the tyrant, and wrested away his sceptre. He descended into the prison-house, knocked off the fetters of the captives; and when he came up again, left the door of every cell open, that they might follow him. He has gone over into our promised inheritance, and his glory illuminates the mountains of immortality; and through the telescope which he has bequeathed us, we "see the land that is very far off."

I recollect reading in the writings of Flavel this sentiment—that the souls in paradise wait with intense desire for the reanimation of their dead bodies, that they may be united to them in bliss for ever. O, what rapture there shall be among the saints, when those frail vessels, from which they escaped with such a struggle, as they foundered in the gulf of death, shall come floating in, with the spring-tide of the resurrection, to the harbor of immortality! How glorious the reunion, when the seeds of affliction and death are left behind ·in the tomb! Jacob no longer lame, nor Moses slow of speech, nor Lazarus covered with sores, nor Paul troubled with a thorn in the flesh!

"It doth not yet appear what we shall be; but we know that when he shall appear, we shall be like him; for we shall see him as he is." The glory of the body of Christ is far above our present conception. When he was transfigured on Tabor, his face shone like the sun, and his raiment was white as the light. This is the pattern shown to his people in the mount. This is the model after which the bodies of believers shall be fashioned in the resurrection. " They that be wise shall shine as the brightness of the firmament ; and they that turn many to righteousness, as the stars for ever and ever."

In conclusion :—The angel said to the women—" Go quickly, and tell his disciples that he is risen from the dead ; and behold, he goeth before you into Galilee ; there shall ye see him; lo! I have told you. And they departed quickly from the sepulchre, with fear and great joy; and did run to bring his disciples word."

Brethren! followers of Jesus! be ye also preachers of a risen Saviour! Go quickly—there is no time for delay—and publish the glad tidings to sinners! Tell them that Christ died for their sins, and rose again for their justification, and ascended to the right hand of the Father to make intercession for them, and is now able to save unto the uttermost all that come unto God by him!

And you, impenitent and unbelieving men! hear this blessed message of salvation! Do you intend ever to embrace the proffered mercy of the gospel? Make haste! Procrastination is ruin! Now is the accepted time! O, fly to the throne of grace! Time is hastening; you will soon be swallowed up in eternity! May the Lord have mercy upon you, and rouse you from your indifference and sloth! It is my delight to invite you to Christ; but I feel more pleasure and more confidence in praying for you to God. I have besought and entreated you, by every argument and every motive in my power; but you are yet in your sins, and rushing on toward hell. Yet I will not give you up in despair. If I cannot persuade you to flee from the wrath to come, I will intercede with God to have mercy upon you for the sake of his beloved Son. If I cannot prevail in the pulpit, I will try to prevail at the throne!

Sermon 14

THE ASCENSION

Whom the heaven must receive until the times of restitution of all things (Acts 3:21).

THESE words are part of St. Peter's sermon to the people of Jerusalem, on occasion of the cure of the lame man, at the "Beautiful Gate" of the temple, shortly after the day of Pentecost.

This, and the sermon recorded in the preceding chapter, were perhaps the most effective ever delivered on earth. As the fruit of Peter's ministry in these two discourses, about five thousand souls were converted to Christianity.*

It is recorded, that, on the day of Pentecost, the hearers "were pricked in their hearts, and said unto Peter and the rest of the apostles—Men and brethren, what shall we do?" An inquiry which indicates the utmost solicitude and distress. A sense of sin overwhelmed them, especially of their guilt in rejecting the Son of God; and they pressed around the preacher and his colleagues with this earnest interrogative.

The answer was ready. True ministers of Christ are never at a loss in answering the inquiries of awakened sinners. When the Philippian jailer came trembling to Paul and Silas, and fell down before them, exclaiming—"What must I do to be saved?" "Believe on the Lord Jesus Christ, and thou shalt be saved," was the prompt and appropriate answer.

So Peter, on the day of Pentecost, when three thousand conscience-smitten and heart-broken hearers cried out under the sermon—"What shall we do?" immediately replied—"Repent

---

* Acts iv. 4.

and be baptized, every one of you, in the name of Jesus Christ, for the remission of sins, and ye shall receive the gift of the Holy Ghost; for the promise is unto you, and to your children, and to all that are afar off, even as many as the Lord our God shall call."

And so in the sermon whence we have taken our text, when he saw that the truth had found its way to the understanding, and the conscience, and the heart—that many were awakened, and convinced of sin—he exhorted them to repentance and faith in Christ, as the condition of salvation:—"Repent ye, therefore, and be converted, that your sins may be blotted out, when the times of refreshing shall come from the presence of the Lord; and he shall send Jesus Christ, who before was preached unto you; whom the heaven must receive until the times of restitution of all things."

The doctrine of this text is—the necessity of Christ's return to heaven till the consummation of his mediatorial work.

It is generally admitted, that the twenty-second psalm has particular reference to Christ. This is evident from his own appropriation of the first verse upon the cross:—"My God! my God! why hast thou forsaken me?" The title of that psalm is—"Aijeleth Shahar;" which signifies—A hart, or—the hind of the morning. The striking metaphors which it contains are descriptive of Messiah's peculiar sufferings. He is the hart, or hind of the morning, hunted by the black prince, with his hell-hounds—by Satan, and all his allies. The "dogs," the "lions," the "unicorns," and the "strong bulls of Bashan," with their devouring teeth, and their terrible horns, pursued him from Bethlehem to Calvary. They beset him in the manger, gnashed upon him in the garden, and wellnigh tore him to pieces upon the cross. And still they persecute him in his cause, and in the persons and interests of his people.

The faith of the church anticipated the coming of Christ, "like a roe or a young hart," with the dawn of the day promised in Eden; and we hear her exclaiming in the Canticles—"The voice of my beloved! behold, he cometh, leaping upon the mountains, and skipping upon the hills!" She heard him announce his advent in the promise—"Lo, I come to do thy will, O God!" and with prophetic eye, saw him leaping from the mountains of eternity to the mountains of time, and skipping from hill to hill throughout the land of Palestine, going about doing good. In the various types and shadows of the law, she beheld him "standing by the wall,

looking forth at the windows, showing himself through the lattice;"
and then she sung—"Until the day break, and the shadows flee
away, turn, my beloved, and be thou like the roe or the young hart
upon the mountains of Bether!" Bloody sacrifices revealed him to
her view, going down to the "vineyards of red wine;" whence she
traced him to the meadows of gospel ordinances, where "he feedeth
among the lilies"—to "the gardens of cucumbers," and "the beds
of spices;" and then she sung to him again—"Make haste"—or,
flee away—"my beloved! be thou like the roe or the young hart
upon the mountains of spices!"

Thus she longed to see him, first "on the mountain of Bether,"
and then "on the mountain of spices." On both mountains she
saw him eighteen hundred years ago, and on both she may still
trace the footsteps of his majesty and his mercy. The former he
hath tracked with his own blood, and his path upon the latter is
redolent of frankincense and myrrh.

Bether signifies division. This is the craggy mountain of Calvary; whither the "Hind of the morning" fled, followed by all the
wild beasts of the forest, and the hunting-dogs of hell; summoned
to the pursuit, and urged on, by the prince of perdition; till the
victim, in his agony, sweat great drops of blood—where he was
terribly crushed between the cliffs, and dreadfully mangled by sharp
and ragged rocks—where he was seized by Death, the great grey-
hound of the bottomless pit—whence he leaped the precipice, without breaking a bone; and sunk in the dead sea, sunk to its utmost
depth, and saw no corruption.

Behold the "Hind of the morning" on that dreadful mountain!
It is the place of skulls, where death holds his carnival in compa-
nionship with worms, and hell laughs in the face of heaven. Dark
storms are gathering there—convolving clouds, charged with no
common wrath. Terrors set themselves in battle-array before the
Son of God; and tempests burst upon him, which might sweep all
mankind in a moment to eternal ruin. Hark! hear ye not the sub-
terranean thunder? Feel ye not the tremor of the mountain? It is
the shock of Satan's artillery, playing upon the Captain of our salvation. It is the explosion of the magazine of vengeance. Lo,
the earth is quaking, the rocks are rending, the graves are opening,
the dead are rising, and all nature stands aghast at the conflict of
divine mercy with the powers of darkness. One dread convulsion

more, one cry of desperate agony, and Jesus dies—an arrow has entered into his heart. Now leap the lions, roaring, upon their prey; and the bulls of Bashan are bellowing; and the dogs of perdition are barking; and the unicorns toss their horns on high; and the devil, dancing with exultant joy, clanks his iron chains, and thrusts up his fettered hands in defiance toward the face of Jehovah!

Go a little farther upon the mountain, and you come to "a new tomb hewn out of the rock." There lies a dead body. It is the body of Jesus. His disciples have laid it down in sorrow, and returned weeping to the city. Mary's heart is broken, Peter's zeal is quenched in tears, and John would fain lie down and die in his Master's grave. The sepulchre is closed up and sealed, and a Roman sentry placed at its entrance. On the morning of the third day, while it is yet dark, two or three women come to anoint the body. They are debating about the great stone at the mouth of the cave. "Who shall roll it away?" says one of them. "Pity we did not bring Peter or John with us." But arriving, they find the stone already rolled away, and one sitting upon it, whose countenance is like lightning, and whose garments are white as the light. The steel-clad, iron-hearted soldiers lie around him, like men slain in battle, having swooned with terror. He speaks:—"Why seek ye the living among the dead? He is not here; he is risen; he is gone forth from this cave victoriously."

It is even so; for there are the shroud, and the napkin, and the heavenly watchers; and when he awoke, and cast off his grave-clothes, the earthquake was felt in the city, and jarred the gates of hell. "The Hind of the morning" is up earlier than any of his pursuers, "leaping upon the mountains, and skipping upon the hills." He is seen first with Mary at the tomb; then with the disciples in Jerusalem; then with two of them on the way to Emmaus; then going before his brethren into Galilee; and finally, leaping from the top of Olivet to the hills of Paradise; fleeing away to "the mountains of spices," where he shall never more be hunted by the black prince and his hounds.

Christ is perfect master of gravitation, and all the laws of nature are obedient to his will. Once he walked upon the water, as if it were marble beneath his feet; and now, as he stands blessing his people, the glorious form so recently nailed to the cross, and still more recently cold in the grave, begins to ascend like "the living creature" in Ezekiel's vision, "lifted up from the earth," till nearly out of sight; when "the chariots of God, even thousands of angels," receive him, and haste to the celestial city, waking the thrones of eternity with this jubilant chorus—" Lift up your heads, O ye gates! and be ye lifted up, ye everlasting doors! and the King of glory shall come in!"

Christ might have rode in a chariot of fire all the way from Bethlehem to Calvary; but he preferred riding in a chariot of mercy, whose lining was crimson, and whose ornament the malefactor's cross. How rapidly rolled his wheels over the hills and the plains of Palestine, gathering up everywhere the children of affliction, and scattering blessings like the beams of the morning! Now we find him in Cana of Galilee, turning water into wine; then treading the waves of the sea, and hushing the roar of the tempest; then delivering the demoniac of Gadara from the fury of a legion of fiends; then healing the nobleman's son at Capernaum; raising the daughter of Jairus, and the young man of Nain; writing upon the grave at Bethany—" I am the resurrection and the life;" curing the invalid at the pool of Bethesda; feeding the five thousand in the wilderness; preaching to the woman by Jacob's well; acquitting the adulteress, and shaming her accusers; and exercising everywhere, in all his travels, the three offices of Physician, Prophet, and Saviour, as he drove on toward the place of skulls.

Now we see the chariot surrounded with enemies—Herod, and Pilate, and Caiaphas, and the Roman soldiers, and the populace of Jerusalem, and thousands of Jews who have come up to keep the Passover, led on by Judas and the devil. See how they rage and curse, as if they would tear him from his chariot of mercy. But Jesus maintains his seat, and holds fast the reins, and drives right on through the angry crowd, without shooting an arrow, or lifting a spear upon his foes. For in that chariot the King must ride to Calvary—Calvary must be consecrated to mercy for ever. He sees the cross planted upon the brow of the hill, and hastens forward to embrace it. No sacrifice shall be offered to Justice on this day, but the one sacrifice which reconciles heaven and earth. None of those children of Belial shall suffer to-day. The bribed witnesses, and clamorous murderers, shall be spared—the smiters, the scourgers, the spitters, the thorn-platters, the nail-drivers, the head-shakers; for Jesus pleads on their behalf—" Father, forgive them! they know not what they do. They are ignorant of thy truth and grace They are not aware whom they are crucifying. O, spare them' Let Death know that he shall have enough to do with me to-day! Let him open all his batteries upon me! My bosom is bare to the stroke! I will gather all the lances of hell in my heart!"

Still the chariot rushes on, and "fiery darts" are falling thick and fast, like a shower of meteors, on Messiah's head, till he is covered with wounds, and the blood flows down his garments, and leaves a crimson track behind him. As he passes, he casts at the dying malefactor a glance of benignity, and throws him a passport into Paradise, written with his own blood; stretches forth his scepter, and touches the prison-door of death, and many of the prisoners come forth, and the tyrant shall never regain his dominion over them; rides triumphant over thrones and principalities, and crushes beneath his wheels the last enemy himself, and leaves the memorial of his march engraven on the rocks of Golgotha!

Christ is everywhere in the Scriptures spoken of as a blessing; and whether we contemplate his advent, his ministry, his miracles, his agony, his crucifixion, his interment, his resurrection, or his ascension, we may truly say, "all his paths drop fatness." All his travels were on the road of mercy; and trees are growing up in his footsteps, whose fruit is delicious food, and whose " leaves are for the healing of the nations." He walketh upon the south winds, causing propitious gales to blow upon the wilderness, till songs of joy awake in the solitary place, and the desert blossoms as the rose.

If we will consider what the prophets wrote of Messiah, in connection with the evangelical history, we shall be satisfied that none like him, either before or since, ever entered our world, and departed from it. Both God and man—at once the Father of eternity and the son of time—he filled the universe, while he was imbodied upon earth; and ruled the celestial principalities and powers, while he wandered—a persecuted stranger—in Judea. " No man," saith he, " hath ascended up to heaven, but he that came down from heaven—even the Son of man, who is in heaven."

Heaven was no strange place to Jesus. He talks of the mansions in his Father's house as familiarly as one of the royal family would talk of Windsor Castle, where he was born; and saith to his disciples—" I go to prepare a place for you; that where I am, there ye may be also." The glory into which he entered was his own glory—the glory which he had with the Father before the world was. He had an original and supreme right to the celestial mansions; and he acquired a new and additional claim by his office as mediator. Having suffered for our sins, he "ought to enter into his glory." He ought, because he is "God, blessed for ever"—he ought, because he is the representative of his redeemed people. He has taken possession of the kingdom in our behalf, and left on record for our encouragement this cheering promise—"To him that overcometh will I grant to sit with me in my throne; even as I also have overcome, and am set down with my Father in his throne."

The departure of God from Eden, and the departure of Christ from the earth, were two of the sublimest events that ever occurred, and fraught with immense consequences to our race. When Jehovah went out from Eden, he left a curse upon the place for man's sake, and drove out man before him into an accursed earth. But when Jesus ascended from Olivet, he lifted the curse with him, and left a blessing behind him—sowed the world with the seed of eternal blessings; "and instead of the thorn shall come up the fir-tree; and instead of the briar shall come up the myrtle-tree; and it shall be to the Lord for a name, and an everlasting sign, that shall not be cut off." He ascended to intercede for sinners, and reopen paradise to his people; and when he shall come the second time, according to the promise, with all his holy angels, then shall we be "caught up to meet the Lord in the air, and so shall we ever be with the Lord."

"The Lord is gone up with a shout," and has taken our redeemed nature with him. He is the head of the church, and her representative at the right hand of the Father. "He hath ascended on high; he hath led captivity captive; he hath received gifts for men; yea, for the rebellious also, that God may dwell among them." "Him hath God exalted, with his own right hand, to be a Prince and a Saviour, to give repentance to Israel, and remission of sins." This is the Father's recognition of his "Beloved Son," and significant acceptance of his sacrifice. "Wherefore God also hath highly exalted him, and given him a name which is above every name; that at the name of Jesus every knee should bow, of things in heaven, and things in the earth, and things under the earth; and that every tongue should confess that Jesus Christ is Lord, to the glory of God the Father."

The evidence of our Lord's ascension is ample. He ascended in the presence of many witnesses, who stood gazing after him till a cloud received him out of their sight. And while they looked steadfastly toward heaven, two angels appeared to them, and talked with them of what they had seen. Soon afterward, on the day of Pentecost, he fulfilled, in a remarkable manner, the promise which he had made to his people:—"If I go away, I will send you another Comforter, who shall abide with you for ever." Stephen, the first of his disciples that glorified the Master by martyrdom, testified to his murderers—"Lo, I see the heavens opened, and the Son of Man standing on the right hand of God!" And John, "the beloved disciple," while an exile "in Patmos, for the word of God, and the testimony of Jesus Christ," beheld him "in the midst of the throne, as a Lamb that had been slain!" These are the evidences that our Lord is in heaven; these are our consolations in the house of our pilgrimage.

The apostle speaks of the *necessity* of this event:—"Whom the heaven *must* receive."

Divine necessity is a golden chain, reaching from eternity to eternity, and encircling all the events of time. It consists of many links, all hanging upon each other; and not one of them can be broken, without destroying the support of the whole. The first link is in God, "before the world was;" and the last is in heaven, when the world shall be no more. Christ is its Alpha and Omega, and Christ constitutes all its intervenient links. Christ in the bosom of the Father, receiving the promise of eternal life, before the foundation of the world, is the beginning; Christ in his sacrificial blood, atoning for our sins, and pardoning and sanctifying all them that believe, is the middle; and Christ in heaven, pleading the merit of his vicarious sufferings, making intercession for the transgressors, drawing all men unto himself, presenting the prayers of his people, and preparing their mansions, is the end.

There is a necessity in all that Christ has done as our Mediator, in all that he is doing on our behalf, and all that he has engaged to do—the necessity of Divine love manifested, of Divine mercy exercised, of Divine purposes accomplished, of Divine covenants fulfilled, of Divine faithfulness maintained, of Divine justice satisfied,

of Divine holiness vindicated, and of Divine power displayed.
Christ felt this necessity while he tabernacled among us, often declared it to his disciples, and acknowledged it to the Father in the
agony of the garden.

Behold him wrestling in prayer, with strong crying and tears:—
" Father, save me from this hour! If it be possible, let this cup
pass from me!" Now the Father reads to him his covenant engagement, which he signed and sealed with his own hand before the
foundation of the world. The glorious Sufferer replies:—" Thy
will be done! For this cause came I unto this hour. I will drink
the cup which thou hast mingled, and not a dreg of any of its
ingredients shall be left for my people. I will pass through the
approaching dreadful night, under the hidings of thy countenance,
bearing away the curse from my beloved. Henceforth, repentance
is hidden from mine eyes!" Now, on his knees, he reads the
covenant engagements of the Father, and adds:—" I have glorified
thee on the earth. I have finished the work which thou gavest me
to do. Now glorify thou me, according to thy promise, with thine
own self, with the glory which I had with thee before the world was.
Father, I will also that they whom thou hast given me, be with me
where I am, that they may behold my glory. Thine they were,
and thou hast given them to me, on condition of my pouring out
my soul unto death. Thou hast promised them, through my righteousness and meritorious sacrifice, the kingdom of heaven, which
I now claim on their behalf. Father, glorify my people, with him
whom thou lovedst before the foundation of the world!"

The intercession of Christ for his saints, begun on earth, is continued in heaven. This is our confidence and joy in our journey-
ings through the wilderness. We know that our Joshua has gone
over into the land of our inheritance, where he is preparing a place
of habitation for Israel, for it is his will that all whom he has redeemed should be with him for ever!

The text speaks of the period when the great purposes of our
Lord's ascension shall be fully accomplished:—" until the times of
restitution of all things."

The period here mentioned is " the dispensation of the fulness of
time," when " the fulness of the gentiles shall come in," and " the
dispersed of Judah" shall be restored, and Christ shall " gather together in himself all things in heaven and in earth," overthrow hi

enemies, establish his everlasting kingdom, deliver the groaning creation from its bondage, glorify his people with himself, imprison the devil and his angels in the bottomless pit, and punish with destruction from his presence them that obey not the gospel.

To this glorious consummation, the great travail of redemption, and all the events of time, are only preparatory. It was promised in Eden, and the promise was renewed and enlarged to Abraham, to Isaac, and to Jacob. It was described in gorgeous oriental imagery by Isaiah, and "the sweet psalmist of Israel;" and "spoken of by all the prophets, since the world began." Christ came into the world to prepare the way for his future triumph—to lay on Calvary the "chief corner-stone" of a temple, which shall be completed at the end of time, and endure through all eternity. He began the great restitution. He redeemed his people with a price, and gave them a pledge of redemption by power. He made an end of sin, abolished the Levitical priesthood, and swallowed up all the types and shadows in himself. He sent home the beasts, overthrew the altars, and quenched the holy fire; and, upon the sanctifying altar of his own divinity, offered his own sinless humanity, which was consumed by fire from heaven. He removed the seat of government from Mount Zion in Jerusalem, to Mount Zion above, where he sits—"a priest upon his throne"—drawing heaven and earth together, and establishing "the covenant of peace between them both." Blessed be God! we can now go to Jesus, the mediator; passing by millions of angels, and all the spirits of just men made perfect; till we "come to the blood of sprinkling, which speaketh better things than that of Abel." And we look for that blessed day, when "this gospel of the kingdom" shall be universally prevalent; "and all shall know the Lord, from the least even to the greatest"—when there shall be "a new heaven, and a new earth, wherein dwelleth righteousness"—when both the political and the moral aspects of our world shall be changed; and a happier state of things shall exist than has ever been known before—when the pestilence, the famine, and the sword shall cease to destroy; and "the saints of the Most High shall possess the kingdom," in "quietness and assurance for ever." "Then cometh the end," when Emmanuel "shall destroy in this mountain the vail of the covering cast over all people, and swallow up death in victory!"

But what will it avail you to hear of this glorious restitution, if you are not partakers of its incipient benefits, and happily interested in its consummation? Has it begun in your own hearts? Are you restored to God in Christ? Have you a place in his house, and a name among his people? Are your feet running the way of his commandments, and your hands diligent in doing his work? If not, "it is high time to awake out of sleep." "Repent and believe the gospel!" "Let the wicked forsake his way, and the unrighteous man his thoughts; and let him return unto the Lord, who will have mercy upon him · and to our God, for he will abundantly pardon!"

Sermon 15

TRIBULATION CONQUERED

These things have I spoken unto you, that in me ye might have peace. In the world ye shall have tribulation; but be of good cheer; I have overcome the world (John 16:33).

THE last sayings of those we love are not soon forgotten. These words form the conclusion of our Lord's valedictory to his disciples. They did not yet understand that the redemption of man was to be obtained by the death of their Master. When Christ was put to death, he descended to the lower parts of the earth, in order to raise up sinners; but their faith could not follow him into the deep. Nicholas Pisces sunk into the sea to raise a golden cup, but neither he nor the cup ever came up again. A man clothed in glass went down to prepare for raising the Royal George; the man came up, but the ship remains in the bottom. But our blessed Redeemer, clothed in humanity, descended to the deeps of death, and raised the church from the pit of perdition, and founded her upon a rock, against which the gates of hell cannot prevail.

We would notice, *first*, the peace that is in Christ, in opposition to the tribulation that is in the world ; and *secondly*, the victory of Christ over the world, as the source of comfort and joy to believers.

I. " These things have I spoken unto you, that in me ye might have peace. I know what you will have in the world—mountains of tribulation—nothing but tribulation. I will put my peace in the other end of the scale."

Peace in Christ is " the peace of God which passeth all understanding"—an ocean sufficiently deep and large to swallow up millions of fiery mountains. See the awakened sinner, overwhelmed with the terrors of God. His inflexible justice and spotless holiness seem to him like a mountain of flame, which he cannot approach without being consumed. But the Holy Spirit shows him the reconciling blood of the cross. He sees the crucified God-man rising from the grave, and ascending on high, "to be a Prince and a Saviour, to give repentance and remission of sins." Instantly the terrible mountain sinks and is lost in the sea of his Redeemer's merit. His faith has conquered his fears. His burden of guilt is gone. He is a new creature in Christ Jesus, and in Christ Jesus there is no condemnation. The deluge of tribulation may swell and roar around him, but he is securely enclosed in the ark.

A man in a trance saw himself locked up in a house of steel, through the walls of which, as through walls of glass, he could see his enemies assailing him with swords, spears, and bayonets; but his life was safe, for his fortress was locked within. So is the Christian secure amid the assaults of the world. His "life is hid with Christ in God."

The psalmist prayed—"When my heart is overwhelmed within me, lead me to the Rock that is higher than I." Imagine a man seated on a lofty rock in the midst of the sea, where he has every thing necessary for his support, shelter, safety, and comfort. The billows heave and break beneath him, and the hungry monsters of the deep wait to devour him; but he is on high, above the rage of the former, and the reach of the latter. Such is the security of faith.

But why need I mention the rock and the steel house? for the peace that is in Christ is a tower ten thousand times stronger, and a refuge ten thousand times safer. Behold the disciples of Jesus exposed to famine, nakedness, peril, and sword—incarcerated in dungeons; thrown to wild beasts; consumed in the fire; sawn asunder; cruelly mocked and scourged; driven from friends and home, to wander among the mountains, and lodge in dens and caves of the earth; being destitute, afflicted, tormented; sorrowful, but always rejoicing; cast down, but not destroyed; an ocean of peace within, which swallows up all their sufferings.

"Neither death," with all its terrors; "nor life," with all its allurements; "nor things present," with all their pleasure; "nor things to come," with all their promise; "nor height" of prosperity; "nor depth" of adversity; "nor angels" of evil; "nor principalities" of darkness; "shall be able to separate us from the love of God, which is in Christ Jesus." "God is our refuge and strength ; a very present help in trouble. Therefore will not we fear, though the earth be removed, and though the mountains be carried into the midst of the sea—though the waters thereof roar and be troubled—though the mountains shake with the swelling thereof." This is the language of strong faith in the peace of Christ. How is it with you amid such turmoil and commotion ? Is all peaceful within? Do you feel secure in the name of the Lord, as in a strong fortress—as in a city well supplied and defended?

" There is a river, the streams whereof shall make glad the city of God, the holy place of the tabernacles of the most high. God is in the midst of her ; she shall not be moved. God shall help her, and that right early." " Unto the upright, there ariseth light in the darkness." The bright and morning star, shining upon their pathway, cheers them in their journey home to their Father's house. And when they come to pass over Jordan, the Sun of Righteousness shall have risen upon them, with healing in his wings. Already they see the tops of the mountains of immortality, gilded with his beams, beyond the valley of the shadow of death. Behold, yonder, old Simeon hoisting his sails, and saying—" Lord, now lettest thou thy servant depart in peace, according to thy word ; for mine eyes have seen thy salvation." Such is the peace of Jesus, sealed to all them that believe, by the blood of his cross.

When we walk through the field of battle, slippery with blood, and strewn with the bodies of the slain—when we hear the shrieks and the groans of the wounded and the dying—when we see the country wasted, cities burned, houses pillaged, widows and orphans wailing in the track of the victorious army, we cannot help exclaiming—O, what a blessing is peace ! When we are obliged to witness family turmoils and strifes—when we see parents and children, brothers and sisters, masters and servants, husbands and wives, contending with each other like tigers—we retire as from a smoky house, and exclaim as we go—O, what a blessing is peace ! When duty calls us into that church, where envy and malice prevail, and the spirit of harmony is supplanted by discord and contention— when we see brethren, who ought to be bound together in love, full of pride, hatred, confusion, and every evil work—we quit the unhallowed scene with painful feelings of repulsion, repeating the exclamation—O, what a blessing is peace !

But how much more precious in the case of the awakened sinner! See him standing, terror-stricken, before mount Sinai. Thunders roll above him—lightnings flash around him—the earth trembles beneath him, as if ready to open her mouth and swallow him up. The sound of the trumpet rings through his soul—" Guilty! guilty! guilty!" Pale and trembling, he looks eagerly around him, and sees nothing but revelations of wrath. Overwhelmed with fear and dismay, he cries out—" O wretched man that I am! Who shall deliver me! What shall I do?" A voice reaches his ear—penetrates his heart—" Behold the Lamb of God, that taketh away the sin of the world!" He turns his eyes to Calvary. Wonderous vision! Emmanuel expiring upon the cross! the sinner's Substitute satisfying the demand of the law against the sinner! Now all his fears are hushed, and rivers of peace flow into his soul. This is the peace of Christ.

How precious is this peace, amid all the dark vicissitudes of life! How invaluable this jewel, through all the dangers of the wilderness! How cheering to know that Jesus, who hath loved us even unto death, is the pilot of our perilous voyage; that he rules the winds and the waves, and can hush them to silence at his will, and bring the frailest bark of faith to the desired haven! Trusting where he cannot trace his Master's footsteps, the disciple is joyful amid the darkest dispensations of Divine Providence; turning all his sorrows into songs, and all his tribulations into triumphs. "Thou wilt keep him in perfect peace, whose mind is stayed on thee, because he trusteth in thee."

II. The victory of Christ over the world, the source of comfort and joy to believers. "In the world ye shall have tribulation; but be of good cheer; I have overcome the world."

The world is the great castle of Belial, containing three temples; "the lust of the flesh, the lust of the eye, and the pride of life;" in one or another of which every unconverted soul is a worshipper. But Jesus has demolished that castle, and abolished the service of its several temples.

The world has two modes of warfare. Sometimes it puts on the apparent mildness of a lamb, and allures to destruction with the song of a siren. Again it leaps upon its prey like an angry lion, or pursues its victim like an exasperated dragon. Its frown has destroyed thousands; its smile, tens of thousands.

A certain man has laid it down as a rule, that all must take the world as it is. But all general rules have their exceptions. Christ is the exception here. Christ conquered the world. The Prince of this world met him in the wilderness, when he was alone, in poverty and distress—weary, hungry, and thirsty—and offered him all the kingdoms of the world, for which have been fought so many battles. But Jesus refused the offer; choosing rather to be poor, that we might be made rich. He detected the lion in his affectation of the lamb, and stripped from the angel of darkness his garment of light.

Then the enemy assumed another aspect—assailed him with the rage of a wild beast, and the malice of a fiend. No sooner had he preached his first sermon, than there was an attempt to hurl him down the precipice. "The archers sorely grieved him, and shot at him, and hated him." Judea became to him a mountain of leopards, and humanity seemed infernalized. He was stigmatized as a hypocrite—an impostor—a demoniac. He was falsely accused before rulers, and insult was added to perjury. "But his bow abode in strength, and the arms of his hands were made strong by the hands of the mighty God of Jacob." "He was tempted in all things like as we are, yet without sin." "He did no iniquity, neither was guile found in his mouth." He went through the wilderness without contracting any of its defilement.

But this was comparatively a small part of his victory. A more glorious conquest of the world was achieved by his death upon the cross, and his resurrection from the grave. It is here we behold him "glorious in his apparel, traveling in the greatness of his strength," trampling the hosts of hell, till his raiment is red with blood. It is here we behold him "spoiling principalities and powers, and making a show of them openly—triumphing over them" in his atonement. It is here we behold the Prince of this world cast out and judged. The Prince of Peace has broken his sceptre, demolished his throne, and established upon the ruins of his empire an everlasting kingdom of grace.

Caiaphas rejoiced that Christ was under the king's seal in the grave; but his unholy joy was brief as "the crackling of thorns under a pot." At the dawning of the third day, Cæsar's seal is broken, the stone rolled away, the tomb deserted of its occupant, Caiaphas' feast of joy turned to lamentation and mourning, and the eternal power and Godhead of him whom they crucified engraved for ever on the rent rocks of Calvary.

Alexander conquered the world, but did not live to enjoy the fruits of his victory. But the Captain of our salvation, though he was dead, is alive for evermore. He shall prosecute his conquests, and put all enemies under his feet, and retain his dominion for ever. "He shall see of the travail of his soul, and be satisfied." He lives to confer upon his people the riches which he procured for them by his death. He lives to defend his redeemed, and draw all men unto himself. He lives to perpetuate in the church the peace which he bequeathed to her in his last will and testament.

A servant of Julian the Apostate asked one of the martyrs—" What is thy God, the carpenter, doing now in heaven?" He answered —"Making a coffin for thy master!" Julian was soon afterward mortally wounded by an arrow from one of the Scythians. When he was expiring, he waved his hand sorrowfully, and exclaimed— " O Galilean, thou hast conquered!"

"Be of good cheer," therefore, ye trembling disciples! Christ has vanquished all your enemies. Ye are more than conquerors, through him that loved you, and gave himself for you. "In those things wherein they were proud, he was above them." When Pharaoh exulted to overtake Israel, shut in between Pi-hahiroth and Baal-zephon, with the sea before them, Jehovah was higher than the Egyptian. His sight was clearer—his arm was stronger—his purpose was firmer. He said to his people—"Stand still! you are not able to raise this rampart. I must do it for you. I will divide the sea, and lead you through on dry land, and drown those who have drowned so many of your infants. Every one of them shall perish, from the king to the last footman." Thus the Prince of Peace has triumphed over your foes, and you may conquer through faith in his conquest. "Whatsoever is born of God overcometh the world; and this is the victory that overcometh the world, even our faith."

John in the Apocalypse saw the army of the victors—a great multitude, out of all nations, and kindreds, and peoples, and tongues —standing before the throne, and before the Lamb; clothed with white robes, and palms in their hands; and crying with a loud voice—"Salvation to our God, who sitteth upon the throne, and unto the Lamb!" And one of the elders asked him—"Who are these, and whence came they?" But so wonderfully were they changed, since he saw them on earth—in exile, in prison, in torture and death—that he confessed he knew them not. Then answered the elder—" These are they that came out of great tribulation, and have washed their robes, and made them white in the blood of the Lamb. Therefore are they before the throne of God, and serve him day and night in his temple; and he that sitteth on the throne shall dwell among them. They shall hunger no more, neither thirst any more; neither shall the sun light on them, nor any heat. For the Lamb, who is in the midst of the throne, shall feed them, and shall lead them unto living fountains of waters; and God shall wipe away all tears from their eyes."

Thus, ye saints, shall you " overcome by the blood of the Lamb;" "for greater is he that is in you than he that is in the world;" and your sorrows shall be lost in unspeakable joy, and your disgrace in eternal glory!

Sermon 16

THE GLORY OF THE GOSPEL

According to the glorious gospel of the blessed God (1 Timothy 1:11).

THE being of God, and some of his attributes, are revealed to us by natural religion. The proof is seen in all his works, commending itself to the reason and conscience even of pagan nations. "Because that which may be known of God is manifest in them, for God hath showed it unto them; for the invisible things of him, from the creation of the world, are clearly seen, being understood by the things that are made, even his eternal power and godhead; so that they are without excuse, because that when they knew God, they glorified him not as God, neither were thankful, but became vain in their imaginations, and their foolish heart was darkened."*

Paul's sermon in Athens was founded on the revelations of natural religion:—" Then Paul stood in the midst of Mars' hill, and said, Ye men of Athens, I perceive that in all things ye are too superstitious; for as I passed by, and beheld your devotions, I found an altar with this inscription, TO THE UNKNOWN GOD; whom therefore ye ignorantly worship, him declare I unto you. God that made the world and all things therein, seeing that he is Lord of heaven and earth, dwelleth not in temples made with hands; neither is worshipped with men's hands, as though he needed any thing, seeing he giveth to all life, and breath, and all things; and hath made of one blood all nations of men for to dwell on all the face of the earth, and hath determined the times before appointed, and the bounds of their habitation; that they should seek the Lord, if haply they might feel after him, and find him, though he be not far from every one of us; for in him we live,

---

* Rom. i. 19 21.

and move, and have our being; as certain also of your own poets
have said, For we are also his offspring."*

But natural religion, though it reveals the being and attributes of
God, cannot teach the way of salvation, nor lead us in the path of
holiness. It may excite a thousand fears, not one of which can it
allay; and suggest a thousand questions, not one of which can it
answer. It leaves us, with the deist, in a region of doubt and perplexity; and neither of its four oracles—creation, providence, reason,
and conscience—can satisfy the soul that inquires, "What must I
do to be saved?" Its light affords us no guidance in the path of
virtue; no certain indications of duty, either to God or man. Our
understandings are so darkened, our wills so perverted, our affections so carnal, that we can depend upon no suggestions of external
nature, or of reason and conscience, for the regulation of our moral
conduct. God, therefore, of his infinite mercy, has given us his
written word—a perfect rule both of faith and practice—a law by
which we ought to live, and by which we shall be judged—a revelation of the mystery which had been hidden for ages, but is now
made manifest to the saints, dispelling the fears of conscience, sooth-
ing the sorrows of the heart, and bringing life and immortality to
light.

Divine revelation, though infinitely above human reason, does
not in the least oppose it. That God should clearly make known
his will to man, is so far from being contrary to reason, that we may
truly say, nothing is more reasonable. The deductions of reason
from the insufficiency of natural religion strongly indicate the necessity of such a revelation; and as to its possibility, we know that
there can be no impossibility on the part of God to give it, and there
is no impossibility on the part of man to receive it. God is able to
communicate his will to his creatures in any way he pleases. He
can stamp it on the mind, and make us know that it is he who
speaks to us. But he has chosen another method. He has given
us a record of his will in the Holy Scriptures. "God who, at sundry times, and in divers manners, spake in time past unto the fathers
by the prophets, hath in these last days spoken unto us by his Son,
whom he hath appointed heir of all things, by whom also he made
the worlds. Therefore we ought to give the more earnest heed to

* Acts xvii. 22—28.

the things which we have heard, lest at any time we should let them slip."

Is the gospel the truth of God or not? Much has been written on this question. The arguments that have been advanced in support of the affirmative have never been overthrown, and never can be, by all the skeptics in the world. The revelation of the method of salvation was given in the garden of Eden to our first parents. Since that period great talents have been employed, talents worthy of a better cause, in ridiculing the Bible; but to very little purpose. The character of the Book of God stands firm as a mountain amid the clouds, the thunders, and the whirlwinds; and all the opposition of infidels and blasphemers, instead of tarnishing, have only brightened its lustre; and from every trial through which it has passed, it has come forth as fine gold from the furnace. The religions of the world, the vices and virtues of the world, all its wisdom and sagacity, and all its power and authority, in league with the demons of the pit, have not been able to destroy the gospel, or stay the wheels of its chariot. Though they were headed by the prince of darkness —the prince of this world—the prince of the power of the air, that worked mightily in the children of disobedience, in Palestine, in Greece and Rome, and all over the world; yet the gospel has proved triumphant. Its enemies, human and infernal, may wonder and be amazed at its prosperity; but let them remember that its author is the living God, and liveth for ever. Though its ministers have been persecuted and imprisoned, stoned, sawn asunder, slain with the sword, and burnt in the flames; yet the word of the Lord is not bound, but is freely preached in many parts of the world, and its doctrines and practices maintained in their purity by multitudes of Christians, notwithstanding the most dreadful attempts that have been made at different times to corrupt and destroy them. "For all flesh is as grass, and all the glory of man as the flower of grass. The grass withereth and the flower thereof falleth away; but the word of the Lord endureth for ever. And this is the word which by the gospel is preached unto you."

We would now call your attention to the Divine authority of the gospel, and its characteristic glory.

I. It is "the gospel of the blessed God"—a message from God to man—a revelation of God's gracious method of saving sinners through the death of his Son—a declaration of his sovereign love and mercy to the utterly wretched and perishing children of men. It testifieth of the coming of the promised Messiah; of the glory of his person as God-man; of the excellency of his offices, as our Prophet, Priest, and King; the honor which he has conferred upon the law that we have violated, and the satisfaction which he has given to the Divine justice that we have insulted. It records the sufferings and death of Christ, his victory over the powers of darkness, his resurrection from the grave, his ascension to glory, his session at the right hand of the Father, and his intercession for sinners on the ground of his vicarious sufferings; and predicts his second coming in glory, on the clouds of heaven, to judge the quick and the dead.

I do not mean to say that there is no other truth necessary to be preached and believed, but all the truths of Divine revelation are immediately connected with the doctrine of the cross. This is the testimony that the Father hath testified of his 'Son. This is the glad tidings of great joy which shall be unto all people. This is the faithful saying, or true report, that is worthy of all acceptation, that Christ Jesus came into the world to save the chief of sinners. This is " the glorious gospel of the blessed God;" emanating from his spirit, and conducting to his kingdom. Let us consider the evidences of its Divine authority.

The perfections of God, in some degree, are manifested in all his works and words; his character is stamped on every thing that his hands hath formed, and his mouth hath spoken; so that there is a vast difference between the work and language of God, and the work and language of men. This is especially the case in reference to the Christian revelation. It is " the gospel of the blessed God," and bears throughout the impress of its author. When John saw the Lamb in the midst of the throne, he had no difficulty in determining that he was a proper object of adoration and praise. As soon as any one sees the stone with seven eyes laid before Zerubabel, he knows that it is not a common stone. When you look to the book of the firmament, the fingers of the Creator's eternal power and Godhead are evidently seen in the sun, the moon and the stars. So, in the Bible, we trace·the same Divine hand. As often as I read it, I see eternity, with its flaming eye, gazing upon me. It unfolds to me the mysteries of creation and providence. It informs me who made, and still sustains and governs the universe. It leads me to the spring and original cause of all things; and places me immediately before the eyes of the eternal God; and I find myself, in his presence, both killed and made alive —most dreadfully oppressed, and set at perfect liberty—sunk in the valley of repentance and humiliation, and lifted upon the top of Pisgah—full of fears, and full of joy—desiring to hide myself from his sight, yet wishing to abide in the light of his countenance for ever!

I see the eye of Omniscience looking out upon me from every chapter of the Bible—from every doctrine, every precept, every promise, every ordinance of the gospel—penetrating alike the darkness and the light—searching me through and through, till I can hide nothing from its gaze—giving me a faithful representation of my conscience and my heart—making me hate myself, and confess my uncleanness, and cry out for the creation of a right spirit within me. And then I see it looking far into futurity—discovering, many hundreds of years beforehand, the smallest circumstances in the life and death of Jesus, even to the price of his betrayal, the gall mingled with his drink, and the lot cast for his vesture. How can I doubt that this is the eye of God?

Again: I see Holiness, Justice, and Truth, gazing upon me from the very heart of the gospel, like so many eyes of consuming fire. I tremble before them, like Moses before the burning bush, or Israel at the base of Sinai. Yet do I wish to behold this terrible glory, for it is mingled with milder beams of mercy. I take off my shoes, and approach that I may contemplate. "Truly, God is in this place!" I cannot live in sin under the intense blaze of his countenance. But here also I find the cleft of the Rock, even the Rock of Ages, wherein he hides me with his hand, while he makes all his goodness pass before me, and proclaims to me his name—"The Lord, the Lord God, merciful and gracious, forgiving iniquity, and transgression, and sin, and by no means clearing the guilty!"

"The word of God is quick and powerful, sharper than a two-edged sword; piercing to the dividing asunder of soul and spirit, and of the joints and marrow; and discerning"—revealing—condemning—correcting—"the thoughts and intents of the heart." It unlocks my soul, and sits upon its throne; an infallible judge over all my secret imaginations, purposes, and feelings; bringing them under its own perfect law; examining them in the light of spotless holiness, inflexible justice, and eternal truth. And when I shrink from the scrutiny, overwhelmed with a sense of my corruption, and confessing my guilt with a broken and contrite heart, then it speaks to me of the boundless love of God, and the infinite merit of Christ; and "a still small voice" directs my sight to the holy of holies; where I see, through the rent vail, the King of Zion, sitting upon his throne of grace, more glorious than the ancient Shekinah upon the mercy-seat. I approach with joyful confidence, and find him invested with my own nature, "God manifest in the flesh," his royal garments red with sacrificial blood; and again I hear the still small voice—"Thy faith hath saved thee; go in peace!" And when the dark mountains of tribulation rise up before me, I see their tops gilded with beams of love; and when I look into the valley of the shadow of death, I see it brightening with the footsteps of the Son of God; and when the soul sits solitary and dejected in her mortal prison, longing for the wings of a dove, that she may fly away and be at rest, she sees the eyes of her Deliverer looking through the crevices of the wall, and hears his voice at the grated window—"Fear not, for I am with thee; be not dismayed, for I am thy God!"

Thus the gospel commends itself to my conscience and my heart, as "the gospel of the blessed God." But there is other, and if possible still stronger, proof of its divinity; namely, its power to renew the human soul, and reform the human character. The Earl of Rochester was a great skeptic, and one of the most witty and sarcastic men of his age. In his last sickness, he was reading the fifty-third chapter of Isaiah; where the prophet, in so graphic and touching a manner, describes the vicarious sufferings of Christ. It scattered all his deistical doubts, as the sun scatters the mist of the morning; led him with a broken and believing heart to the atoning Lamb of God; and converted his death-bed into a vestibule of heaven. This is not a solitary case. Thousands and millions have been, in like manner, awakened and converted through the gospel, and brought to the knowledge of the truth as it is in Jesus. It is "mighty through God, to the pulling down of strong-holds; casting down imaginations, and every high thing that exalteth itself against the knowledge of God; and bringing into captivity every thought to the obedience of Christ"—turning men from darkness to light, and from the power of Satan to God, that they may receive remission of sins, and an inheritance among all them that are sanctified through faith in Jesus. Matthew at the custom-house, the woman of Samaria at Jacob's well, the dying malefactor upon the cross, the penitent jailor at Philippi, the blasphemous persecutor on the road to Damascus, and three thousand souls under Peter's preaching at the Pentecost, all found it "the power of God unto salvation." And still it retains its convincing and quickening virtue. Wherever it is proclaimed in its purity, and accompanied with the power of the Holy Ghost, proud and hardened sinners are pricked in their hearts, and forced to cry out—"Men and brethren, what must we do?" It answers the question. It points to the crucified and saith—"Believe and be saved!" It reconciles the enemy unto God. It makes the blasphemer a man of prayer, the sensualist a man of purity, the inebriate a man of sobriety; and where sin abounded, grace much more abounds. The dead whom Jesus quickened had no time to inquire into the mysterious process by which the work was wrought. They sprang instantly into life by the power of God. Yet the evidence of the change was clear and incontestible. So it is with the transforming effects of the gospel. We cannot rationally doubt its power to raise the soul from death in trespasses and sins. Suppose I have been long afflicted with a cancer, or have been bitten by a mad-dog, or a rattlesnake; and I find a sovereign and instantaneous remedy; but after I am cured, a skeptic calls upon me, and tries to convince me that the remedy is good for nothing, insists that it is a cheat lately invented by a villain, demands of me to prove that such things were used before the deluge, and asks me a thousand questions about the cure which Solomon could not answer; how can I look upon such a man as better than a maniac? I have tried the experiment, and found it successful; and all his pretended philosophical reasoning rings in my ears like a sounding brass, or a tinkling cymbal. The wisdom of men has invented many remedies for the guilt and the love of sin; but the vain philosophy of the world has never, like the gospel, restored a single soul to peace, purity, and happiness. I can truly say, after the most careful self-examination, and millions more can testify the same thing, that the gospel, in the hand of the Spirit of God, has subdued the love of sin, and quenched the fire of guilt within me; and has taken away the sting of death, and the terrors of the grave. If the infidel will allow that I am a sane man, and a man of truth, what farther proof does he want that this is " the gospel of the blessed God?"

Once more : The character of God, as exhibited in the gospel, is perfect, every way worthy of himself, infinitely above any original conception of the human mind. The gods of Homer and Virgil are cruel and revengeful. The god of Mohammed delights in pollution and crime. The god of Voltaire is a buffoon, and the god of Paine a tyrant. But the gospel represents the Deity in his true character, as the concentration and the fountain of all moral excellence.

All this evidence of the Divine authority of the gospel is corroborated by an overwhelming array of external proof. It was certainly written by the men whose names it bears. They were men of irreproachable character. Their declarations were confirmed by the testimony of miracles, and the fulfilment of prophecy. Jesus of Nazareth was crucified on Calvary, rose from the dead the third day, and ascended to heaven, according to the Scriptures. These were facts believed by the primitive Christians, and admitted by their enemies. They were received with the most perfect confidence by the immediate successors of the original witnesses; and farther corroborated by the testimony of neutrals, apostates, and the most inveterate opponents. The question therefore is settled; all is admitted that is necessary to prove that the Christian's gospel is " the gospel of the blessed God."

II. It is " the *glorious* gospel"—emphatically and pre-eminently glorious; and this is our second topic of discourse.

It is a wonderful exhibition of the glory of God—the most perfect revelation of the Divine attributes ever granted to man—displaying the sovereign mercy of the Father, in the gift of his beloved Son; the infinite compassion of Christ, in offering himself upon the cross for our sins; and the gracious power of the Holy Spirit, in turning us from darkness to light, and renewing us in righteousness and true holiness after the image of God.

But it is chiefly from a comparison of the gospel with the law, both in its dispensation and its character, that we see its transcendant glory. On this point let us fix our attention.

" The law was given by Moses, but grace and truth came by Jesus Christ." The ministration of the law brought the angels from heaven to earth, but the ministration of the gospel required the incarnation of the God of angels. The Mediator of the new covenant is Jehovah enshrined in humanity—"Emmanuel"—"God with us"—"God manifest in the flesh"—"the fulness of the Godhead," that "filleth all in all," imbodied and made visible in the lowly Son of David.

This is the foundation of the apostle's argument, by which he convicts the despisers of the gospel of greater guilt than the transgressors of the law. "If the word spoken by angels"—that is, the law given upon Sinai—"was steadfast, and every transgression and disobedience received a just recompense of reward; how shall we escape"—we who have heard the glad tidings of the gospel—"if we neglect so great salvation; which at first began to be spoken by the Lord, and was confirmed unto us by them that heard him; God also bearing them witness, with signs, and wonders, and divers miracles, and gifts of the Holy Ghost?" If God is greater than man, then the gospel is greater than the law; and its superior excellence constitutes for it a superior claim upon our faith and our affections; and the strength of that claim graduates the guilt of its rejection. There is a fire more intense than that which flamed on Sinai, and a judgment more terrible than that of Korah and his confederates. "He that despised Moses' law died without mercy, under two or three witnesses; of how much sorer punishment, suppose ye, shall he be thought worthy, who hath trodden under foot the Son of God, and hath counted the blood of the covenant an unholy thing, and hath done despite to the Spirit of grace!"

The ceremonial law contained many a type and shadow of Messiah; but the gospel is the history of his advent and mediatorial work. The ceremonial law pointed to the coming Prince of Peace; but the gospel brings him to his throne, and puts the crown upon his head. Christ is "the brightness of the Father's glory, and the express image of his person;" and Moses and Aaron are lost in his light, as the moon and the stars in the blaze of the rising sun. The excellence of his person, the merit of his sacrifice, and the utility of his offices, give him an immense superiority. The many prophets, priests, and kings, of the former dispensation, were but the shadows cast by the one great Prophet, Priest, and King, which indicated his coming. A light arose from the cross of Calvary, which turned the black cloud on Sinai into a pillar of glory.

Typical blood shielded the children of Israel from the arm of the destroying angel, healed the leper, anointed to holy offices, atoned for ceremonial sins, and sealed the covenant of God with his people; but never cancelled the sinner's debt, nor satisfied his conscience, nor sanctified his affections, nor calmed his trembling spirit in the hour of death. All these blessings, however, flow from the blood of Christ—these, and infinitely more—more than tongue can tell, or heart conceive.

The gospel is emphatically the ministration of mercy—the covenant of grace, " ordered in all things and sure"—a goodly ship, freighted with the bread of life, and commanded by the Son of God, who has steered into the harbor of our famishing world, and is dispensing the precious provision to all who will accept. These are " the sure mercies of David."

The law is only a partial revelation of the Divine attributes, which, in the gospel, are all equally exhibited, and all equally glorified. Here, " Mercy and Truth are met together; Righteousness and Peace have kissed each other." The justice of God looks more terrible at the cross of Christ than at the gate of hell; and is more glorified in the sufferings of his Son than in the eternal agonies of all the damned ; while his mercy is more beautiful, because more honorable to his administration, than if sinners had been saved without an atonement.

Thus, while the law reveals the righteousness of God, the gospel brightens the revelation of his righteousness, and adds the revelation of his grace. While the law imprisons the sinner, the gospel liberates him, yet liberates him according to law. While the law shows the malignity of sin, and dooms the sinner to death, the gospel assents to both, but conquers the one and counteracts the other.

The law convinces us of our fall; the gospel assures us of our redemption. The law shows us what we are, and what we ought to be ; the gospel tells us what we may become, and how the change must be effected. The law tears open our wounds ; the gospel pours in the healing balm. The law makes known our duty; the gospel aids us to perform it. The law plunges us in the ditch ; the gospel opens to us the purifying fountain. The law is a mirror in which we behold our own filthiness and deformity; the gospel is a mirror which reflects the glory of God in Christ, and transforms the believer into the same image.

The law has no fellowship with the sinner—offers no pardon to the sinner—cannot cure the love of sin in his heart—cannot give a spark of life, without perfect obedience, and full satisfaction for past offences. Therefore some accuse the law of cruelty—cannot set forth the superior glory of the gospel, without representing the law as a tyrant or a vagrant. But it is not the cruelty of the law, but the righteousness of the law, that condemns the sinner. This is the reason that it has no alms-house, nor city of refuge, in its dominion. Yet " the law is our schoolmaster, to bring us to Christ." By convincing us of sin, it shows us our need of a Saviour. It meets the sinner on his way to hell, and drives him back to Calvary!

But the gospel is more glorious. It enters the sinner's heart, and casts out the love of sin, and scourges the traffickers from the temple of God. It enters the prisoner's cell, knocks off his fetters, and bids him go free. It descends into the valley of dry bones, makes the mouldering skeletons living men, and leads them to Mount Zion with songs of everlasting joy. It gives eyes to the blind, ears to the deaf, feet to the lame, tongues to the dumb, health to the sick, life to the dead, and revives such as are fainting under the terrors of the law. It is " the power of God unto salvation to every one that believeth."

The Moravian missionaries in Greenland preached several years on the great doctrines of natural religion, and the requirements of the moral law, without producing any visible reformation in their hearers; but under the very first sermon which exhibited " Jesus Christ and him crucified," many " were pricked in their hearts, and led effectually to repentance.

We have a striking illustration of the distinguishing glory of the gospel—its mercy—in the parable of the prodigal son. The young man, having received his portion from his Father, went into a far country, and spent all his substance in drunkenness and debauchery. Reduced to the last extremity of want, the proud young nobleman hired himself to a citizen of that country, and became a feeder of swine—the meanest employment to which a Jew could be degraded. On the very verge of starvation, we see him snatching the husks from the mouths of the detested animals to satisfy his hunger. Now he contrasts the present with the past. " My father's house! O, my father's house!" A trembling hope springs up in his bosom. "I will arise and go!" I see him coming, full of guilt and shame— halting—trembling—ready to turn back, or lie down by the way-

side and die. While yet a great way off, the father beholds him—
O, not with an eye of anger and revenge! and runs to meet him—
O, not with a drawn sword, or an uplifted rod! He feels within
him the yearning of a father's heart, leaps to embrace the prodigal,
and pours upon him a mingled shower of kisses and tears. Not a
reproachful word is uttered—not the slightest censure—nothing but
love. " Father, I have sinned! I am not worthy to be"—"Peace,
my son! Servants, bring a robe, a ring, a pair of shoes; and haste
to kill the fatted calf; and let us eat and be merry; for this my son
was dead and is alive, was lost and is found!" "And they began
to be merry."

Such, my brethren, is the unspeakable mercy of the gospel, which
constitutes its distinguishing glory. It is the law that creates the
famine in the "far country" of sin. The poor prodigal goes about,
begging for bread; but none will give him a crust, or a crumb.
The desert of Mount Sinai is a poor country for a starving soul.
There is no bread in all that region, and no toleration for beggars.
If the sinner offers to work for any of the citizens—either for Mr.
Holiness, or Mr. Justice, or Mr. Truth—he is sent into the fields to
feed swine, till he is thoroughly convinced of the nakedness of the
land, and the misery of his lot; and if he faints through famine or
fatigue, and fails to perform his task, he is thrust into the house of
correction, and placed upon the tread-wheel of remorse, till the
ministers of mercy come to his relief. It is the gospel that whis-
pers—" Return to thy father!" It is the gospel that inspires the
hope of acceptance. It is the gospel that meets him with more than
paternal welcome, and rains upon him the baptism of blessings
and tears. It is the gospel that brings its robe of righteousness,
and its ring of favour, and spreads its feast of joy, and calls the angels to merry-making " over one sinner that repenteth."

O, the love of God! O, the riches of Christ! His salvation is
more than a restoration to the joys of Eden. He came that we
might have life, and that we might have it more abundantly. Where
sin abounded under the law, grace hath much more abounded under
the gospel. It is an ocean of blessings—" blessings of the heaven
above, and of the deep that lieth under"—the blessings of Jacob,
" prevailing above the blessings of his progenitors, unto the utmost
bound of the everlasting hills"—blessings which cannot be circum-
scribed by time, passing over the mountains which now divide us

from the promised land, and flowing down on the other side into the pacific vales of immortality!

Such is "the glorious gospel of the blessed God." You have seen the evidence of its divinity, and the peculiar excellence of its character. Suffer me to ask, do you believe its doctrines? do you obey its precepts? do you enjoy its blessings? do you delight in its promises? It commends itself every way to your faith, and your affections. It is worthy of all acceptation. It is the light of the world—walk ye in it! It is a feast for the soul—eat and be satisfied! It is a river of living water—drink and thirst no more!

How miserable is that man who rejects alike its evidences and its offers! How miserable in the hour of death! As Thistlewood said of himself, when on the drop at Newgate, he is "taking a leap in the dark!" How miserable in the day of judgment! God saith —"Because I have called, and ye refused; I have stretched out my hands all the day long, and no man regarded; but ye have set at naught my counsel, and would none of my reproof; therefore I also will laugh at your calamity, I will mock when your fear cometh— when your fear cometh as desolation, and your destruction cometh as a whirlwind—when distress and anguish cometh upon you!"

THE SONG OF THE ANGELS

Glory to God in the highest, and on earth peace, good will toward men (Luke 2:14).

THE most important event recorded in the annals of time, is the incarnation of the Son of God. Anointed to be "the Apostle and High Priest of our profession," it was necessary that he should humble himself, to assume our degraded nature, and enter into our suffering condition. Had he appeared on earth in the unmitigated glory of his Godhead, the children of men could not have borne the revelation, and could not have been benefited by his personal ministry; neither could he have been "touched with the feeling of our infirmities," nor have offered himself a sacrifice for our sins. His manifestation in the flesh was essential to the great objects of his advent; and no wonder the heavenly host descended to announce his coming, and poured forth their delight in this joyful strain;— "Glory to God in the highest, and on earth peace, good will toward men."

Let us consider, *first*, The incarnation of the Eternal Word; and, *secondly*, The song of the angels on the occasion of his birth.

I. Though it is impossible for the immutable God to be made a creature, yet the Divine nature was so closely and mysteriously joined to the human, that the same person was "a child born," and "the Mighty God"—"a son given," and "the Everlasting Father." The Divinity did not become humanity, and the humanity did not become Divinity; but the two were so united as to constitute but one glorious Mediator.

Though his incarnation did not destroy, or even tarnish in the least, the essential glory of the Deity; yet was it a mighty and marvellous condescension, for him who is "over all, God, blessed for ever," thus to assume our frail and suffering flesh. Solomon asked —"Will God in very deed dwell with men upon the earth?" A question which neither men nor angels could answer. But God hath answered it himself, and answered it in the affirmative. "The Word" that "was in the beginning with God, and was God," in the fulness of time, "was made flesh, and dwelt among us, and we beheld his glory, the glory as of the only begotten of the Father, full of grace and truth."

We can form no idea of the natural distance between God and man. But the infinite vacuum is filled up by the Messiah. He is "Emmanuel"—"the true God," and "the Son of Man." "He thought it not robbery to be equal with God, but made himself of no reputation, and took upon himself the form of a servant, and was made in the likeness of sinful flesh." Passing by the nobler nature of angels, "he took on him the seed of Abraham." Nor did he join himself to humanity in its original perfection and glory. He came into the mean condition of fallen creatures, sharing with us our various infirmities and sufferings. Yet he was free from all moral contamination. He was "holy, harmless, undefiled, and separate from sinners." He "knew no sin." He "did no iniquity, neither was guile found in his mouth."

But notwithstanding the humility of his appearance in Bethlehem, such was the dignity of his person, and such the magnitude and grandeur of the work for which he came into the world, that angels descended from heaven to publish the glad tidings to the children of men. True, no ambassadors were sent to the Sanhedrim at Jerusalem—none to the Senate of Rome, to proclaim the coming of the Prince of Peace; but never was there such an embassage on earth, to announce the birth of a royal son, as that which came to the shepherds of Bethlehem. When he appeared among men, the order was given in heaven, that all the angels of God should worship him; and their example was followed by wise men upon earth. The prophet Isaiah said that his name should be called Wonderful; and the angel informed Mary that he should be great, and should be called the Son of the Highest; and that God should give unto him the throne of his father David, and he should reign over the house of Jacob for ever. "Though he was rich, yet for our sake he became poor, that we through his poverty might be rich." He humbled himself that we might be exalted—was bruised and wounded that we might be healed—died the most shameful death that men could inflict, that we might live the most glorious life that God can confer!

II. Let us now consider the import of the anthem, sung by the heavenly host, when he was born in Bethlehem. "Glory to God in the highest, and on earth peace, good will toward men."

1. "Glory to God in the highest." The shining light between the cherubim, on the mercy-seat, was called "the glory of the Lord," being a supernatural representation of his presence in the sanctuary. Three of the apostles saw the same glory upon the mount of trans-figuration, and all believers have seen it by faith. The word "glory," in the anthem of the angels, refers to the divine honor and praise resulting from the humiliation of Christ. The redemp-tion of sinners, through the blood of the cross, and by the grace of the Holy Spirit, is not only consistent with the glory of God, but highly promotive of his glory, as our Creator and Lawgiver. It brightens all the gems previously visible in his crown, and reveals others that were concealed. His glory, as seen in the works of creation and providence, is the glory of wisdom, power, and love. His glory, as seen in his law and its administration, is the glory of holiness, justice, and truth. These are essential to his nature and his government. But in the incarnation and the cross of Christ, we behold a new glory, a glory nowhere else displayed, the glory of mercy. God was known before to be the friend of saints, but here he shows himself the friend of sinners. His character as pre-viously revealed was matter of admiration and praise in earth and heaven, but this new revelation occasions new wonder and rejoicing to men and angels. Angels delighted to bear the joyful news to men, and this was the burden of their message:—"Behold, we bring you glad tidings of great joy, which shall be unto"—the righteous? the benevolent and charitable? no; but—"unto all people." And what are these tidings? "To you is born, this day, in the city of David, a Saviour, who is Christ the Lord." Here is the Lawgiver embracing the rebels; his the glory, theirs the benefit; while angels participate the joy of both, singing— "Glory to God in the highest, and on earth peace."

2. "On earth peace." Not by a compromise with Satan, as he

proposed when he tempted the Son of God in the wilderness. Not at the expense of the Divine law, but by magnifying and making it honorable. Not a peace with enmity, for Christ hath slain the enmity by his cross. Our peace flows from the reconciling blood of Jesus. Nothing else could satisfy the claims of Divine justice, and procure pardon for the penitent believer.

Without the atonement, there is no peace for sinners. There is an accusing witness within. Behold that king in the banqueting-house! Why changes his countenance? Why tremble his knees? Have the wise men of Babylon interpreted the mystic writing upon the wall? No; but conscience has. Conscience has given dreadful intimations of its meaning, before Daniel comes into the presence of the king, and the Hebrew prophet only confirms the previous interpretation. Every sinner bears about with him that internal tormentor. It may be bribed; but not for ever. It may be lulled to sleep; but it will awake with increased energy, and augmented wrath. The gnawing worm may be stupified for a season, but cannot be killed. The devouring fire may be temporarily stifled, but cannot be quenched. How dreadful are its torments, when it wreaks all its anger upon the guilty! To be drowned in the Red Sea, like Pharaoh—to be swallowed up by the earth, like Korah—to be hewn in pieces, like Agag—to be eaten of worms, like Herod—is nothing in the comparison.

Where shall we find peace? We have heard of a stone which nothing but blood can dissolve. Such a stone is the human conscience. But all the blood shed on Jewish altars could never effect the work. It must be the blood of Jesus. He is "the Lamb of God that taketh away the sin of the world." At his cross, the believer's conscience finds assurance and repose. He is the good physician, and his blood is the sovereign balm. Come to his extended arms! Come, for he waits to be gracious!

3. "Good will toward men." The "good will" of whom? Of God, blessed for ever. The funds of a benevolent society may be exhausted, so that its members in distress can receive no benefit. But in the "good will" of God we find unsearchable riches of grace, sufficient to pay off our whole debt to the law, and restore our forfeited inheritance; to bring forth the prisoners, and them that sit in darkness, out of the prison-house; to support the believer through life, and comfort him in death, and raise him from the grave not a

beggar, or a pensioner, but a prince, clothed in white, and entitled to an everlasting kingdom.

Did I possess the nature of angels, with my present sinfulness, I should have no hope of salvation, for God hath provided no mercy for fallen angels; but, in his infinite wisdom, he hath devised a method for the consistent display of his "good will toward men," by assuming their nature, and in that nature atoning for their sins. This is a wonderful scheme, whereby God can be just, and yet justify the ungodly. His law is honoured, though its violater be acquitted; and his government is secure, though the rebel be forgiven.

Methinks I hear the Infant in Bethlehem, speaking from the manger, in the strain of the Evangelical Prophet:—"Is my hand shortened at all, that I cannot redeem; or have I no power to deliver? Behold, at my rebuke I dry up the sea, and make the rivers a wilderness; I clothe the heavens with blackness, and make sackcloth their covering. Though ye see me in human flesh, I am still Lord of all, and can save unto the uttermost. Though ye do not hear me, I have the tongue of the learned, to speak a word in season to him that is weary. I have taken upon myself your nature, that I may be able to sympathize in your sufferings, and make satisfaction for your sins. For you will I give my back to the smiters, and my cheek to them that pluck off the hair; and I will not hide my face from shame and spitting. Calvary and Joseph's grave shall manifest my benevolence, and it shall be seen that my mercy is mightier than death. Who will contend with me? Let him come near! Let us stand together! I challenge all the powers of darkness to defeat the purposes of my grace. I will triumph by suffering. I will dash them in pieces as a potter's vessel. Hell shall tremble at the report; and on every gate and door-post, in all my journey from this place to Golgotha, and thence home to my Father's house, shall be inscribed the record of my good will toward men!"

"This is a faithful saying, and worthy of all acceptation, that Christ Jesus came into the world to save sinners." Behold him pressing the wine of eternal life for us from the cup of his own mortality; demolishing the kingdom of darkness on earth, and establishing in its stead the kingdom of heaven; destroying the works of the devil, delivering the captives from his iron yoke, and uniting sinners to himself in everlasting fellowship and love. The whole economy of Divine grace, based on the incarnation of the Son of God, is like a complicated piece of machinery, consisting of many wheels, all revolving in harmony, and impelled by the same power. Salvation is a river, flowing from the manger in Bethlehem, conveying eternal life to millions, and bearing away many a precious gem from the dominions of death and hell. It has already swept from the earth more false gods than would have filled the Roman Pantheon; and carried multitudes of human souls, pardoned and purified, to Abraham's bosom. No opposition of men or devils can stand before "the glorious gospel of the blessed God." O that its light may shine into the heart and the conscience of every hearer! May the goodness of God lead you all to repentance, and fill you with peace in believing! Then will you go forth with joy, and publish his "good will toward men;" and when the purposes of his mercy are accomplished in your hearts, you shall be removed from grace to glory—from peace to perfect love—and sin and sorrow shall be shut out for ever! Amen.

Sermon 18
STONE OF ISRAEL

Behold the stone that I have laid before Joshua. Upon one stone shall be seven eyes. Behold, I will engrave the graving thereof, saith the Lord of hosts, and I will remove the iniquity of that land in one day (Zechariah 3:9).

AMID all the tribulations which the church has suffered, she has ever been preserved and sustained by the gracious providence of God; like the bush in Horeb—burning, yet unconsumed.

In the days of this prophet, the church was feeble and afflicted. Having just returned from the captivity in Babylon, by which she had been greatly reduced, she resembled the myrtle among the oaks, the firs, and the cedars. But the Messiah appears to the prophet, standing among the myrtle-trees, and encouraging the children of Israel to proceed in rebuilding Jerusalem and the temple. The good success of Zerubbabel is represented by a golden candlestick, with a bowl at the top, and seven lamps for the light, and seven pipes to convey the oil to the lamps, and two olive-trees —one on each side—pouring the oil into the pipes. This was intended also to set forth the relation of Christ to his church, as her head, and the fountain whence she derives strength and nourishment, enabling her to grow in grace, and the saving knowledge of God. As they bring forth the foundation and the corner-stones with joy, wondering at the Divine goodness and mercy, Jehovah shows them that he is about to lay in Zion the foundation and chief corner-stone of a spiritual temple: "Behold the stone that I have laid before Joshua. Upon one stone shall be seven eyes. Behold I will engrave the graving thereof, saith the Lord of hosts, and I will remove the iniquity of that land in one day."

Let us consider the important truths taught us in this metaphorical description of Christ and his mediatorial work.

I. Christ is the foundation and chief corner-stone of his church. This figure is often used in the Holy Scriptures. "From hence is the Shepherd, the Stone of Israel"—said Jacob in the blessing of Joseph. "The stone which the builders refused," said the Psalmist, "is become the head-stone of the corner." And Isaiah said— "Thus saith the Lord God : Behold, I lay in Zion, for a foundation, a stone, a tried stone, a precious corner-stone, a sure foundation." All these predictions were appropriated by Messiah, to whom they were intended to apply. Christ is the foundation and chief corner-stone. "Other foundation can no man lay than that which is laid, which is Jesus Christ." "Ye are built upon the foundation of the apostles and prophets"—that is, the foundation which they recognised and recommended—"Jesus Christ himself being the chief corner-stone." He is indeed the foundation of the world ; and in the fulness of time, was declared the foundation of the church. All the buildings of mercy that have ever been erected stand firm and immovable on this Rock of Ages.

In the architecture of the first covenant in Eden, there was a Stone under one end, and earth under the other. "The first man was of the earth, earthy." And when the storm and the flood came, the earth gave way, and the building fell. But in the architecture of the second covenant upon Calvary, God laid help upon one that was mighty. "The second man is the Lord from heaven." A stone suitable for the foundation of a royal palace is very valuable, because the safety of the building depends upon the firmness of the foundation. This Stone is "chosen of God and precious." It is long and broad enough for the whole edifice, stretching from eternity to eternity ; and sufficiently strong to sustain it, though millions of living stones be built into the spiritual temple ; and such is its firmness, that time, with all its storms, shall never destroy it, or injure its beauty. It is a tried and precious stone, composed of all that is excellent on earth, and all that is glorious in heaven—a sinless specimen of humanity, possessing "all the fulness of the Godhead bodily." As a foundation, it is laid deep in the earth ; as a corner-stone, it rises above the stars, and binds the whole building in heaven and earth together.

II. This Stone is "laid before Joshua." God has revealed his

Son, as the only foundation, and chief corner-stone, to the wise master-builders of his church, in every age of the world. The seed was promised in Eden. Holy men of old beheld the promises afar off. Abraham desired to see his day; he saw it, and was glad. This was the foundation of the prophets and apostles. As Moses found so much of God in the rod that was in his hand, that he could think of no other means for working a miracle; so the prophets and apostles saw and felt so much of Christ in the revelations of which they were made the media, that they could never think of salvation from sin and hell but through his meritorious death; and the most dreadful tortures, and even martyrdom itself, lost their terrors in "the light of the knowledge of the glory of God in the face of Jesus Christ."

This Stone was laid also before Wickliff and Luther. The office and work of Christ had been lost sight of, in the intercession of saints, and the merit of human works. But "the foundation of God standeth sure;" and all the rubbish which Roman monks had heaped upon it could not hide it from the reformers, whose vision had been cleared and quickened by light from heaven. And it was laid before Wesley and Whitefield in England, who built upon it "gold, silver, and precious stones;" and before Powell, Erbery, and Wroth—before Rowlands, Harris, Jones, Evans, Thomas, and Francis—as the foundation of that wonderful revival in Wales, the blessed effects of which we feel to this day.

We are now endeavoring to exhibit the glory and excellency of this Stone, as the foundation of your hopes. Will you build upon Christ? Can you venture your eternal salvation upon the merit of his sacrifice? "He that believeth on him shall not be ashamed."

III. It is said that "upon one stone shall be seven eyes;" by which we may understand, either seven eyes of others, looking upon the stone; or seven eyes in the stone, looking upon others.

If we take the former idea, there are many eyes looking upon this "One Stone;" some from envy, malice, and wrath; others from astonishment, gratitude, and love. It attracts the gaze of heaven, earth, and hell. The eternal Lawgiver looks to Messiah for satisfaction on behalf of guilty man. Mercy and Truth look upon him as the foundation of their palaces. Righteousness and Peace look upon him as the only place where they can salute each other with a kiss. The devil and his angels, sin, death, and the

grave, look upon him with eyes of anger and revenge; determined, if possible, to bruise him with their weapons, and cast him
among the rubbish, into the pit of corruption. Celestial spirits look
upon him with eyes of wonder and delight; announce his coming
to Joseph and Mary, sing his advent to the shepherds of Judea,
accompany him through all his pilgrimage of sorrow, minister to
him after the temptation in the wilderness, talk with him on the
mount of transfiguration, sustain him in the agony of the garden,
gather unseen around his cross, roll away the rock from the entrance
of his tomb, and attend him with songs as he ascends to glory.
And believers look upon him with eyes of faith and love, as the
foundation of all their hopes, in this world, and that which is to
come—as their "wisdom, righteousness, sanctification, and redemption."

The other interpretation refers these "seven eyes" to the perfection of our Lord's mediatorial character. The priest under the
law was to sprinkle the blood seven times upon the mercy-seat,
and seven times upon the leper; the first to typify a perfect atonement for sin; the second, a perfect application of its benefits to the
believer. When the Lamb of God revived from the ashes on the
altar of Calvary, he appeared "in the midst of the throne," having
seven horns and seven eyes, to denote the completeness of his prophetic wisdom, and the fulness of his regal authority. He sustains
to his people the threefold relation of high-priest, prophet, and
king. He is our high-priest, not after the order of Aaron, whom
death robbed of his sacerdotal vesture; but "a high-priest for
ever, after the order of Melchizedec." He is our prophet, speaking with the tongue of the learned, and as one having authority—
speaking to the conscience and the heart, and the dead hear his
voice and live. He is our king, according to the decree, "on the
holy hill of Zion;" exalted by the right-hand of the Father, and
"declared to be the Son of God with power by the resurrection
from the dead." Methinks I hear the Father speaking to Caiaphas:—"Have you a law, and do you say that by your law he
ought to die? I will read to you the law on the morning of the
third day, and you shall see that he is the resurrection and the life
—that I have made him both Lord and Christ!" And methinks I
hear the voice of the risen Messiah:—"I have travelled through
the forest of the world's temptations, through the dens of lions, the

mountains of leopards, the dark haunts of devils, and the dominions of death and the grave; and have opened, through all the desert, a new and living way to my Father's house. The powers of darkness thought to strip me of my official regalia, and bind me for ever in the grave; but I have broken Cæsar's seal, and rent the rocks of Joseph's sepulchre, and am alive for evermore—the high-priest, prophet, and king of Israel. Though I gave myself up to death upon the cross, death could not deprive me of my threefold office. I died with my vesture on, my miter and breastplate, as high-priest over the house of God. I died with the book of the mysteries of the kingdom of heaven in my hand, as a prophet to instruct my people, and lead them into all truth. I died with the crown upon my head, and all my enemies beneath my feet, as a king, whose dominion is everlasting, and whose glory shall never end. Death and hell could not take from me my triple diadem; and I came forth from the place of the dead in the power of an endless life; and will continue to wear my robes unspotted, till I have finished my mediatorial work, and gathered all the saints unto myself!"

IV. This stone is fitted and prepared by God himself. "I will engrave the graving thereof, saith the Lord of hosts."

This figure evidently refers to the sufferings of Christ, by which he was made perfect for his mediatorial work. Many hammers and chisels were upon him from Bethlehem to Calvary; but they were all appointed of God, as the instruments of his preparation to be the sure foundation and chief corner-stone of the church. The Scribes and the Pharisees, Caiaphas, Judas, Pilate, the Jewish populace, and the Roman soldiery, whatever their malicious designs, only accomplished "the determinate counsel and foreknowledge of God" upon his well-beloved Son. All was appointed by the Father; all was understood by the Messiah; all was necessary to secure the great objects of his advent. It pleased the Father to bruise him, and put him to grief; and he cheerfully submitted to suffer, that we might be spared. O, wonder of wonders! Emmanuel wounded, that sinners might be healed! the Golden Vessel marred, that the earthen vessels might be saved! the Green Tree dried up, that the dry tree might grow as the lily, and cast forth its roots like Lebanon! According to another metaphor, "the plowers plowed upon his back; they made long their furrows." And they were deep as well as long. They plowed into his very heart, and his body was covered with blood, and his cry of agony pierced the supernatural gloom of Golgotha, and soured the wine of dragons throughout the region of Gehenna!

Thus the foundation was fitted and prepared; and wicked men and devils but blindly did the work which God had before determined to be done. It is fixed in its place, firm and immovable; and the chief Architect is raising other stones from the quarry, and building them thereon, "for a habitation of God through the Spirit." Brethren, "look unto the rock whence ye are hewn, and the hole of the pit whence ye are digged"—even the flinty rock of impenitence, and the horrible pit of corruption. I have known men relinquish the hewing of stones from the quarry, because it was more expense than profit; and I have known men abandon the digging of ore from the mine, because it was too deep in the mountain. But Christ "descended into the lower parts of the earth," and imbibed the gas of death. He carried in his hand the hammer of the word, which breaketh the flinty rock in pieces. He expelled the deadly vapour, blasted the solid adamant, and prepared the way for the workmen; and when he ascended, he sent down the apostles, to gather stones for his spiritual temple; while he stands at the top of the shaft, and turns the windlass of intercession, by which he draws up all to himself.

The work was gloriously begun on the day of Pentecost, and men and demons have never yet been able entirely to stop its progress. The pope and the devil tried their best, for a long time, to keep the digging and hewing tools of the twelve wise master-builders concealed in the vaults of the monasteries; but Luther, with the lamp of God in his hand, discovered them, brought them forth, and set them at work; and millions of lively stones have since been dug out, and sent up from the pit, to be placed in the walls of "God's building."

And still the gospel is mighty in the salvation of souls, of which we have abundant evidence in the principality. What multitudes were converted at Langeiththo in the days of Rowlands and Williams; when two thousand communicants in the winter, and three thousand in the summer, met every month in the same place around the table of the Lord! And there are now in Wales hundreds of large and flourishing churches among the Baptists and Independents.

Glory to God, that I have in my own possession the register of hundreds, who have been hewn from the flinty rock, and raised from the horrible pit, to a place in the Lord's holy temple—from drunkenness to sobriety, from unbelief to faith in Christ, from enmity to reconciliation to God, from persecution to patient suffering for righteousness' sake, from disobedience to the filial temper of "sons and daughters of the Lord Almighty;" and many of them I have seen going home, rejoicing, to their Father's house above!

Hark! what do I hear? The hammers and chisels of mercy all over the mountain of the militant church. The great Architect is building up Zion. He is gathering his materials from Europe, and Asia, and Africa, and America. Glory to God! I hear his footsteps to-day in this mountain; I see his hand in this congregation. Brethren in the ministry, we are workers together with him. Delightful work! How easy it is to preach, when the hand of God is with us! Let us labour on! The topstone will soon be brought forth with shouting, the sound of the building shall cease, and we shall receive our reward!

V. The gracious design for which this Divine Foundation is prepared, is the justification and sanctification of sinners. "I will remove the iniquity of that land in one day."

Christ came to destroy the works of the devil—to take away sin by the offering of himself. As the moon is illuminated by the sun, so the rites and ceremonies of the old testament are illustrated by the facts and doctrines of the new. The priesthood of Jesus explains the priesthood of Aaron. The one sacrifice of Calvary explains all the sacrifices that went before. The glory of God in the face of Jesus Christ enters the windows of Solomon's temple, and penetrates the Holy of Holies within the vail. All the bloody offerings of the Mosaic ritual were intended only as types of him who "removed the iniquity of that land in one day."

What land? Emmanuel's land—a garden enclosed, and measured by the line of God's eternal purpose; including all the redeemed of the Lord, who will ultimately be brought to glory. The map of "that land" was in the mind of Jehovah, when he made this promise through the prophet. He remembered his covenant engagement before the foundation of the world in reference to its redemption. He saw it encumbered by mountains of sin, and blasted by the fiery curse of the law; and in the fulness of time, he sent his Son to deliver it.

To remove iniquity is to remove its penalty and its pollution Christ hath accomplished both for believers. He " bore our sins in his own body on the tree!" He carried upon his own shoulder the burden which must have sunk the whole human race to eternal perdition. By enduring our punishment, he provided for our purification. In his own wounds a fountain was opened wherein we may wash and be clean. From his own heart the balm was extracted whereby our moral leprosy may be cured. " Behold the Lamb of God, that taketh away the sin of the world." See how our great High-priest removes the iniquity of his people ; not, like Aaron, by many sacrifices; but by the single offering of himself, " in one day."

The word which is here rendered " remove" is in the original the same as that which is used to express the translation of Enoch. As Enoch was removed from the earth, beyond the sight of man, and the power of death ; so sin is removed by the Mediator—removed for ever from the believer's heart and conscience—blotted out—cast into the depth of the sea—carried away into the land of forgetfulness. The removal is perfect and everlasting.

This was a work which Jewish sacrifices were too weak to accomplish. For two thousand years the victims bled upon the altar, and not a single sin was actually removed. Every year the goat of the burnt-offering must bleed afresh, and the scape-goat must be sent away into the wilderness. But Jesus, the great ante-type of all these emblems, removed in one day, by a single offering, the iniquities of all who believe in him, from the fall to the end of time.

All the sacrifices that preceded his coming were intended only to remind men that they were sinners, that they needed an atonement, and that justification and eternal life could flow only from the meritorious sufferings of the future Christ. But when the substance came, the shadows passed away, and the promised work was at once accomplished ; and all our iniquities were lost in the sea of mercy, which rose to a full tide in the Mediator's merit.

Sinners, do you expect ever to be made free from sin ? Would you have your leprosy cured, your impurity cleansed, and the curse removed ? Come to our great High-priest ! Lo, he stands by the altar, and the blood is on his hands ! He waits to be gracious ! Come, for he has virtually removed your iniquity, and it requires in you but a simple act of faith to realize the benefit ! " Believe in the Lord Jesus Christ, and thou shalt be saved !"

Sermon 19

JUSTIFICATION BY FAITH

But how should man be just with God? (Job 9:2).

THE Almighty proclaimed himself to Moses, "the Lord, merciful and gracious;" and in the New Testament, he is called "the God of all grace." "Where sin abounded, grace did much more abound; that as sin reigned unto death, even so might grace reign, through righteousness, unto eternal life, by Jesus Christ our Lord." God is determined to glorify the unsearchable riches of his grace in the salvation of sinners. But how can this be done, without casting a cloud over the Divine throne, and bringing into contempt the Divine law? How can the guilty be considered and treated as innocent, without an apparent indifference to the evil of sin, and a total disregard of the claims of eternal justice? How can the rebel be acquitted in the court of Heaven, with honor to the character of God, and safety to the interests of his moral government? This is a question which angels could not answer; but it has been answered by the God of angels. The light of nature and reason is too feeble to afford us any aid in this inquiry; "but we have a more sure word of prophecy, whereunto we do well that we take heed, as unto a light that shineth in a dark place;" for " God hath shined in our hearts, to give the light of the knowledge of the glory of God, in the face of Jesus Christ."

Following, then, the guidance of the New Testament, let us consider the nature and the ground of a sinner's justification with God.

I. To justify is the public act of a judge, declaring a person innocent, not liable to punishment. "It is God that justifieth" the ungodly. Justification, in its strict sense, and remission of sins, are two very different things. Job could forgive his friends; but he could not justify them. But in the gracious economy of the gospel, these are always immediately connected; nor these alone, but other and superior mercies—mercies infinite and unspeakable. Those whom God justifieth are not only forgiven, but also purified and renewed—not only delivered from condemnation, but also entitled to eternal life—not only redeemed from the curse of the law, but also blessed with the spirit and the privilege of adoption —not only liberated from bondage and imprisonment, but also constituted heirs " to an inheritance that fadeth not away." They are " heirs of God, and joint-heirs with Christ." They are kings and priests, and shall reign for ever and ever. God having given his Son as our surety, and published " the law of the spirit of life in Christ Jesus," and taken his seat upon the throne of grace in the character of a merciful judge, he proclaims the believer free from condemnation, and " accepted in the Beloved."

In a human court, a man may be either justified or forgiven. Sometimes the jury find the prisoner innocent, and he is acquitted; sometimes they find him guilty, and he is forgiven. The former is an act of justice; the latter, an act of mercy. No earthly court can go farther; no earthly court can justify the guilty. But God is able, through the wonderful economy of substitution and atonement revealed in the gospel, in the same court, from the same throne, by the same law, and in the same sentence, to proclaim full pardon and free justification to the sinner. By virtue of the obedience and suffering of Christ on his behalf, he is at once forgiven and justified. Faith unites us to Christ, and gives us an interest in him, as our Mediator, who " bore our sins in his own body on the tree." " Even as David also describeth the blessedness of the man to whom God imputeth righteousness without works:—Blessed are they whose iniquities are forgiven, and whose sins are covered; blessed is the man to whom the Lord will not impute sin."

The righteousness by which the sinner is justified infinitely transcends all other righteousness in earth or heaven. It is the righteousness of the Second Adam—an invaluable pearl, to which all the members of Christ's mystical body are equally entitled. It is the pure gold of the gospel, which cannot be mixed with the works of the law, or derive any increase of value from human merit. It lies upon the very surface of evangelical truth, like oil upon the water. It is the righteousness finished upon the cross—a complete wedding garment furnished by the Son of God, which the sinner has only to put on to be prepared for the marriage supper of the Lamb.

How cold and cheerless is the doctrine of the mere moralist, leaving the poor sinner wallowing in the mire, and weltering in his blood, with nothing but his own works to depend upon for salvation! But the doctrine of justification through the satisfying righteousness of Jesus Christ warms the heart, and quickens the soul of the believer into a new and heavenly life. Here is our deliverance from the curse of the law. Here the relation between us and Adam is annihilated, and another relation is established between us and Christ. Here is the sea into which our sins are cast to rise no more. "There is, therefore, now no condemnation to them who are in Christ Jesus, who walk not after the flesh, but after the spirit;" and they may boldly say—"O Lord, I will praise thee; for though thou wast angry with me, thine anger is turned away, and thou comfortest me!"

II. The ground of our justification now claims a more particular attention.

This is a subject of the greatest importance; for if we build upon the sand, the whole superstructure inevitably falls, and great must be the fall thereof. The Jews, being ignorant of God's righteousness—the righteousness of faith—went about to establish their own, which was by the works of the law. Let us examine these two foundations—the righteousness which is of the law, and that which is of faith.

What sort of righteousness does the law demand, as the ground of our acceptance with God? It must originate in the heart. It must be commensurate with life, and not a broken link in the chain, for he that offendeth in one point is guilty of all. It must be so comprehensive as to include all your duties to God, your neighbor and yourself. It must engage all the powers of your mind, without the least imperfection, in thought, word, or deed. The coin must be pure gold, of full weight and measure, and bearing the right and lawful stamp. "Cursed is every one that continueth not in all things written in the book of the law to do them."

"But what saith the righteousness which is of faith?" "Believe in the Lord Jesus Christ, and thou shalt be saved." "He that believeth shall never be confounded." "Christ is the end of the law for righteousness to every one that believeth." "He hath magnified the law, and made it honorable." "He hath redeemed us from the curse of the law, being made a curse for us." This is the doctrine which answers all our questions, removes all our guilty fears, and opens to us a path of hope in the valley of the shadow of death. The justifying righteousness of Christ is as deep as the misery of man, as high as the requirements of God, as broad as the commandment, and as long as eternity. It is sufficient for all them that believe, and able to save unto the uttermost. It is a deluge which covers the mountains of transgression, and bears the believer securely in the ark. It comes to the sinner, shut up under the judgment of God, and reads to him the article of his manumission. I hear it addressing the guilty in the following language :—

"I saw the Son of God coming forth from the bosom of the Father, and uniting himself to the nature of man. I saw the mighty God manifested in the Son of Mary, and lying in a manger. I beheld some of his blood shed, as an earnest to the law, when he was eight days old. I stood in the garden of Gethsemane, when he drank the cup of trembling mingled and presented by his Father's justice. I was with him on Calvary, when he blotted out the handwriting of Eden and Sinai, and nailed it to his cross— when he finished the redemption of man, and spoiled the powers of darkness, and sealed with his own blood the covenant of peace. I beheld him descending to the lower parts of the earth, and lying under the sinner's sentence in the grave. I beheld him rising in the same human nature, with the keys of death and hell in his hand, and the crown of the mediatorial kingdom upon his head. I beheld him ascending to the right-hand of the Father, leading thy captivity captive, and entering into heaven itself, there to appear in the presence of God for thee. And now I see him in the midst of the throne, as a lamb newly slain ; and the merit of his sacrifice, as a sweet-smelling savor, fills the heaven of heavens. On thy behalf he has honored the law, satisfied the claims of justice, and opened a new and living way, whereby God can be just, and the justifier of him that believeth in Jesus."

Thus the question is answered—"How should man be just with God?" Sinners are "justified freely by his grace, through the redemption that is in Christ Jesus." "Therefore we conclude

that a man is justified by faith, without the deeds of the law."
This is the key-stone of the gospel, and the strength of the arch of
salvation. The only way to obtain acceptance with God is by
grace; "and if by grace, then it is no more of works." In the
justification of the sinner, Divine grace and human works can no
more be mixed together than oil and water, for they belong to different covenants. Christ came into the world, not to repair the
old covenant, but to be the mediator of a new covenant, established
upon better promises—not to mend the leaky and sinking vessel of
the law, but to build and launch a new ark of salvation, and rescue
the shipwrecked and the drowning. The law could not save.
The law is holy, but we are unclean. The law is spiritual, but
we are carnal. The law is righteous, but we are guilty. The law
is good, but every imagination of the thoughts of the heart of man
is evil, and only evil, and that continually. The law will not consent to a compromise with the sinner, will not relax its claims upon
him, nor in any way accommodate itself to his fallen condition.
Its power to condemn is commensurate with its authority to command.

Thus we see how it is that no man can be justified by the deeds
of the law. We are not under the law, but under grace. Were
we under the law, the deeds of the law would be sufficient for our
justification. The law demands obedience; obedience satisfies
the law. Between obedience and the law there is perfect correspondence and harmony; the one gives what the other asks. There
is also a perfect agreement between grace and faith. Grace bestows
freely, without money and without price; and faith, having nothing
to pay, receives humbly and thankfully. Grace, by bestowing,
acquires great glory; faith, by receiving, obtains great happiness.
God confers blessings according to the riches of his grace; sinners receive according to the strength of their faith. Faith and the
law cannot agree at all, for both are seeking and receiving; neither
can works and grace agree, for both live by communicating.
Therefore " by grace are ye saved, through faith; and that not of
yourselves, it is the gift of God; not of works, lest any man should
boast." Ye are justified through the righteousness and merit of
Christ, who became your substitute, and both obeyed the law and
suffered the penalty in your stead.

This view of the ground of a sinner's justification is everywhere sustained in the Holy Scriptures. "By the obedience of one, shall many be made righteous." "By the righteousness of one, the free gift came upon all men, unto justification of life." "The obedience of one," and "the righteousness of one," in these two sentences, signify the same thing. Again: "He who knew no sin was made sin for us, that we might be made the righteousness of God in him." "In whom we have redemption through his blood, the forgiveness of sins, according to the riches of his grace." "All we like sheep have gone astray, and the Lord hath laid on him the iniquity of us all. He was wounded for our transgressions; he was bruised for our iniquities; the chastisement of our peace was upon him, and with his stripes we are healed."

The perfect obedience of Christ, and his meritorious death, were both necessary, as the ground of a sinner's justification. Neither would have been sufficient without the other. His obedience would not answer without his death; for the law which had been broken must be honored; and the penalty which had been incurred by the sinner must be endured by the Substitute. Neither would his death answer without his obedience; for it is the obedient, and not the punished, that the law justifies; he who keeps the precept, and not he who endures the penalty. It is only by satisfying both claims on our behalf, that Christ "of God is made unto us wisdom, and righteousness, and sanctification, and redemption."

When it is said we are justified by faith, it is not meant that there is any merit in faith, any justifying efficacy; but that faith is the condition on which we are justified for the sake of him who obeyed and suffered for us—the Divinely appointed means by which we appropriate the merit of his obedience and suffering. It is by the eye of faith we see the excellency and adaptation of Christ's righteousness and merit; and it is by the hand of faith we take and put on the wedding garment provided for us, and thus prepare ourselves for the marriage supper of the Lamb. Faith is the bond which unites us to Christ, by virtue of which union we are justified. Faith is the wedding ring by which the poor daughter of the old Amorite is married to the Prince of Peace. She is raised from the greatest poverty and degradation to unspeakable opulence and honor, not because of the intrinsic value of the ring, though it is a golden one; but on account of the union which it signifies between her and her Beloved. "He that hath the Son hath life"

" But faith, if it hath not works, is dead, being alone. Yea, a man may say—Thou hast faith, and I have works. Show me thy faith without thy works, and I will show thee my faith by my works. Thou believest that there is one God; thou doest well; the devils also believe, and tremble. But wilt thou know, O vain man, that faith without works is dead? Was not Abraham our father justified by works, when he had offered Isaac his son upon the altar? Seest thou how faith wrought with his works? And by works was faith made perfect; and the scripture was fulfilled which saith—Abraham believed God, and it was imputed unto him for righteousness, and he was called the friend of God. Ye see, then, how that by works a man is justified, and not by faith only. Likewise also was not Rahab the harlot justified by works, when she had received the messengers, and sent them out another way? For as the body without the spirit is dead, so faith without works is dead also."*

We have noticed the nature and ground of justification; in these words of the Apostle, we have the evidence of justification. The same doctrine was preached by our Saviour:—" For by thy works thou shalt be justified, and by thy works thou shalt be condemned." Works justify only as the fruit of faith. A faith that does not produce good works is inefficient and worthless. It is not the faith which justifies the ungodly. What is it that justifies a man in a court of law? The goodness of his cause? No, verily. A man of common sense will not think of making a long speech to the jury, without adducing any evidence of the truth of his statements. My fellow sinners, if your cause is good, why do you not prove it? Why not bring forward your evidence? Why not act in this supremely important case as in every other? If you have justifying faith, let us see the fruit in a sanctified life. " Let your light so shine before men, that they may see your good works, and glorify your Father which is in heaven."

In this world, every man receives according to his faith; in the world to come, every man shall receive according to his works. " Blessed are the dead who die in the Lord, for they rest from their labors, and their works do follow them." Their works do not go before them to divide the river Jordan, and open the gates

---

* James ii. 17—26.

of heaven. This is done by their faith. But their works are left
behind, as if done up in a packet, on this side of the river. John
saw the great white throne descending for judgment, the Son of
Man sitting thereon, and all nations gathered before him. He is
dividing the righteous from the wicked, as the shepherd divideth
the sheep from the goats. The wicked are set on the left-hand,
and the awful sentence is pronounced—" Depart from me, ye accursed, into everlasting fire, prepared for the devil and his angels!"
But the righteous are placed on the right-hand, to hear the joyful
welcome—" Come, ye blessed of my Father, inherit the kingdom
prepared for you from the foundation of the world!" The books
are opened, and Mercy presents the packets that were left on the
other side of Jordan. They are all opened, and the books are
read wherein all their acts of benevolence and virtue are recorded.
Justice examines the several packets, and answers—" All right.
Here they are. Thus it is written—' I was hungry, and ye gave
me meat; I was thirsty, and ye gave me drink; I was a stranger,
and ye took me in; I was naked, and ye clothed me; I was sick,
and ye visited me; I was in prison, and ye came unto me.' "
The righteous look upon each other with wonder, and answer—
" Those packets must belong to others. We knew nothing of all
that. We recollect the wormwood and the gall. We recollect
the strait gate, the narrow way, and the Slough of Despond.
We recollect the heavy burden that pressed so hard upon us, and
how it fell from our shoulders at the sight of the cross. We recollect the time when the eyes of our minds were opened, to behold
the evil of sin, the depravity of our hearts, and the excellency of
our Redeemer. We recollect the time when our stubborn wills
were subdued in the day of his power, so that we were enabled
both to will and to do of his good pleasure. We recollect the
time when we obtained hope in the merit of Christ, and felt the
efficacy of his blood applied to our hearts by the Holy Spirit. And
we shall never forget the time when we first experienced the love
of God shed abroad in our hearts. O, how sweetly and powerfully it constrained us to love him, his cause, and his ordinances!
How we panted after communion and fellowship with him, as the
hart panteth after the water-brooks! All this, and a thousand
other things, are as fresh in our memory as ever. But we recollect nothing of those bundles of good works. Where was it?

Lord, when saw we thee hungry, and fed thee; or thirsty, and gave thee drink; or a stranger, and took thee in; or naked, and clothed thee? We have no more recollection than the dead, of ever having visited thee in prison, or ministered to thee in sickness. Surely, those bundles cannot belong to us." Mercy replies —"Yes, verily, they belong to you; for your names are upon them; and besides, they have not been out of my hands since you left them on the stormy banks of Jordan." And the King answers —"Verily, I say unto you, inasmuch as ye have done it unto one of the least of these my brethren, ye have done it unto me."

If the righteous do not know their own good works; if they do not recognise, in the sheaves which they reap at the resurrection, the seed which they have sown in tears on earth, they certainly cannot make these things the foundation of their hopes of heaven. Christ crucified is their sole dependence for acceptance with God, in time and in eternity. Christ crucified is the great object of their faith, and the centre of their affections; and while their love to him prompts them to live soberly, and righteously, and godly, in this present evil world, they cordially exclaim—"Not unto us, not unto us, but to thy name, O Lord, give glory!" Amen.

Sermon 20
THE SHIELD OF FAITH

Above all, taking the shield of faith, wherewith ye shall be able to quench all the fiery darts of the wicked (Ephesians 6:16).

THE Christian is engaged in a warfare, "not against flesh and blood, but against principalities and powers, against the rulers of the darkness of this world, against spiritual wickedness"—or wicked spirits—"in high places;" who go about like roaring lions, seeking whom they may devour; assailing the servants of Christ even on their high places—their Pizgahs, their Tabors, their Olivets; swarming up from the sea of corruption within and around us, like the frogs in Egypt, and entering into our very bed-chambers and closets of devotion.

These spiritual adversaries must be opposed with spiritual armor; and the apostle has here given us a complete set of weapons for fighting, and a complete panoply for defence. The Roman armor consisted of several parts, all of which St. Paul makes use of figuratively, to represent the several Christian graces by which we resist our subtle, deceitful, and invisible enemies. As the articles to which he alludes constituted a complete coat of arms, and the soldier was not prepared for the field without the whole; so the Christian graces which they represent are all of them important, "that the man of God may be perfect, thoroughly furnished unto every good work." Some of these heavenly qualities may appear brighter at particular times in one Christian than in another; but the whole list is indispensable to every spiritual warrior. Abraham may excel in faith, Moses in meekness, Job in patience, Daniel in courage, Peter in zeal, Paul in humility, and John in love; but each must have the entire armor, though different occasions may require the use of different articles in the catalogue. That you may be able to stand in the evil day, you must have the shoes of peace, to preserve your feet; the girdle of truth, to strengthen your loins; the helmet of hope, to defend your heads; the breastplate of right-eousness, to cover your hearts; the sword of the Spirit, to cut your way through the columns of the foe; "And above all, taking the shield of faith, wherewith ye shall be able to quench all the fiery darts of the wicked."

It is only to this article last mentioned, that we would now call your attention; in the consideration of which, let us notice, *first*, The nature of faith; and *secondly*, Its importance and utility as a shield.

I. There are many passages in the word of God which show the excellency of faith; but there is only one passage which contains an exact definition of faith; and that you will find in the first verse of the eleventh chapter of Paul's epistle to the Hebrews:—" Now faith is the substance of things hoped for, the evidence of things not seen"—or, as it may be read—the confidence of things hoped for, the conviction of things not seen. I am surprised that divines have taken so little notice of this passage, in treating of the nature of faith. Generally, they wander in the wilderness without a guide; they put out to sea without compass, chart, or helm. Some of them make faith every thing, and others make it almost nothing. According to the apostle's definition, it consists of these two things:—a conviction of the truth of the gospel testimony relative to things invisible, and a confidence in the character and word of the invisible Testifier. This is a common-sense definition. Here is no mystification or obscurity. In this way the term faith is understood by all men. In the ordinary transactions of business, we seldom mistake each other on this subject; why should we in the great concern of salvation pending between us and God?

Here is a man who has a note for an amount sufficient to support him comfortably, were he to live a thousand years. Still he appears very unhappy—full of doubts and fears about his future subsistence. Ask him—" Friend, what think you of that note? is it genuine?" " O yes," he replies, " I am perfectly satisfied that it is genuine." " What is the reason, then, that you are not more cheerful and happy?" "Alas, I have no confidence in the bank." The man is without faith. True, he believes—he believes that the note is not a counterfeit—he is well satisfied of its genuineness; but such a belief is not sufficient, while he is suspicious of the bank—produces no change in his feelings or his conduct. But if, in addition to his conviction of the genuineness of the note,.he could be satisfied of the goodness of the bank, then you should find him quite another man. These two things united constitute faith:—Believing the truth of the gospel respecting things unseen; and trusting in the power and faithfulness of God, through our Lord Jesus Christ, to fulfil his promises. This is the faith that justifieth the ungodly; this is the faith that overcometh the world.

Now every one of you believes the truth of the gospel; but the promises of the gospel, which are worthy of all acceptation, some of you have not accepted—are no more influenced by them than if they did not belong to you. The gospel contains a pearl of great price—"an inheritance incorruptible, undefiled, and that fadeth not away;" but your confidence in the promise is feeble and inefficient—does not lead you to prayer—does not influence your conduct, so as to bring you in possession of this heavenly treasure. You have no faith. You have one of the elements of faith, but not the other. You have the belief, but not the confidence—that part of faith which belongs to the intellect, but not that which belongs to the heart. Therefore you are still poor, and naked, and miserable.

The Holy Scriptures record many admirable instances of true faith; in which confidence in the character, the providence, and the promises of God, rises into the most perfect assurance. Behold those women on the bank of the Nile. They are making a basket of bulrushes, and plastering it with bitumen. Placing the infant Moses therein, they commit the frail ark to the floods. Jochebed, why dost thou not fear that the child will be drowned? "I believe the promises of God, I believe that he will do good unto his people. I trust in him for the salvation of Israel."

See that old man on mount Moriah. He has built a rude altar, and laid fire and wood thereon. He has bound his own son—his only son—his well-beloved Isaac, and is about to offer him as a sacrifice. Abraham, stay thy hand. Wilt thou slay thy only son? Then what will become of the promise? "My mind is easy. I will obey God. I believe he is able to raise Isaac from the dead. I feel assured that he will return home with me alive, and that from him will spring the Messiah." So Abraham determined to offer Isaac upon the altar, for he confided in the promise—"In Isaac shall thy seed be called."

We have another instance in the Centurion whose servant was healed by our Lord. He had perfect confidence in the word of Christ, even though Christ had given him no promise. "Only say in a word," said he, "and my servant shall be healed. Thy word created the world; thy word has quickened the dead; and thy word can accomplish a cure without a journey to my house." This is an instance of remarkable faith; and our Lord testified— " I have not found so great faith, no, not in Israel."

Whatever the object of faith, it is always the same in its nature, though not always the same in degree. Christ said to his disciples —" O ye of little faith!" and the apostle saith of Abraham—" He was strong in faith, giving glory to God." Faith is represented in the Scriptures by a variety of expressions, such as—believing the testimony of God—relying or staying upon the Lord—waiting upon him—trusting in him—looking unto him—coming to Christ—putting on the Lord Jesus—committing the keeping of the soul to him, as unto a faithful Creator. These different expressions denote the several modifications of faith, and its several degrees of intensity ; but they all fall under the apostolical definition noticed above.

The language of the law was—" Do this and live." The language of the gospel is—" Believe on the Lord Jesus Christ, and thou shalt be saved." Faith in Christ is the prescribed and only condition of acceptance with God. Christ is the way, and the truth, and the life ; no man cometh unto the Father but by him. Faith is the eye with which we behold his mercy ; faith is the hand by which we receive his blessings ; faith is the golden chain which binds us to him for ever. The necessity of faith in the merit and righteousness of our Divine Mediator, as the condition of salvation, is a truth which lies scattered over the surface of inspired Scripture. God has always owned and blessed its proclamation in the conversion of souls. It was the article of Luther's emancipation from legal bondage. It was the master-key which unlocked the iron gates of Antichrist, and poured the true light over all Europe ; so that neither pope nor council, nor both together, could hide it again under a bushel. And in the church of England, even in its present weak and languid state, whenever one of its ministers preaches clearly and faithfully this blessed doctrine, souls are given him as the seals of his ministry.

There is no end to the praises of faith. Faith is the glass that draws fire from the Sun of Righteousness. Faith is the wedding ring that joins the sinner to Christ in an everlasting covenant. Faith is the living principle of all holy obedience, working by love, and purifying the heart. If God command a man to leave his country and his kindred, and go into a strange land—to offer his beloved son as a sacrifice upon the altar—to build an ark on dry ground—to go to the fiery furnace, or the lions' den—to face his exasperated foes at Jerusalem, or hide from them in the caves of the mountains—it is faith that prompts him to the painful duty, and sustains him therein, in spite of improbabilities; and amidst difficulties, dangers, and deaths.

II. This brings us to notice the importance and utility of faith as a shield. "And above all, taking the shield of faith, wherewith ye shall be able to quench all the fiery darts of the wicked."

Faith is in some respects the first of all the Christian graces. It is the beginning of spiritual life in the soul—the originating and sustaining principle of all evangelical holiness. Having faith, we have nothing to do but to add to it all the rest of our lives. "Add to your faith virtue, and to virtue knowledge, and to knowledge temperance, and to temperance patience, and to patience godliness, and to godliness brotherly kindness, and to brotherly kindness charity."

Love is in some respects superior to faith, and shall live and rejoice before the throne when faith shall have finished its work; but faith is an impenetrable shield, such as love cannot furnish, on the field of battle. The shield was a broad piece of defensive armor, worn ordinarily on the left arm; and which, being movable, might be used to defend any part of the body. According to Homer, the shields of some of the warriors at the siege of Troy were made of sevenfold thick bull-hides, covered with brass.

The value of "the shield of faith" is seen in the case of David. Look down there in the valley. There is Goliath of Gath, the chief of the giants, blaspheming, and defying the armies of the living God. His spear is as a weaver's beam, and his armor

bearer carries before him an enormous shield. And there is a fine-
looking young man going down to meet him, without any visible
weapons, except his shepherd's sling, and five smooth stones from
the brook. David! hast thou no fear? Rash youth! is thy unpractised hand able to cope with the mailed champion of Philistia?
" I will go and meet him in the name of my God, for I know that
the Lord will deliver him into my hand. God will avenge his
people, and vindicate his own honor against the insults of his enemies. He who defended me against the lion and the bear will save
me from the hand of the blasphemer, and glorify himself this day
before the thousands of Israel." He moves on, invincibly shielded
by his faith, and the next moment Goliath is slain with his own
sword.

Let us look again at the case of Abraham. God said unto him
—" Take now thy son, thine only son Isaac, whom thou lovest,
and get thee into the land of Moriah, and offer him there for a
burnt offering, upon one of the mountains that I will tell thee of."
Now the enemy assails him, in the persuasive language of natural
affection, and carnal reasoning; and every word is like a flaming
arrow in the patriarch's heart:—" Abraham! if thou obey this command, thou wilt disobey thereby many other commands. God hath
said—' Thou shalt not kill;' and wilt thou shed the blood of thy own
child? Canst thou so trample upon the law of God, and all the
tender instincts of human nature? How will thy servants regard
thee—how will the world look upon thee, after so horrible a deed?
What will they think of thy God, when they hear that he has required at thy hand the immolation of thy only son? Will it not
bring everlasting dishonor upon his name? And what will become
of the Divine promise upon which thy faith is built—that from
Isaac's loins shall spring the Messiah, the hope of the world?
Besides, thou wilt certainly break poor old Sarah's heart; she will
never be able to survive the loss, in so dreadful a manner, of her
darling boy. If thou hast any feelings of humanity in thy heart,
any fear of God before thine eyes, any regard for the glory of his
name among men, refrain from that deed of blood!"

Such were the " fiery darts" which " the wicked one" hurled
at the good man's heart, but they fell harmless upon his " shield
of faith." " He staggered not at the promise through unbelief."
" He conferred not with flesh and blood." He rose up early in

the morning, took Isaac and the servants, and set out for the appointed place of sacrifice. He travelled three days toward Moriah, with a settled purpose to cut Isaac's body in pieces, and shed the blood of his heart upon the altar, and burn it to ashes in the consuming flames. He loved his son as his own soul, but the command of God was dearer to his heart. " And Abraham said unto his young men—Abide ye here with the ass, and I and the lad will go yonder, and worship, and come again to you;" for he firmly believed that God would raise his son from the ashes of the altar, and that they would return together. I see them ascending the hill—O, what an ascent was that! Never was there a walk so sorrowful, till the great Antitype of Isaac ascended the same mountain to " make his soul a sacrifice for sin." The altar is built, the fire and the wood are placed thereon ; and O for words to describe the feelings of both father and son, when Abraham laid hold on Isaac, and took the knife to plunge it into his heart! There is a pause. The patriarch's arm is stretched aloft, with the instrument of death. God of mercy! is there no help for a father? Earth cannot speak; but there comes a voice from heaven; and O, with what melody it rings through Abraham's heart!—" Abraham! Abraham! lay not thine hand upon the lad ; for now I know that thou fearest God, seeing thou hast not withheld thy son, thine only son, from me."

There was the triumph of faith. " By faith Abraham, when he was tried, offered up Isaac ; and he that had received the promises offered up his only begotten son, of whom it was said—In Isaac shall thy seed be called ; accounting that God was able to raise him up even from the dead, from whence also he received him in a figure." The patriarch's faith quenched " all the fiery darts of the wicked one," which were cast at him in this dreadful trial.

The arrows of the orientals were often poisoned at one end, and ignited at the other. It is to this circumstance the apostle alludes in the phrase—" the fiery darts of the wicked," or the wicked one. Satan has his quiver full of impoisoned and flaming arrows, from which the servants of Christ would be much endangered without " the shield of faith." He shot one of them at Eve in Paradise, and set the whole world on fire, " and it is set on fire of hell." He shot an arrow of lust at David, and an arrow of fear at Peter; and both of them were dreadfully wounded in the back. He shot an arrow of covetousness at Judas, and another at Ananias and Sapphira; and having no "shield of faith," they were smitten, and dropped down into hell.

The devil is a fierce and malicious enemy, "going about as a roaring lion, seeking whom he may devour." Fain would he destroy all the holy from the earth. His "fiery darts" inflame the heart with the love of sin, the fear of man, the torments of remorse, and the apprehensions of judgment and fiery indignation. But when the heart is shielded by the faith of the gospel—when we clearly understand the truth as it is in Jesus, cordially assent to it, appropriate it experimentally, and surrender ourselves to its sanctifying influence—they have no power to injure, and the Christian is more than conqueror.

"Cast not away, therefore, the beginning of your confidence, which hath great recompense of reward." Grasp firmly the shield. Whatever the aspect of the fight, hold it fast till the end. You will need it through all the campaign. You will need it especially in your contest with "the last enemy, which is death." "Be steadfast, immovable, always abounding in the work of the Lord." So shall you be able to testify with Paul, when he anticipated the termination of the warfare—"I have fought a good fight; I have finished my course; I have kept the faith; and henceforth there is laid up for me a crown of righteousness, which the Lord—the righteous judge—shall give unto me in that day."

Sermon 21

THE PARACLETE

And I will pray the Father, and he shall give you another Comforter, that he may abide with you forever; even the Spirit of Truth, whom the world cannot receive, because it seeth him not, neither knoweth him; but ye know him, for he dwelleth with you, and shall be in you (John 14:16, 17).

THE Bible is a most wonderful book. It came to us from heaven, and is stamped with the Spirit and the character of heaven. It assails our favorite maxims and customs, and declares that he who will be the friend of this world is the enemy of God. It will consent to no compromise with sin. It will not in the least accommodate itself to the carnal inclinations of the human heart. What is written is written, and not one jot or tittle can be altered till heaven and earth shall pass away. It is the sword of God, by which he conquers the nations—the instrument of his grace, by which he renovates the world. Like the ark in the land of the Philistines, which was mightier than all their lords, and Dagon their god, it is more than a match for the cunning and prowess of the Prince of Darkness and his hosts. He who disobeys it kindles a volcano; he who obeys opens to himself a fountain of living waters. And the secret of all its wonderful qualities and achievements is found in its Divine inspiration, and the power of the Holy Ghost which accompanies its truths. It is "the sword of the Spirit," and the Spirit that brought it into the world continues in the world to wield it, and render it quick and powerful.

These remarks introduce to our consideration the mission and office of the Holy Ghost, of which our Saviour speaks in the language of the text. And,

I. We remark, that the Holy Ghost is evidently not a Divine attribute merely, but a Divine person.

His personality is proved by the terms applied to him in the text—the " Comforter," and " the Spirit of Truth;" and by many other passages where he is spoken of in similar language—language wholly incompatible with the idea of his being a mere attribute, and not a person.

The doctrine of his Divinity is sustained by so many texts that their mere quotation would be an irrefutable argument in its favor. David says—" The Spirit of the Lord spake by me, and his word was in my tongue; the God of Israel said," &c. Here the Holy Ghost is called "the Spirit of the Lord," and "the God of Israel." When Ananias "lied to the Holy Ghost," it is said he "lied to God." The ordinance of Baptism is ordered to be administered "in the name of the Holy Ghost," as well as "the name of the Father and the Son;" and his "fellowship" is equally invoked with the love of the former, and the grace of the latter, in the apostolical benediction. Besides, every attribute that belongs to the Deity belongs to him. He is omnipresent, omniscient, and eternal. He is the Spirit of truth, the Spirit of grace, and the Spirit of life. His works also are the works of God. He creates and quickens, which is the prerogative of God alone. He renovates the soul. He raised the body of Jesus, and will raise the bodies of all men in the last day. Finally: Blasphemy against the Son may be forgiven; but " blasphemy against the Holy Ghost hath never forgiveness, neither in this world nor in that which is to come." If, then, the Father is God, and if the Son is God, so also is the Holy Spirit.

II. The Holy Ghost is the messenger and representative of Jesus Christ in the Church.

Two promises, like heavenly merchant-vessels, brought salvation to our world. The first was given in Eden, and fulfilled on Calvary. The Son of God descended from heaven, suffered in our stead the curse of the law, spoiled the powers of death and hell, and returned to his Father, leaving another promise, shortly to be fulfilled upon his people. With what supernatural power and unction the Holy Spirit manifested himself on the day of Pentecost! Divine Comforter! what treasure bringest thou in thy vessel of grace? " The things of Christ; and I will unload them to-day in

the region of Calvary. I have come to fulfil the promise, to en-
dow the disciples with power from on high, and finish the work
which the Son of God has begun." See those tongues of flame
sitting upon the fishermen of Galilee ; while strangers from many
different countries hear from them, each in his own language, "the
wonderful works of God." Only think of three thousand conversions in a day—under a single sermon. Three thousand hearts
were wounded by the arrows of Divine love, through the strongest
breastplate ever made in hell. This was the work of the Holy
Spirit, taking of the things of Christ and showing them to the
disciples. It was Christ himself, manifesting himself through his
agent. The first promise brought the Messiah into the world in
the flesh ; the second, in the Spirit—the first, to be crucified ; the
second, to crucify the sins of his people—the first, to empty himself ; the second, to fill the believer with heavenly gifts and
graces—the first, to sanctify himself as a sin-offering upon the
altar ; the second, to give repentance and pardon as a Prince and
a Saviour.

The Holy Spirit is still on earth, prosecuting his gracious work,
and communicating his heavenly gifts. He strives with sinners,
and quickens believers into spiritual life. He dwells in the saints,
leads them into all truth, and bears witness with their spirits that
they are the Children of God. He illuminates their understanding; subdues their will, purifies their thoughts, and plants within
them all holy principles and affections. And this he does, not by
an audible voice from heaven, but through the instrumentality of
the word, and by secret impressions upon the soul. " The wind
bloweth where it listeth, and thou hearest the sound thereof, but
canst not tell whence it cometh, nor whither it goeth ; so is every
one that is born of the Spirit." The operations of the Holy Ghost
are seen only in their effects. It is a drop of water becoming a
fountain " that springeth up unto everlasting life." It is a spark
of fire, kindling a conflagration, which all the rivers of Belial cannot quench.

III. The Holy Ghost is the Paraclete ; that is, the Counselor
and Consoler. In our text, he is called the " Comforter." " And
I will pray the Father, and he shall give you another Comforter,"
—according to the original, one to plead your cause. The word
is the same as that used to designate the Roman ambassadors, who

were sent to other countries, as representatives of the Roman power, to persuade enemies to submit, or offer terms of peace.

A certain author observes, that the office of the Comforter is to reconcile enemies, and invigorate friends—to console the dejected, strengthen the enfeebled, and support the people of God in all the conflicts and trials of life. It is by his grace that the believer's youth is renewed as the eagle's, and all his languishing virtues are revived, so that he can "run and not weary—walk and not faint."

Another part of his office in the Church is intercession. As he pleads with sinners on behalf of Christ in the gospel, so he pleads for believers in the court of heaven; not personally, like our blessed Lord, but by inspiring the spirit of supplication in their hearts. "Likewise the Spirit also helpeth our infirmities, for we know not what we should pray for as we ought; but the Spirit itself maketh intercession for us, with groanings which cannot be uttered; and he that searcheth the hearts knoweth what is the mind of the Spirit, because he maketh intercession for the saints according to the will of God."

When other nations had offended the Romans, it was common for them, fearing the revenge of that mighty empire, to send messengers to Rome, to plead their cause, and treat for peace. "The Spirit of Truth," having brought sinners to repentance by pleading with them for Christ in the gospel, pours down upon them the spirit of grace and supplication, so that they cry out for mercy, and this is virtually the Spirit of God crying out within them. What is the meaning of all that prayer and agony in the congregation? The Spirit of God is there. His hammer has broken the rock—his fire has melted the iron. No other power could conquer those proud rebellious hearts, and turn the blasphemer into a man of prayer. Listen! "If thou shouldst mark iniquity, O Lord, who could stand?" Hark again! "But thou art a God ready to pardon; there is forgiveness with thee, that thou mayest be feared." It is the voice of the Spirit, pleading in the awakened soul. See that publican in the temple, smiting upon his breast, and saying,— "God be merciful to me a sinner!" The Holy Ghost has both convinced him of sin, and inspired him to pray for mercy. No other agency can thus quicken the "dead in trespasses and sins," and turn the hearts of the children of men to the Lord. The gospel, in the hand of the Holy Spirit, "is the power of God unto salvation." The Holy Spirit can convince the world—can rend the veil from the mind, and dissolve the ice around the heart. He applies the truth to the conscience, and makes the guilty read their own sentence of condemnation by the light of the fires of Sinai ; and then he shows them the atoning blood, and prompts them to pray for pardon. He first convinces them that they are sinking in "the horrible pit of miry clay ;" and then lets down to them the rope of the promise, bids them take hold by faith, draws them out, and sets their feet upon a rock, and puts into their mouth the new song of salvation—"O Lord, I will praise thee ; for though thou wast angry with me, thine anger is turned away, and thou comfortest me !"

O that the "Spirit of grace and supplication" may ever rest upon us ! May we plead for ourselves with God, as Jacob, when he wrestled for the blessing ; or Bartimeus, when he besought the Saviour to restore his sight ! May we plead for sinners, as Abraham for Sodom, as Moses for Israel, as Daniel for the captives, as the Centurion for his servant, and as the woman of Canaan for her daughter !

IV. The Holy Ghost is called "another comforter ;" which suggests a difference between his office in the church, and that of our Lord Jesus Christ.

Christ, by his personal ministry on earth, was the Comforter of his little flock ; and by his death upon the cross, the procurer of all the comforts of them that believe ; and when he ascended, "another comforter" came down to take his place in the church, and communicate the blessings which he bought with his blood. "If any man sin, we have an Advocate with the Father, Jesus Christ the righteous ;" who hath "entered into heaven itself, there to appear in the presence of God for us ;" while his agent and representative on earth dwells with his followers, leads them into all truth, and carries on within them the process of sanctification. Both are comforters—both are advocates—Christ above, and the Holy Spirit below—Christ by his personal presence before the Father, and the Holy Spirit by his gracious influence in the believer's heart.

Christ is making intercession on our behalf without us, and independently of us. But the Holy Spirit is making intercession through us—pleading in our prayers " with groanings that cannot be uttered." He never acts without us. True repentance and faith are his gifts, but they are also our exercises. He draws us to Christ, but we must yield to his attractions. He inspires us to pray, but the act of prayer is our own. He " worketh in us to will and to do of his good pleasure," but he does not will and do for us. He gives us the life and the power, but he requires us to use them. He leads us into all truth, but not unless we follow him. He sheds abroad the love of God in our hearts, but not unless we open our hearts to receive the communication. He destroys the old man within us, and creates the new; but not unless we cordially resign ourselves to his influence, and earnestly co-operate with his grace.

Christ in heaven pleads for the reconciliation of sinners to God. The Holy Spirit on earth awakens sinners, convinces them of sin, draws them to the throne of grace, and breathes into them intense prayers for pardon. He renews them, and purifies them, and makes them temples of his grace, and heirs of glory. He opens the blind eyes, and unstops the deaf ears, and makes the lame man leap as an hart, and the tongue of the dumb to sing. All the true conversions ever effected on earth are the results of his gracious power.

Christ has bound up all the covenants, and carried them with him into heaven, and laid them down before the throne, having obtained eternal redemption for us; and the Holy Spirit has taken of the things of God, and brought them down to men. Christ received gifts for us, and the Holy Spirit confers them upon us. Christ receives from the Father; the Spirit receives from Christ; and we receive from the Spirit. Christ bought the church with his own blood, and the spirit prepares and presents her to him as his bride. Christ opened a way into the Holy of Holies, and the Spirit aids us to offer our sacrifices before the mercy-seat. Christ is the appointed medium of our intercourse with God, and the Spirit helps us to avail ourselves of that unspeakable privilege. Christ in heaven is the life of our redemption, and the Spirit upon earth is the life of the gospel and the ordinances. " I will draw all men unto myself"—is the motto of Christ; "I will draw all men unto Christ"—is the motto of the Spirit.

V. The Holy Ghost has taken up his permanent residence among the people of God. " That he may abide with you for ever—for he dwelleth with you and shall be in you."

His miraculous gifts were temporary; being no longer necessary, when the truth was established in the conviction of mankind. But his renovating and sanctifying grace is as much needed now as ever, and therefore has never been taken from the world. The primitive Christians, and Christians of the present day, in this respect, share the same privilege. It is a " common salvation ;" and the streams will never cease to flow, while there remain " vessels of mercy" to be filled.

The church in every age has suffered great loss in the death of her most able and efficient ministers. The strongest pillars in the house have fallen; the tallest trees in the forest have been cut down. " The fathers, where are they? and the prophets, do they live for ever?" Where are the apostles and evangelists? What has become of the great reformers of every age? They have gone the way whence they shall not return. They have ascended in their chariots of fire. Though safe in heaven, they are lost to earth. But the Holy Spirit is a " Comforter" that shall " abide with you for ever." The hands have all departed, one after another, and new crews have been shipped from age to age; but the Captain is still alive; and has remained on board, ever since he first took the register and the compass, on the day of Pentecost; and will never leave the ship, till he brings her in from her last voyage, and lays her up for ever!

Brethren in the ministry! this is our consolation. The Spirit that blessed the labors of David Jones, Daniel Rowlands, and Howell Harris, still " dwelleth with you, and shall be in you." O let us seek his aid in our holy work, and pray for his outpouring upon our congregations!

Delegates of the different churches! be of good courage! You may not have seen as many additions lately as in former times; but the Holy Spirit has not yet departed from the faithful. You have heard of wonderful revivals in America, as well as in some parts of Wales. The " Comforter" is yet at work. The illuminator of souls is yet at hand. The office is yet open. The blessing is yet offered. O, let us all pray for the Holy Spirit! let us look for his coming! let us wait for his salvation!

Sermon **22**

THE FATHER AND SON
GLORIFIED

Howbeit, when he, the Spirit of truth, is come, he will guide you into all truth; for he shall not speak of himself; but whatsoever he shall hear, that shall he speak; and he will show you things to come. He shall glorify me; for he shall receive of mine, and shall show it unto you. All things that the Father hath are mine; therefore, said I, that he shall take of mine, and shall show it unto you (John 16:13-15).

THE wonderful Providence which brought the Children of Israel out of the house of bondage was a chain of many links, not one of which could be omitted without destroying the beauty, and defeating the end of the Divine economy. The family of Jacob come to Egypt in the time of famine—they multiply—they are oppressed—their cries reach to heaven—God manifests himself in the burning bush—Moses is sent to Egypt—miracles are wrought by his hand—Pharaoh's heart is hardened—the first-born are slain—the passover is eaten—the people depart, led by the pillar of God—the sea is divided—and with many signs and wonders, the thousands of Israel are conducted through the wilderness to the Promised Land. Had one of these links been wanting, the chain of deliverance had been defective.

So, in the salvation of sinners by Jesus Christ, all the conditions and preparatives were essential to the completeness and glory of the scheme. The Son of God must consent to undertake our cause, and become our substitute—the promise must be given to Adam, and frequently repeated to the patriarchs—bloody sacrifices must be instituted to typify the vicarious sufferings of Messiah—a long line of prophets must foretell his advent, and the glory of his kingdom—he must be born in Bethlehem, crucified on Calvary, and buried in Joseph's new tomb—must rise from the dead, ascend to the right hand of the Father, and send down the Holy Spirit to guide and sanctify his church. Without all these circumstances, the economy of redemption would have been incomplete and inefficient.

The last link in the chain is the mission and work of the Holy Spirit. This is quite as important as any of the rest. Our Saviour's heart seems to have been much set upon it during all his ministry, and especially during the last few days before his crucifixion. He spoke of it frequently to his disciples, and told them that he would not leave them comfortless, but would send them "another Comforter," who should abide with them for ever; and that his own departure was necessary, to prepare the way for the coming of the heavenly Paraclete. In our text, he describes the office of the Holy Spirit, and the specific relation which he sustains to the work of salvation:—"Howbeit, when he, the Spirit of Truth, is come, he will guide you into all truth; for he shall not speak of himself; but whatsoever he shall hear, that shall he speak; and he will show you things to come. He shall glorify me; for he shall receive of mine, and shall show it unto you. All things that the Father hath are mine; therefore said I, that he shall take of mine, and shall show it unto you."

These words teach us two important truths—*first*, That the Son is equal with the Father; and *secondly*, That the Father and the Son are alike glorified in the economy of salvation.

I. The Son claims equality with the Father. "All things that the Father hath are mine."

This sentence is very comprehensive and sublime—an unquestionable affirmation of Messiah's "eternal power and Godhead." The same doctrine is taught us in many other recorded sayings of Christ, and sustained by all the prophets and apostles; and when I consider this declaration in connection with the general strain of the inspired writers on the subject, I seem to hear the Saviour himself addressing the world in the following manner:—

"All things that the Father hath are mine. His *names* are mine. I am Jehovah—the Mighty God, and the Everlasting Father—the Lord of Hosts—the Living God—the True God, and Eternal Life.

" His *works* are mine. All things were made by me, and I uphold all things by the word of my power. My Father worketh
hitherto, and I work; for as the Father raiseth up the dead, and
quickeneth them, even so the Son quickeneth whom he will. I am
the author of universal being, and my hand moves all the machinery
of providence.

" His *honors* are mine. I have an indisputable right to the
homage of all created intelligences. I inhabit the praises of eternity. Before the foundation of the world, I was the object of
angelic adoration; and when I became incarnate as a Saviour, the
Father published his decree in heaven, saying—' Let all the angels
of God worship him!' It is his will, also, that all men should
honor the Son, even as they honor the Father—in the same manner,
and the same degree. He that honoreth the Son, honoreth the
Father; and he that honoreth not the Son, honoreth not the Father:
for I and my Father are one—one in honor—possessing joint interest and authority.

" His *attributes* are mine. Though as man and mediator I am
inferior to the Father; yet my nature is no more inferior to his, than
the nature of the Prince of Wales is inferior to the nature of the
King of England. You see me clothed in humanity; but in my
original state, I thought it not robbery to be equal with God. I
was in the beginning with God, and possessed the same eternity of
being. Like him, I am almighty, omniscient, and immutable;
infinite in holiness, justice, goodness, and truth. All these attributes, with every other possible perfection, belong to me in the
same sense as they belong to the Father. They are absolute and
independent, underived and unoriginated—the essential qualities of
my nature.

" His *riches of grace* are mine. I am the mediator of the new
covenant—the channel of my Father's mercies to mankind. I have
the keys of the house of David, and the seal of the kingdom of
heaven. I have come from the bosom of the Father, freighted
with the precious treasures of his good will to men. I have sailed
over the sea of tribulation and death, to bring you the wealth of the
other world. I am the Father's messenger, publishing peace on
earth—a peace which I have purchased with my own blood upon
the cross. It hath pleased the Father that in me all fulness should

dwell—all fulness of wisdom and grace—whatever is necessary for the justification, sanctification, and redemption of them that believe. My Father and I are one in the work of salvation, as in the work of creation. We have the same will, and the same intention of mercy toward the children of the great captivity.

" The *objects of his love* are mine. He hath given them to me in an everlasting covenant. He hath given me the heathen for an inheritance, and the uttermost parts of the earth for a possession. They were mine by the original right of creation; but now they are doubly mine by the superadded claim of redemption. My Father, before the world was, gave me a charter of all the souls I would redeem. I have fulfilled the condition. I have poured out my soul unto death, and sealed the covenant with the blood of my cross. Therefore all believers are mine. I have bought them with a price. I have redeemed them from the bondage of sin and death. Their names are engraven on my hands and my feet. They are written with the soldier's spear upon my heart. And of all that the Father hath given me, I will lose nothing. I will draw them all to myself; I will raise them up at the last day; and they shall be with me where I am, that they may behold my glory—the glory which I had with the Father before the foundation of the world."

II. The Father and the Son are equally glorified in the economy of redemption, and the work of the Holy Spirit.

1. The Son glorifies the Father. I hear him praying in the garden:—"Father, I have glorified thee on the earth; I have finished the work which thou gavest me to do." I hear him again, amid the supernatural gloom of Calvary, with a voice that rings through the dominions of death and hell, crying—"It is finished!"

What mighty achievement hast thou finished to-day, blessed Jesus? and how have thy unknown agony and shameful death glorified the Father?

" I have glorified the Father, by raising up those precious things which fell in Eden, and were lost in the abyss.

" I have raised up my Father's *law*. I found it cast down to the earth, and trampled into the dust. I have magnified and made it honorable. I have vindicated its authority in the sight of men and angels. I have satisfied its demands on behalf of my redeemed, and become the end of the law for righteousness to all who will receive me as their surety.

"I have raised up my Father's *name*: I have declared it to my brethren. I have manifested it to the men whom he has given me. I have given a new revelation of his character to the world. I have shown him to sinners, as a just God and a Saviour. I have restored his worship in purity and spirituality upon earth. I have opened a new and living way to his throne of grace. I have written the record of his mercy with my own blood upon the rocks of Calvary.

"I have raised up my Father's *image*. I have imprinted it afresh upon human nature, from which it was effaced by sin. I have displayed its excellence in my own character. I have passed through the pollutions of the world, and the territory of death, without tarnishing its lustre, or injuring its symmetry. Though my visage is marred with grief, and my back plowed with scourges, and my hands and feet nailed to the accursed cross, not one trace of my Father's image has been obliterated from my human soul. It is as perfect and as spotless now as when I lay in the manger. I will carry it unstained with me into heaven. I will give a full description of it in my gospel upon earth. I will change my people into the same image from glory to glory. I will also renovate and transform their vile bodies, and fashion them like unto my own glorious body. I will ransom them from the power of the grave; and because I live, they shall live also—the counterpart of my own immaculate humanity—mirrors to reflect my Father's glory for ever."

2. The Father glorifies the Son. He prayed in the garden:— "And now, Father, glorify thou me with thine own self, with the glory which I had with thee before the world was." Was the petition granted? Answer, ye Roman sentinels, who watched his sepulchre! Answer, ye men of Galilee, who gazed upon his chariot, as he ascended from the Mount of Olives!

The glorification of the Son by the Father implies all the honors of his mediatorial office—all the crowns which he won by his victory over the powers of death and hell. The Father raised him from the dead, and received him up into glory, as a testimony of his acceptance as the sinner's surety—an expression of perfect satisfaction with his vicarious sacrifice upon the cross. It was the just reward of his work; it was the fruit of his gracious travail. He is " crowned with glory and honor for the sufferings of death." " Because he hath poured out his soul unto death," therefore " God also hath highly exalted him, and given him a name that is above every name."

What an honor would it be to a man, to receive eight or ten of the highest offices in a kingdom! Infinitely greater is the glory of Emmanuel. His name includes all the offices and titles of the kingdom of heaven. The Father hath made him " both Lord and Christ"—that is, given him the supreme prerogatives of government and salvation. " Him hath God exalted to be a prince and a Saviour, to give repentance to Israel, and remission of sins." He is " head over all things in the church"—Prime Minister of the kingdom of heaven—Lord Treasurer, dispensing the bounties of Divine grace to mankind—Lord High-Chancellor of the realm, and Keeper of the Great Seal of the living God; holding in his hand the charter of our redemption, and certifying the authenticity of the Divine covenant—Lord Chief Justice of heaven and earth, having all power and authority to administer the laws of Providence throughout the universe—the Chief Prince—the General of the army—the Captain of the Lord's host—the Champion who conquered Satan, Sin, and Death; bruising the head of the first, destroying the power of the second, and swallowing up the third in victory. He hath the keys of hell and of death. He shutteth, and no man openeth; he openeth, and no man shutteth. He bears all the honors of his Father's house; and concentrates in himself all the glories of Supreme Divinity, redeemed humanity, and " mediator between God and man."

3. The Holy Spirit glorifies Father and Son together. He is procured for the world by the blood of the Son, and sent into the world by the authority of the Father; so that both are alike represented in his mission, and equally glorified in his office. The gracious things which the Father gave into the hands of the Son when he descended from heaven, the Son gave into the hands of the Spirit when he returned to heaven. " All things that the Father hath are mine; and he shall take of mine, and shall show it unto you "

This is the object of the Spirit's advent, the communication of the things of Christ to men. What are the things of Christ? His merit, his mercy, his image, his gospel, his promises, all the gifts of his grace, all the treasures of his love, and all the immunities of eternal redemption. These the Father hath given to the Son, as the great Trustee of the church; and the Son hath given them to the Spirit, as the appointed agent of their communication.

A ship was laden in India, arrived safe in London, unloaded her precious cargo, and the goods were soon distributed all over the country, and offered for sale in a thousand stores. The Son of God brought immense riches of Divine grace from heaven to earth, which are all left to the disposal of the Holy Spirit, and freely proffered to the perishing wherever the gospel is preached.

The Holy Spirit came not to construct a new engine of mercy, but to propel that already constructed by Christ. Its first revolution rent the rocks of Calvary, and shook the rocky hearts of men. Its second revolution demolished the throne of death, burst his prison-doors, and liberated many of his captives. Its third revolution carried its builder up into the heaven of heavens, and brought down the Holy Spirit to move its machinery for ever. Its next revolution, under the impulse of this new Agent, was like "the rushing of a mighty wind" among the assembled disciples at Jerusalem, kindled a fire upon the head of every Christian, inspired them to speak all the languages of the babbling earth, and killed and quickened three thousand souls of the hearers.

The Holy Spirit is still on earth, glorifying the Father and the Son. He convinces the world of sin. He leads men to Christ, through the rivers of corruption, the mountains of presumption, and the terrible bogs of despair, affording them no rest till they come to the city of refuge. He continues on the field to bring up the rear; while the Captain of our Salvation, on his white horse, rides victorious in the van of battle. He strengthens the soldiers—"faint, yet pursuing;" raises the fallen; encourages the despondent; feeds them with the bread of life, and the new wine of the kingdom; and leads them on—"conquering, and to conquer."

His work will not be finished till the resurrection. Then will he quicken our mortal bodies. Then will he light his candle, and sweep the house till he find every lost piece of silver. Then will he descend into the dark caves of death, and gather all the gems of redeemed humanity, and weave them into a crown for Emmanuel, and place that crown upon Emmanuel's head, amid the songs of the adoring seraphim !

Thus the Holy Spirit glorifies the Father and the Son. Let us pray for the outpouring of his grace upon the church. In proportion to his manifestation in our hearts, will be our " knowledge of the light of the glory of God in the face of Jesus Christ." Nor is this all ; in proportion to the visitations of the Holy Spirit, will be the purity of our lives, the spirituality of our worship, the ardor of our zeal and charity, and the extent of our usefulness to the cause of Christ. Would you see a revival of religion ? pray for the outpouring of the Holy Spirit upon you, to sanctify your hearts and your lives, that your light may " so shine before men, that others may see your good works, and glorify your Father who is in heaven."

" When thou hearest the sound of a going in the tops of the mulberry trees, then thou shalt bestir thyself; for then the Lord shall go out before thee, to strike the hosts of the Philistines." Brethren, this is the time. The mulberry trees are shaking. God is going before his people, to prepare their way to victory. The hand of Divine Providence is opening a great and effectual door for the gospel. The mountains are levelled, the valleys are exalted, and a highway is cast up in the wilderness for our God. The arts of printing and navigation, the increasing commerce of the world, the general prevalence of the spirit of peace, the rapid march of literature and science, and the correspondence of eminent and leading men in every nation, are so many preparatives for the moral conquest of the world. The Captain of our Salvation, on the white horse of the gospel, can now ride through Europe and America; and will soon lead forth his army to take possession of Asia and Africa. The wings of the mighty angel are unbound, and he is flying in the midst of heaven.

Again : Christians are better informed concerning the moral state of the world than formerly. If my neighbor's house were on fire, and I knew nothing of it, I could not be blamed for rendering him no assistance ; but who could be guiltless in beholding the building in flames, without an effort to rescue its occupants? Brethren, you have heard of the perishing heathen. You have heard of their dreadful superstitions, their human sacrifices, and their abominable rites. You have heard of Juggernaut, and the River Ganges, and the murder of infants, and the immolation of widows, and the worship of idols and demons. You know something of the delusion of Mohammedism, the cruel and degrading ignorance of Popery, and how millions around you are perishing for lack of knowledge. Do you feel no solicitude for their souls—no desire to pluck them as brands from the burning?

What can we do? The Scriptures have been translated into nearly all the languages of the babbling earth. Missionaries have gone into many lands—have met the Indian in his wigwam, the African in his Devil's-bush, and the devotee on his way to Mecca. We can furnish more men for the field, and more money to sustain them. But these things cannot change and renovate the human heart. " Not by might, nor by power, but by my Spirit, saith the Lord." This is the grand regenerating agency. He alone can convince and save the world. His aid is given in answer to prayer; and the Father is more ready to give than we are to ask.

Mr. Ward, one of the Baptist missionaries in India, in a missionary discourse at Bristol, said,—" Brethren, we need your money, but we need your prayers more." O, what encouragement we have to pray for our missionaries! Thus saith the Lord :—" I will pour water upon him that is thirsty, and floods upon the dry ground; I will pour my Spirit upon thy seed, and my blessing upon thine offspring." Let us plead with God for the accomplishment of the promise. " Ye that make mention of the Lord, keep not silence, and give him no rest till he make Jerusalem a praise in the whole earth."

Brethren in the ministry! let us remember that all our success depends upon the aid of the Holy Spirit, and let us pray constantly for his blessing upon the word! Brethren in the church! forget not the connection between the work of the Holy Spirit and the glory of your Best Friend, and earnestly entreat him to mingle his sanctifying unction with the treasures of Divine Truth contained in these earthen vessels! "Finally, brethren, pray for us; that the word of the Lord may have free course and be glorified;" and all the ends of the earth see the salvation of our God!

> " Hasten, Lord, the glorious time,
>   When, beneath Messiah's sway,
> Every tribe, in every clime,
>   Shall the gospel call obey!

> " Then shall wars and tumults cease;
>   Then be banished grief and pain;
> Righteousness, and joy, and peace,
>   Undisturbed, for ever reign !"

EXTRACTS

EXTRACTS

1

THE DEMONIAC OF GADARA

(Luke 8:26-39).

" AND when he went forth to land, there met him out of the city
a certain man, which had devils a long time, and ware no clothes,
neither abode in any house, but in the tombs."

I imagine that this demoniac was not only an object of pity, but
he was really a terror in the country. So terrific was his appearance,
so dreadful and hideous his screams, so formidable, frightful, and
horrid his wild career, that all the women in that region were so
much alarmed that none of them dared go to market.

And what made him still more terrible was the place of his
abode: It was not in a city, where some attention might be paid to
order and decorum—(though he would sometimes ramble into the
city as in this case.) It was not in a town, or village, or any house
whatever, where assistance might be obtained in case of necessity;
but it was among the tombs, and in the wilderness—not far, however, from the turnpike road. No one could tell but that he might
jump at them, like a panther, and scare them to death. The gloomi-
ness of the place made it more awful and solemn. It was among
the tombs—where, in the opinion of some, all witches, corpse-
candles, and hobgoblins abide.

One day, however, Mary was determined that no such nuisance
should be suffered in the country of the Gadarenes. The man must
be clothed, though he was mad and crazy. And if he should at
any future time strip himself, tie up his clothes in a bundle, throw
them into the river, and tell them to go to see Abraham, he must

be tied and taken care of. Well, this was all right—no sooner said than done. But, so soon as the fellow was bound in chains and fetters, Samson-like, he broke the bands asunder, and could not be tamed.

By this time, the devil became offended with the Gadarenes, and in a pout he took the demoniac away, and drove him into the wilderness. He thought the Gadarenes had no business to interfere and meddle with his property ; for he had possession of the man. And he knew, that " a bird in the hand is worth two in the bush." It is probable that he wanted to send him home ; for there was no knowing what might happen now-a-days. But there was too much matter about him to send him as he was ; therefore, he thought the best plan would be to persuade him to commit suicide by cutting his throat. But here Satan was at a nonplus—his rope was too short— He could not turn executioner himself, as that would not have answered the design he has in view, when he wants people to commit suicide ; for the act would have been his own sin and not the man's. The poor demoniac, therefore, must go about to hunt a sharp stone, or any thing that he could get. He might have been in search of such an article, when he returned from the wilderness into the city, whence he came when he met the Son of God.

" Jesus commanded the unclean spirit to come out of the man. And when he saw Jesus he cried out, and fell down before him, and with a loud voice said, What have I to do with thee, Jesus, thou Son of God most high ? I beseech thee torment me not."

Here is the devil's confession of faith. The devils believe and tremble, while men make a mock of sin, and sport on the brink of eternal ruin. To many of the human race, Christ appears as a root out of dry ground. They see in him neither form nor comeliness, and there is no beauty in him that they should desire him. Some said he was the carpenter's son, and would not believe in him ; others said he had a devil, and that it was through Beelzebub the chief of the devils, that he cast out devils ; some cried out, Let him be crucified—let him be crucified ; and others said, Let his blood be on us and on our children. As the Jews would not have him to reign over them ; so many, who call themselves Christians, say that he is a mere man ; as such, he has no right to rule over their consciences, and demand their obedience, adoration, and praise. But Diabolus knows better—Jesus is the Son of God most high.

Many of the children of the devil, whose work they do, differ very widely from their father in their sentiments respecting the person of Christ.

"Jesus commanded the legion of unclean spirits to come out of the man." They knew that out they must go. But they were like Scotchmen—very unwilling to return to their own country. They would rather go into hogs' skins than to their own country. And he suffered them to go into the herd of swine. Methinks that one of the men who fed the hogs, kept a better look out than the rest of them, and said, "What ail the hogs? Look sharp there, boys—keep them in—make good use of your whips. Why don't you run? Why, I declare, one of them has gone over the cliff! There goes another! Drive them back." Never was there such a running, and whipping, and hallooing; but down go the hogs, before they are aware of it. One of them said, "They are all gone!" "No, sure not all gone into the sea!" "Yes, every one of them, the black hog and all! They are all drowned!—the devil is in them! What shall we do now?—what can we say to the owners?" "What can we say?" said another. "We must tell the truth—that is all about it. We did our best—all that was in our power. What could any man do more?"

So they went their way to the city, to tell the masters what had happened. "John, where are you going," exclaimed one of the masters. "Sir, did you know the demoniac that was among the tombs there?" "Demoniac among the tombs! Where did you leave the hogs?" "That madman, sir——" "Madman!—Why do you come home without the hogs?" "That wild and furious man, sir, that mistress was afraid of so much——" "Why John, I ask you a plain and simple question—why don't you answer me? Where are the hogs?" "That man who was possessed with the devils, sir—" "Why, sure enough, you are crazy!—you look wild!—tell me your story, if you can, let it be what it may." "Jesus Christ, sir, has cast out the unclean spirits out of the demoniac; they are gone into the swine; and they are all drowned in the sea; for I saw the tail of the last one!" The Gadarenes went out to see what was done, and finding that it was even so, they were afraid, and besought Jesus to depart from them.

How awful must be the condition of those men who love the things of this world more than Jesus Christ!

The man out of whom the unclean spirits were cast, besought Jesus that he might be with him. But he told him to return to his

222 / Sermons and Memoirs of Christmas Evans

own house, and show how great things God had done unto him. And he went his way and published throughout the whole city of Decapolis, how great things Jesus had done unto him. The act of Jesus casting so many devils out of him, was sufficient to persuade him that Jesus was God as well as man.

I imagine I see him going through the city, crying—"O yes! O yes! O yes!—Please to take notice of me, the demoniac among the tombs. I am the man who was a terror to the citizens of this place —that wild man, who would wear no clothes, and that no man could bind. Here am I, now, in my right mind. Jesus Christ, the friend of sinners, had compassion on me. He remembered me when I was in my low estate—when there was no eye to pity, and no hand to save. He cast out the devils and redeemed my soul from destruction."

Most wonderful must have been the surprise of the people, to hear such proclamation. The ladies running to the windows, the shoemakers throwing their lasts one way and their awls another, running out to meet him and to converse with him, that they might be positive there was no imposition, and found it to be a fact that could not be contradicted. "O, the wonder of all wonders! Never was there such a thing!"—must, I think, be the general conversation.

And while they are talking and everybody having something to say, homeward goes the man. As soon as he comes in sight of the house, I imagine I see one of the children running in, and crying, "O, mother! father is coming—he will kill us all!" "Children, come all into the house," says the mother. "Let us fasten the doors. I think there is no sorrow like my sorrow!" says the broken-hearted woman. "Are all the windows fastened, children?" "Yes, mother." "Mary, my dear, come from the window—don't be standing there." "Why, mother, I can hardly believe it is father! That man is well-dressed." "O yes, my dear children, it is your own father. I knew him by his walk the moment I saw him." Another child stepping to the window, says, "Why, mother, I never saw father coming home as he does to-day. He walks on the footpath and turns round the corner of the fence. He used to come towards the house as straight as a line, over fences, ditches, and hedges; and I never saw him walking as slow as he does now."

In a few moments, however, he arrives at the door of the house, to the great terror and consternation of all the inmates. He gently tries the door, and finds no admittance. He pauses a moment, steps towards the window, and says in a low, firm, and melodious voice—

" My dear wife, if you will let me in, there is no danger. I will not hurt you. I bring you glad tidings of great joy." The door is reluctantly opened, as it were between joy and fear. Having deliberately seated himself, he says : " I am come to show you what great things God has done for me. He loved me with an eternal love. He redeemed me from the curse of the law and the threatenings of vindictive justice. He saved me from the power and the dominion of sin. He cast out the devils out of my heart, and made that heart, which was a den of thieves, the temple of the Holy Spirit. I cannot tell you how much I love the Saviour. Jesus Christ is the foundation of my hope, the object of my faith, and the centre of my affections. I can venture my immortal soul upon him. He is my best friend. He is altogether lovely—the chief among ten thousand. He is my wisdom, righteousness, sanctification, and redemption. There is enough in him to make a poor sinner rich, and a miserable sinner happy. His flesh and blood is my food—his righteousness my wedding garment—and his blood is efficacious to cleanse me from all my sins. Through him I can obtain eternal life ; for he is the brightness of the Father's glory, and the express image of his person : in whom dwelleth all the fullness of the Godhead bodily. He deserves my highest esteem and my warmest gratitude. Unto him who loved me with an eternal love, and washed me in his own blood, unto him be the glory, dominion, and power, for ever and ever ! For he has rescued my soul from hell. He plucked me as a brand out of the burning. He took me out of the miry clay, and out of a horrible pit. He set my feet upon a rock, and established my goings, and put in my mouth a new song of praise and glory to him ! Glory to him for ever !—Glory to God in the highest !—Glory to God for ever and ever ! Let the whole earth praise him !—Yea, let all the people praise him !"

It is beyond the power of the strongest imagination to conceive the joy and gladness of this family. The joy of seafaring men delivered from shipwreck ; the joy of a man delivered from a burning house ; the joy of not being found guilty to a criminal at the bar ; the joy of receiving pardon to a condemned malefactor ; the joy of freedom to a prisoner of war, is nothing in comparison to the joy of him who is delivered from going down to the pit of eternal destruction. For it is a joy unspeakable and full of glory.

2
ENTERING PORT

For so an entrance shall be ministered unto you abundantly into the everlasting kingdom of our Lord and Saviour Jesus Christ (2 Peter 1:11).

THIS language seems to be borrowed from the case of a ship bringing her passengers to port on a pleasant afternoon, her sails all white and whole, and her flags majestically waving in the breeze; while the relatives of those on board ascend the high places, to see their brothers and their sisters returning home in safety from the stormy main. How pleasant to a man who is about to emigrate to the new world, America, when he meets with some one that has been there, and who is well acquainted with the coast, knows the best landing-place, and will accompany him on his passage. "Though I walk through the valley and the shadow of death, I will fear no evil: for thou art with me; thy rod and thy staff they comfort me." He who passed through death himself, and is Lord of the sea, is our High-priest; and, with his priestly vestments on, he will stand in Jordan's current till the feeblest in all the tribes shall be safely landed on Canaan's shore. How delightful must be the feelings of the dying Christian, the testimony of whose conscience unites with the witness of the spirit, to assure him that Jesus has paid his fare: and who knows he carries in his hand the white stone with the new name, to be exhibited on the pier-head, the other side, hard by his Father's house. This is an abundant entrance, on a fair day, over a fine sea, with a pleasant breeze swelling every sail. " Now lettest thou thy servant depart in peace, for mine eyes have seen thy salvation."

O how different the entrance ministered to the careless professor— the fruitless and idle—who keeps his hand in his bosom, or leaning upon his implements! Though he may reach the shore with his life, it will be at midnight, surrounded by roaring tempests, full of bitter remembrances and most tormenting fears. Yet, with tattered sails and broken ropes, peradventure he may gain the port; "for the Lord is good, and his mercy endureth for ever." But who shall describe the condition of the ungodly, driven out to sea in all their wickedness; not even allowed a quarantine within sight of the heavenly Jerusalem, but obliged to drift about, dismantled and disabled, amid the darkness of eternal storms! Oh! to be forced from their moorings at midnight, when they cannot see a handbreadth before them; the thunders rolling; the lightnings flashing; strange voices of wrath mingling with every blast; and the great bell of eternity tolling a funeral knell for the lost soul, through all its dismal, and solitary, and everlasting voyage! Let us flee for refuge, to lay hold on the hope set before us, which hope is as an anchor of the soul, sure and steadfast, grasping the Rock of Ages within the vail!

3
THE UNCLEAN SPIRIT IN DRY PLACES

I SEE the wicked spirit, like a winged dragon, having a long tail, drawing circles and flying in the air, in search of a dwelling-place. Casting his fiery look upon a certain neighborhood, he spies a young man, in the bloom of his days, and in the strength of his powers, sitting on the box of his cart, going for lime. "There he is," says the old hellish dragon; "his veins are full of blood, and his bones are full of marrow; I will cast the sparks into his bosom, and will set all his lusts on fire; I will lead him on from bad to worse, until he commit every sin. I will make him a murderer, and will plunge his soul for ever beneath the boiling billows of the great fiery furnace." With this, I see him descending in all the vehemence of his character—but when close by the lad, the dragon hears him sing,

> "When on the cross the Saviour hung,
> The mid-day sank in midnight gloom;
> When guilty sinners were redeemed,
> The midnight burst in mid-day bloom."

Upon which the dragon cries out, "This place is too dry for me," —and away he flies.

I see him again, a second time, hovering in the air, and seeking for a resting-place. In a flowery meadow, by a river of clear water, he sees a maiden, eighteen years of age, among the kine, picking up some beautiful flowers, here and there. "Behold her," says Apollyon, full of hellish joy; "I will poison her mind, and lead her astray from the paths of the Almighty enemy; I will make her a harlot, and will ultimately cast her over the precipice, until she sink for ever in the furnace of divine wrath." He hastens down; and, approaching the maiden, finds her singing the following stanzas, in a heavenly, transporting frame of mind, and with a voice that might almost melt the rocks:

> "Unto the righteous will arrive,
> A day of rest serene,
> When to their joy they see the Lord,
> Without a vail between.

"Then from the grave I shall arise,
And take my joyful stand
Among the saints who dwell on high,
Received at God's right hand."

" This place is too dry for me," says the dragon, and off he flies.

From the meadow he ascends like a great balloon, with renewed rage, blowing smoke and fire from his mouth, and threatening damnation to all creation. " I will have a place to rest and dwell in," says Apollyon, " in spite of the purpose, covenant, and grace of God!" With this he espies an aged woman, sitting at the door of her cot, and spinning on her little wheel. " Ah, she is ripe for destruction," says the dragon; " I will give her a taste of the burning gall of damnation, and will cast her into the lake that burneth with fire and brimstone." With this he descends on the eaves of the cot, and hears the old woman, with a trembling voice, but with heavenly feelings, repeat the following beautiful passage: " For the mountains shall depart, and the hills be removed, but my kindness shall not depart from thee, neither shall the covenant of my peace be removed, saith the Lord that hath mercy on thee!" " This place is too dry for me," says the dragon, and is off again.

It might be thought that all these disappointments would discourage him from prosecuting his infernal designs farther; but not so: he is determined, if possible, to find a dwelling-place. For this purpose he rises again, to mark some spot where he may alight and find a welcome. He sees in a small village a neat and decent house of refreshment. " There," says he, " will I dwell, and lead to bondage every one that shall cross the threshold, and make him fast in eternal fetters." He flies down like lightning, enters the house, and walks into the parlor; but there he finds a company of ministers of the New Testament, returning from an Association, who are talking about the victory of Calvary, and exchanging appointments with each other. The wicked spirit cannot stay within the sound of their voice, but retreats with hasty steps, muttering and growling as he goes,—" This place is too dry for me, I will return to my house from which I came out!"

4

THE YOUNG CHILD

HEROD said to the wise men, "Go and search diligently for the young child." The magi immediately commenced their inquiries, according to the instructions they received. I see them approaching some village, and when they come to the gate they inquire, "Do you know any thing of the young child?" The gateman comes to the door; and, supposing them to have asked the amount of the toll, says, "O, three halfpence an ass is to pay." "We do not ask what is to pay," reply they, "but, do you know any thing of the young child?" "No; I know nothing in the world," answers he; "but there is a blacksmith's shop a little farther on; inquire there, and you will be very likely to obtain some intelligence concerning him."

The wise men proceed, and when they come to the blacksmith's shop, they ask, "Do you know any thing of the young child?" A harsh voice answers, "There is no such thing possible for you, as having the asses shod now; you shall in two hours hence." "We do not ask you to shoe the asses," say they; "but inquire for the young child, if you know any thing of him?" "Nothing in the world," says the blacksmith; "but inquire at the tavern that is on your road, and probably you may hear something of him there."

On they go, and stand opposite the door of the tavern, and cry, "Do you know any thing of the young child?" The landlord, thinking they call for porter, bids the servant attend, saying, "Go, girl; go with a quart of porter to the strangers." "We do not ask for either porter or ale," say the wise men; "but something about the young child that is born." "I know nothing in the world of him," says the landlord; "but turn to the shop on the left hand; the shopkeeper reads all the papers, and you will be likely to hear something respecting him there."

They proceed accordingly towards the shop, and repeat their inquiry, "Do you know any thing of the young child, here?" The shopkeeper says to his apprentice, "Reach half a quarter of tobacco to the strangers." "We do not ask for tobacco," say the wise men; "but for some intelligence of the young child." "I do not know any thing of him," replies the shopkeeper; "but there is an old Rabbi living in the upper end of the village; call on him, and very probably he will give you all the information you desire respecting the object of your search."

They immediately direct their course towards the house of the Rabbi; and having reached it, they knock at the door; and being admitted into his presence, they ask him if he knows any thing of the young child. "Come in," says he; and when they have entered and are seated, the Rabbi refers to his books and chronicles, and says he to the wise men, "There is something wonderful about to take place; some remarkable person has been or is to be born; but the best thing for you is to go down yonder street; there is living there, by the river side, the son of an old priest; you will be sure to know all of him."

Having bid the old Rabbi a respectful farewell, on they go; and reaching the river's side, they inquire of the by-standers for the son of the old priest. Immediately he is pointed out to them. There is a "raiment of camel's hair about him, and a leathern girdle about his loins." They ask him if he knows any thing of the young child. "Yes," says he, "there he is: behold the Lamb of God, that taketh away the sin of the world! There he is; he will bruise the dragon's head, and bring in everlasting righteousness to every one that believeth in his name."

5
VARIETIES OF PREACHING

I PERCEIVE four strong men on their journey toward Lazarus' grave, for the purpose of raising him to life. One of them, who is eminent for his piety, says, "I will descend into the grave, and will take with me a bowl of the salt of duties, and will rub him well with the sponge of natural ability." He enters the grave, and commences his rubbing process. I watch his operations at a distance, and after a while inquire, "Well, are there any symptoms of life there? Does he arise, does he breathe, my brother?" "No such thing," replies he, "he is still quiet, and I cannot salt him to *will*— and besides this, his smell is rather heavy."

"Well," says the second, "come you out; I was afraid that your means would not answer the purpose; let me enter the grave." The second enters, carrying in his hand a whip of the scorpions of threatening; and, says he, "I will make him feel." He directs his scorpion and fiery ministry at the dead corpse; but in vain, and I hear him crying out, "All is unsuccessful; dead he is after all."

Says the third, "Make room for me to enter, and I will see if I cannot bring him to life." He enters the grave, and takes with him a musical pipe; it is melodious as the song of love; but there is no dancing in the grave.

The fourth says, "Means of themselves can effect nothing, but I will go for Jesus, who is the resurrection and the life." Immediately he leaves to seek for Christ, and speedily returns, accompanied by the Saviour. And when the Lord came, he stands in the door of the sepulchre, and cries out, "Lazarus, come forth!" and the dead body is instantaneously instinct with life.

Let our confidence be in the voice of the Son of God. And let us turn our faces toward the wind, and say, "O breath, come from the four winds, and breathe upon these slain, that they may live!"

6

THE SIX CROCODILES

EVERY church-member should learn to hunt a crocodile. The first crocodile is a spirit to search closely for faults, instead of hiding them with brotherly love, according to the directions of the gospel. This is Ham, the old crocodile, that exposed the nakedness of his father, instead of hiding it like Shem and Japheth; for which his father banished him to the river Nilus, where he still remains in Africa, under the curse of his father.

Old pious Eli erred greatly, by allowing his children to enter the sanctuary as crocodiles, by sparing them, and suffering them in their sins, which brought, through these crocodiles, destruction on his house: and in the same manner since upon many congregations,—as the churches of Asia. This is an evil spirit in the mount.

Another crocodile is the spirit of preference. This is the crocodile Judas, who was offended with Jesus in Bethany on account of Mary's ointment, which she poured on the head of Jesus; and that only because they did not consult him; in revenge for which he turned traitor. He was a selfish miser; and ultimately hung himself, and went to his own place. This crocodile still lurks among the reeds. There are many like him, ready to blame every act of discipline in the church; not that they care so much for the interests of the church, or any belonging to it, but they wish to swallow all up themselves.

Another crocodile is the spirit of Ahithophel, who plotted a cunning artifice to dethrone a person whose heart was with God, and raise Absalom, a wicked man like himself, to the throne in his stead. God turned his counsel into foolishness. He was disappointed— his heart failed—he saddled his ass, and went and hung himself. This was the end of that crocodile.

Another is a spirit to trample and destroy, for the sake of being head. This is the crocodile Joab, who killed Abner, who was better than himself. This crocodile strikes every one who may be in his way under the fifth rib, for the sake of being head himself. But his end came; he lost his life at the horns of the altar, by the sword with which he himself destroyed another.

But, upon looking again, we see the sixth crocodile, and his name is Cain, who would triumph over God and man; without grace, or talents, or faith, or love; and without any sacrifice that has blood in it; and because God will not regard him without faith, he opens his mouth, and sets himself to swallow pious Abel. God delivers him over to the possession of the wicked one.

O brethren, let us prove the spirits, whether they are of God, or of the devil!

I will tell you an anecdote of Mr. Rowlands, of Llangeitho. When he wished to crush the spirit of calumny (the crocodile Ham) which lurked in the church, he said to the slanderer: "Thou sayest, man, that sins must be hunted and exposed, because they are too numerous in the church—and that they ought not be hidden. Be quiet, man. Who art thou? I think I know thy family, and thy eldest brother, even Ham, the son of Noah. His two brothers wished to hide their father's nakedness, but he would expose it. What reward did they receive for covering their father's nakedness? The blessing of God and their father. And what reward did thy brother receive? The curse of God and their father. And I doubt not thy reward will be nothing better."

7

ENVIOUS AMBITIONS

The forest of Lebanon once held a consultation to choose a king, upon the death of the king, the Yew-tree. They agreed to offer the crown to the Cedar; and if the Cedar should refuse, to invite the Vine and the Olive to office. They all refused the honors for the following reasons. The Cedar refused, " because," said he, " I am sufficiently high as I am."—" I would rather," said the Vine, " yield wine to cheer others, than receive for myself." And in the same manner, the Olive preferred giving its oil to honor others rather than receive any honors to itself.

All these having refused the honors offered them, they next agreed to call the Thorn to the government; and if he should decline, to choose the Bramble. The White Thorn, in its beautiful dress, received the honor, speaking thus to itself:—" I have nothing to lose but the white coat, and some red berries; and I have prickles enough to hurt the whole forest." But the Bramble instigated a rebellion against the White Thorn, and kindled the fire of pride in the forest, so that all the trees were set on flame.

Two or three vain and proud men in a peaceful congregation, have, by contending for the preference, disturbed the peace, and obstructed the prosperity of many a church, while there was no more virtue in them than there is of value in the white thorn or prickly bramble.

8
THE DOVE, THE RAVEN, AND THE EAGLE

A NOBLEMAN had a Dove, a Raven, and an Eagle, belonging to his palace. There was no sociability or fellowship prevailing among them. The Dove fed on its own food, and hid herself in the clefts of the rocks, or in the dove-house near the palace. The Raven fed upon dead carcasses, and sometimes picked out the eyes of little innocent lambs, if she could pounce upon them in a chance place;— she also nestled in the top of the trees. The Eagle was a royal bird, flying very high, but yet of a rapacious character. Sometimes he would not mind eating some half a dozen of the Doves for his breakfast. He thought himself the king of birds because he flew higher than they all. The Doves greatly dreaded his strong beak, his wrathful eyes, and his sharp grappling claws. When the gentleman threw wheat for the Dove on the pavement, the Raven would have a piece of an ear or the foot of a lamb in its beak; and the Eagle was for taking up some little child from the cradle to his nest.

The Dove is the pious diligent Christian; the Raven is the dissolute and difficult to be managed; and the proud, selfish professor is the Eagle. These three characters are too frequently to be found together, and there is no denomination, in church or chapel, without these three birds, if there are any birds at all there. It is impossible for three birds, so different in their dispositions, ever to be happy together. Brethren, pray for the unity of the Spirit in the bond of peace.

MEMOIRS

and

PORTRAITURE

of

CHRISTMAS EVANS

INTRODUCTION

THE introduction of Christianity into Britain is said to have taken place about sixty-three years after the crucifixion. By whose agency it was effected, cannot now be satisfactorily determined. Tradition has ascribed it to Joseph of Arimathea. This, however, is exceedingly doubtful. It has also been attributed to the apostle Paul. That the apostle Paul visited Britain, is quite probable, from the testimony of Theodoret and Jerome. That he was the first preacher of the gospel in Britain, is certainly a mistake. The weight of evidence seems to be in favour of Claudia, a Welsh lady, belonging to Cæsar's household. The circumstances were these:—

The Romans invaded Britain about fifty years before the incarnation. Failing to conquer the Welsh, they made peace with them, and dwelt among them in amity. Many Welsh soldiers joined the Roman army, and several Welsh families went and resided at Rome. Among the latter were Claudia and her husband. Saint Paul was then a prisoner under Nero; dwelling, however, "in his own hired house," and receiving all who came to hear the word of God. Under his ministry, Claudia was converted to Christianity. She soon returned to her native country, and scattered "the Seed of the Kingdom" among her own people. This was in the year of our Lord sixty-three.

About a century after this, Faganus and Daminicanus went to Rome, were converted there, and became "able ministers of the New Testament." In the year of our Lord 180, they were sent back to Wales, to preach to their own countrymen. They were zealous and successful laborers. They opposed the pagan superstitions of the Welsh with wonderful energy. They pursued Druidism to its dark retirements, and poured upon it the withering blaze of the gospel. Through their preaching, Lucius, king of Wales, was brought to embrace Christianity. He was the first king that ever bowed to the Prince of Peace. The royal convert was exceedingly zealous in the propagation of the truth. The Macedonian cry issued from the throne of Wales, an earnest appeal to Eleutherius for help. Then "the word of the Lord had free course, and was glorified."

Under the reign of Dioclesian, about the year 300, the Welsh Christians suffered a dreadful persecution. Their books were burned, their houses of worship were destroyed, and multitudes obtained the crown of martyrdom. The first three were Alban, Aaron, and Julius. They were all excellent men, and greatly beloved by their brethren. They died in triumph, and their blood became the seed of the church. Many others soon followed them in the same path. Dioclesian gave strict orders for their destruction. Not a Christian was to be spared, not a Christian church, not a book or a scrap of writing that could transmit their faith and history to future generations. This was the tenth persecution. The great dragon had sent forth his flood to destroy the church. But "mightily grew the word of God and prevailed." The bush still lived,

"And flourished unconsumed in fire."

The first Christian king, we have said, was a Welshman. So, in part, was the first Christian emperor. Constantine the Great was born in Britain. His father was Roman; his mother Welsh. Having resided some time in Britain, they removed to Rome. Constantine ascended the Imperial throne. Converted, he made Christianity the religion of the empire. The intolerant edicts of his predecessors were abolished; and the absurd rites of paganism, as far as possible, suppressed. The emperor employed all his energies and resources in spreading the gospel. But his course, if honest, was injudicious. In the end, he dishonoured Christianity more by his imprudence than he glorified her at first by his zeal. He opened the door of the church so wide as to admit Antichrist himself. The "man of sin" came and seated himself in the temple of God.

Intoxicated with her prosperity, the church throughout the empire gradually embraced the grossest superstitions. But the Welsh Christians strenuously resisted all innovations. They adhered firmly to the primitive simplicity of Christian faith and worship. Yet they lost a portion of their spirituality. The storms of tribulation are often more favourable to the growth of vital religion, than the sunshine of prosperity. The church becomes dizzy when placed upon the pinnacle of worldly praise. The boatmen wax careless when their craft glides gently along on a smooth sea, before a pleasant gale. This is the natural tendency of the human mind, in circumstances of prosperity. It was thus with the Christians of Wales.

Other things operated unfavourably. The Pelagian controversy divided and distracted the churches, and destroyed the spirit of Christian meekness and love. The Welsh were soon involved in a civil war with the Picts and Scots. In their distress, they solicited the aid of the Saxons. The Saxons promptly responded to the call. But the ally soon became an enemy. They fell upon the Welsh, drove them to the mountains of Cumry, and took possession of their land.* These disasters threatened the extermination of Christianity in Wales. But there were a few faithful ones, whose ark outrode the deluge. Gildas, Dyfrig, Dynawt, Teil, Padarn, Pawlin, Daniel, Codag, Dewi, and several others, stood firmly against the degeneracy of the times, and were " valiant for the truth upon the earth." Through their labors, the religion of Jesus survived among the hills of Cumry.

In the beginning of the seventh century, Austin came to Britain, under a commission from Gregory the Great, to make proselytes to popery. He succeeded well with the Saxons, but not at all with the Welsh. This is not strange. The Saxons were ignorant idolaters, and the transition was easy from Paganism to popery. The Welsh were enlightened Christians, and it was difficult to seduce them from their allegiance to Christ. They consented, however, to hold a large meeting on the borders of Herefordshire, and hear what Austin had to offer. His doctrine did not suit them. They rejected alike the proposals of the monk and the commands of his master. This awoke the fiend within him. He instigated the Saxons to murder them. Twelve hundred ministers and delegates were slaughtered, and afterward many of their brethren. Their leaders being slain, the majority of the survivors reluctantly purchased peace at the sacrifice of conscience, submitting to the creed

---

* Down to this time, the Welsh inhabited all of what is now denominated England. But henceforth they are confined to the western part of the island, called Cumry, or Wales.

and the usages of Rome. Yet there were some who repudiated the doctrine of the pope's supremacy, and maintained for a season the simplicity of the gospel. But they lived among the mountains, in seclusion from the world, like the inhabitants of the vale of Piedmont. We hear little or nothing of them again till the time of the Reformation.

While the Lord, through the labors of his servant Wickliffe, was preparing his way in England, Wales also was remembered in mercy, and visited with " the day-spring from on high." Walter Brute was a native of the principality. He had been at Oxford, where he had formed an intimate acquaintance with Wickliffe. He entered fully into Wickliffe's views concerning the reformation of the church. His heart was moved with compassion for his country-men. Inspired with apostolic faith and zeal, he left the university, and returned to his native land. He determined to resist, even " unto blood," the delusions and abominations of the papacy. He soon distinguished himself as a courageous reformer. He preached in the streets, in the markets, and from house to house. He blew the trump of God throughout the principality. The temple of Antichrist began to tremble, and its gilded and pampered occupants manifested considerable uneasiness and alarm.

Everybody saw that Brute was generous and disinterested. Friends flocked around him, for the people had long since become disgusted with the corruptions of the church, and heartily sick of ecclesiastical despotism. Men of all classes gathered to his standard. His labors of love soon elicited, of course, the hostility of the clergy. But so numerous and respectable were his friends, that all the attempts of ecclesiastical judicatures, and officers of the civil law, were ineffectual. A petition was at length sent to Richard II., King of England, entreating his interference. The king issued an order to the nobility of Wales, requiring them to assist the Bishop of Hereford in apprehending and punishing the heretic and his adherents. This was in the year 1391. Still Walter Brute went on, preaching the gospel, denouncing the papacy, and exposing the corruptions of the church, without material molestation, till 1393. He was then cited to appear before the Bishop of Hereford, to answer to a charge of heresy. He appeared, defended himself against the allegation, and contended boldly that the pope was Antichrist, and the papal church Babylon.

In this argument, Brute triumphed over his accusers, and made many converts to his cause. Several of the clergy now embraced his views, and became zealous defenders of the faith. One of these, Davydd Ddu of Hiraddug, on the border of Cardiganshire, undertook a translation of the Scriptures into Welsh. Portions of this translation were extensively circulated. Another, John Kent, D. D., of Grismond, in Monmouthshire, was a learned man and a fine poet. He labored incessantly with his pen, to expose the vices of the clergy, and promote a more spiritual religion. These divines were variously opposed and persecuted by ecclesiastical power. They were stigmatized as magicians, and accused of intercourse with evil spirits. But all was unavailing. The zeal of Ddu and Kent was unabated, and the progress of truth was unretarded. The hand of God was with them wherever they went. Revivals occurred in the cloisters, and monks came forth from their seclusion to reinforce the reformers. In the monastery of Margam, Glamorganshire, a large number of the monks were converted. One of them, Thomas Evan ab Rhys, travelled the mountains of the principality, at the constant peril of his life, to remonstrate against popery, and recommend a purer form of Christianity.

In 1580, John Penry, an Episcopal minister, dissented from the established church, and became a Baptist. He was a man of liberal education and fine pulpit talents. After having prosecuted his ministry more than seven years, with remarkable zeal and success, he died a martyr. Penry was the first Baptist preacher in Wales after the Reformation.

In 1620, Erbury and Wroth followed his example. The conversion of the latter was very singular. A nobleman belonging to his parish went to London to attend a law-suit. Hearing that he was successful, Mr. Wroth bought a new violin, and prepared to welcome his return with music and dancing. While these preparations were going on, news came that the nobleman was dead. The joy of the party was suddenly turned into mourning. The vicar fell upon his knees, and poured out his heart in fervent prayer to God. This event occasioned his conversion. Erbury, his friend, was converted about the same time. Both began to preach with wonderful unction. " Jesus Christ and him crucified" was their constant theme. Their zeal drew down upon them a violent storm of persecution. But they were not discouraged. God owned their labors, and many were the seals of their ministry. In 1635 they were ejected from their parishes. But they "cared for none of these things." They went from valley to valley, from mountain to mountain, preaching the word. The recent Welsh translation of the Scriptures proved a powerful auxiliary to their work. People read and investigated for themselves, and found that these were men of God, speaking "the words of truth and soberness."

Erbury and Wroth both organized Baptist churches; the former, on the plan of "strict communion;" the latter, on more liberal principles. These were the first Baptist churches instituted in Wales, after the Reformation from popery. It is said, however, that there existed, even centuries before, many Baptists in the valley of Carleon, the Piedmont of Wales, and among the neighboring mountains. Their origin is, very unfortunately, involved in obscurity. Some pretend to trace them back to the year 63, the time of the introduction of Christianity into Britain. This is a very convenient theory for those who wish to show that the first Christians were exclusive immersionists; and who deem it of primary importance to establish a regular succession of such Christians, from the apostles of our Lord, down to the present day. But it is unsustained by a single shadow of evidence, beyond the bare assertion of interested witnesses.

During the ministry of Erbury and Wroth, arose that morning-star of the Baptist church in Wales, Vavasor Powell. He was born in Radnorshire, South Wales. He was educated for the ministry of the established church. For some time he officiated at Clun, on the borders of Shropshire. While there, his conscience was awakened by a reproof from a Puritan for violating the Sabbath. He was soon afterwards converted, under the preaching of Walter Caradock, a noted preacher among the Independents. In 1636, he joined the Baptists, and shortly became a very popular preacher among them. He was a man of great eloquence and power. Many were converted under his ministry. But the red dragon was roused to pursue him. In 1642, he fled his native land for the safety of his life. In four years, however, he returned, and preached boldly throughout the country. The people flocked to hear him, by thousands, to the market-houses, to the fields, the woods, and the tops of the mountains. His ministry was wonderfully blessed to the salvation of souls.

After the death of Cromwell, in 1658, Charles II. returned to England. Now commenced a dreadful persecution of the Baptists in Wales. "Hundreds of them were taken from their beds at night, without any regard to age, sex, or the inclemency of the weather; and were driven to prison, on foot, fifteen or twenty miles; and if they did not keep up with their drivers on horseback, they were most cruelly and unmercifully whipped; and while their drivers stopped to drink at the taverns, they were beaten like cattle, during the pleasure of the king's friends; and all their property was forfeited to the king, except what was deemed necessary to defray the expenses of their drivers. But all this was only the beginning of sorrows, and nothing to what they suffered for the space of six - and-twenty years afterward."

In these persecutions, Vavasor Powell bore his part. He was immured, at different times, in thirteen prisons. Indeed, he was a prisoner most of the time till his death, which happened in 1670. On his tomb is this inscription:—"He was, to the last generation, a successful preacher; to the present generation, a faithful witness; to the next generation, an excellent example."

Contemporary with Vavasor Powell, and immediately succeeding him, were many faithful laborers in the cause of Christ in Wales. One of them was the noted Roger Williams, who subsequently removed to New England, and founded the Baptist sect in America. But after the death of Powell and his coadjutors, the revival in Wales declined, and the churches gradually settled into a spiritual sleep, in which they remained a century, when they were roused by the trumpet-tongued eloquence of Harris and Rowlands.

Harris and Rowlands were Methodists. While Whitefield and Wesley were rekindling the fires of the Reformation on the altars of England, these men of God were scattering some sparks of it among the mountains of Wales. Under their labors commenced such a revival as was never known in that country before. They adhered to the established church; and, on that account, were, for a season, but little opposed. But when the blessed fruits of their ministry began to be developed in the conversion of thousands of souls, the wrath of Satan and his emissaries arose against them. But, as Christmas Evans remarks, it was now too late. The sword of the Spirit was drawn; the gates of the city were opened; the fire was kindled in the stubble, and not all the floods of persecution could stay the progress of the flame. Harris and Rowlands went forward in their work of love, clothed with power from on high. A great and effectual door was opened to their ministry, and the leaven spread rapidly through the lump.

The Baptists shared largely in this work of grace. It was the rising of a new sun upon them, which had been heralded a hundred years before in the powerful ministry of Vavasor Powell. The revival developed whatever of talent and energy lay dormant in the denomination. Many a David went forth to meet the Philistine, and returned in triumph. One of these, and the most successful of them all, was CHRISTMAS EVANS. "He was a man of God," says Dr. Cone, "and eminently useful in his generation." His natural talents were of the highest order, and his Christian graces have not been surpassed in a century. The celebrated Robert Hall regarded him as the first pulpit genius of the age. "Had he enjoyed the advantages of education," writes one who knew him well, and often sat under his ministry, "he might have blended the impassioned declamation of Whitefield with something of the imperial opulence and pomp of fancy that distinguished Jeremy Taylor." His two celebrated "Specimens of Welsh Preaching" have been read throughout Protestant Christendom; and ranked, by universal suffrage, among the most splendid productions of sanctified genius. Who that has seen them does not wish to know more of so remarkable a man? To gratify this desire is a secondary object of the present publication; the primary, is the religious benefit of mankind. The matter of the following memoir and portraiture is compiled from several authentic sources of information. May their perusal afford the reader as rich a harvest of profit and delight as their preparation has afforded the writer!

MEMOIRS

Early Years

CHRISTMAS EVANS, second son of Samuel and Joanna Evans, was born at Ysgarwen, Cardiganshire, South Wales, on the 25th of December, 1776.   His birth happening on Christmas day suggested his Christian name.

Samuel and Joanna Evans were poor, and unable to educate their children; and at the age of seventeen, Christmas could not read a word.   When he was only nine years old, he lost his father and went to live with his uncle, who was a farmer, and a very wicked man.   Here he spent several years of his youthful life, daily witnessing the worst of examples, and experiencing the unkindest of treatment.   He subsequently engaged as a servant to several farmers successively in his native parish.

During these years he met with a number of serious accidents, in some of which he narrowly escaped with his life.   Once he was stabbed in a quarrel.   Once he was so nearly drowned as to be with difficulty resuscitated.   Once he fell from a very high tree, with an open knife in his hand.   Once a horse ran away with him, passing at full speed through a low and narrow passage.

Profession of Christianity

His first religious impressions he dates from his father's funeral.   But they were fitful and evanescent.   To use his own language, "They vanished and recurred once and again."   When he was eighteen years of age, an awakening occurred among the young people of his neighborhood.   Christmas himself was "much terrified with the fear of death and judgment," became very serious in his deportment, and joined the Arminian Presbyterians at Llwynrhydowen.

His Christian experience was evidently very imperfect.   He had a conviction of the evil of sin, and a desire to flee from the wrath to come; but no evidence of acceptance with God, and a very limited knowledge of the plan of salvation. Yet his religious impressions were not entirely fruitless. They produced, at least, a partial reformation of life, and led to many penitential resolutions. He thought much of eternity, and was frequent in secret prayer. He soon felt a strong desire to understand the Scriptures, and with this view began to learn to read. According to his own account, "There was not one in seven in those parts at that time that knew a letter." Almost entirely unaided, he prosecuted his purpose; and in an incredibly short time was able to read his Bible.

He Begins to Preach

He was now called upon to exercise his gifts in public prayer and exhortation. "To this," he says, "I felt a strong inclination, though I knew myself a mass of spiritual ignorance." His first performance was so generally approved, that he felt greatly encouraged to proceed. Shortly afterward, he preached a sermon at a prayer-meeting, in the parish of Llangeler, county of Caermarthen. The discourse, however, was not original, but a translation from Bishop Beveridge. He also committed one of the Rev. Mr. Rowlands' sermons, and preached it in the neighborhood of the church to which he belonged. A gentleman who heard him expressed great astonishment at such a sermon from an unlettered boy. The mystery was solved the next day; he found the sermon in a book. "But I have not done thinking," said he, "that there is something great in the son of Samuel the shoemaker, for his prayer was as good as the sermon." His opinion of the young preacher would probably have suffered some farther abatement, if he had known, what was the fact, that the prayer itself was memorized!

Young Evans now received frequent invitations to preach, in sundry places, for different denominations; especially in the Baptist church, at Penybont, Llandysil. He spoke occasionally in the pulpits of several eminent ministers. All who heard him were delighted with his discourses, and gave him much encouragement. These labors drew him into the society of many excellent Christians. He seems to have profited by their godly conversation, and soon acquired an experimental knowledge of justification by faith, though the witness of the Spirit was not so clear as in many cases, and he could never fix upon any particular time when he obtained the blessing.

Backsliding and Recovery

The young preacher shortly felt the need of a little more learning, to qualify him for his calling. He commenced going to school to the Rev. Mr. Davis, his pastor, and devoted himself for about six months to the study of Latin. This involved him in pecuniary distress. He took a journey into England, to labour during the harvest season, for the purpose of replenishing his purse, and enabling him to continue his studies. While thus engaged, he fell into temptation, and his religious feelings suffered a sad declension. He thought of relinquishing the school and the ministry, and devoting his life to secular pursuits. While revolving this matter in his mind, the children of the wicked one came upon him, and buffetted him back to his duty. He was waylaid by a mob, who had determined to kill him. They beat him so severely, that he lay for a long time insensible; and one of them gave him a blow upon his left eye, which occasioned its total blindness through the rest of his life.

" That night," says he, " I dreamed that the day of judgment was come. I saw Jesus on the clouds, and all the world on fire. I was in great fear, yet crying earnestly, and with some confidence, for his peace. He answered and said: ' Thou thoughtest to be a preacher; but what wilt thou do now? The world is on fire, and it is too late!' On this I awoke, and felt heartily thankful that I was in bed."

This dream produced a deep impression upon his mind, and recovered him from his spiritual declension. He began to preach with renewed energy and success, and all his friends predicted that he would " yet become a great man, and a celebrated preacher."

Doctrinal Changes

There was living, about this time, at Aberduar, a Mr. Amos, who had left the Arminian Presbyterians, and joined the Calvinistic Baptists. He came to visit young Evans, and converse with him on the subject of baptism. The latter was unpractised in argument, and little acquainted with the Scriptures. He strove strenuously for a while, but was at length silenced by the superior skill of his antagonist. Encouraged by his success, Mr. Amos made him another visit, during which he shook his faith in the validity of infant baptism. After this he came again and again. Mr. Evans was at length brought to believe there was no true baptism but immersion by a Baptist minister. Now it was suggested that he ought to be immersed. Other Baptist friends interested themselves in his case, and put into his hands such books as were best adapted to their purpose. He was shortly satisfied what was his duty. "After much struggling," says he, "between the flesh and the spirit, between obedience and disobedience, I went to the Baptist church at Aberduar, in the parish of Llanybyther, in the county of Caermarthen. I was cordially received there, but not without a degree of dread, on the part of some, that I was still a stout-hearted Arminian." He was baptized with several others, by the pastor, Rev. Timothy Thomas, in the river Duar, and admitted to the communion of the church. This was in 1788, when Mr. Evans was about the age of 22.

It is not strange, that, after such a change, he should gradually imbibe the doctrine of election, and its concomitants, as held by the Calvinistic Baptists; but it is quite evident, not only by inference from his own account, but by information from other sources, that he had not yet relinquished his Arminian theology. Whether he would have been more pious and useful, by adhering to his Arminian views, and remaining among his Arminian friends, is a question not for us to answer, and perhaps of little practical importance. It is certain that he became a Calvinist of the highest school, and "a burning and shining light" among his Baptist brethren. That the Calvinistic faith is not incompatible with eminent holiness of life, we have other evidence than that afforded by the history of Christmas Evans. The seraphic piety of a Bunyan, a Baxter, a Whitefield, and a Payson, should silence for ever the clamors of Arminian bigotry!

Depressing Views

For several years after this, Mr. Evans entertained painfully depressing views of his Christian character and ministerial talents He thought every other believer had more light than himself, and every other preacher greater gifts. He called himself " a mass of ignorance and sin." He imagined his discourses entirely useless to his hearers. This he attributed partly to his habit of repeating them *memoriter*. Others appeared to him to speak extemporaneously, and he "thought they received their sermons directly from heaven," while he, by memorizing his, forfeited the aid of the Holy Spirit. " I therefore changed my method," says he, " and took a text without any premeditation, and endeavored to speak what occurred to me at the time. If bad before, it was worse now. I had neither sense nor life, nothing but a poor miserable tone, which produced no effect upon the hearers, and made me really sick of myself. I thought God had nothing to do with me as a preacher. I had no confidence in my own talents and virtues, and the very sound of my voice discouraged me. I have since perceived the great goodness of God herein, preserving me from being puffed up by too good an opinion of my own gifts and graces, which both before and since has proved fatal to many young preachers."

These views of himself often occasioned him deep distress of mind. He entered the pulpit with dread. He conceived that the mere sight of him there was sufficient to becloud the hearts of his hearers, and intercept every ray of light from heaven. He could not ascertain that he had been the means of the salvation of a single soul during the five years of his preaching. It might have been some relief to him, could he have ventured to develope to some judicious Christian friend the disquietude of his soul. But this he dared not do, lest he should be deemed an unconverted man in the ministry, and exposed as a hypocrite to the world. So he wrapped up the painful secret in his heart, and drank his wormwood alone.

From all this, what are we to infer? That Mr. Evans had never been converted, or was not now in favour with God? We think not. All who knew him had full confidence in his piety, and thought him an excellent Christian. Whether his attention to the subject of baptism, or the Calvinistic views he had recently imbibed, had acted injuriously upon his religious enjoyment, would be an unprofitable speculation, if not otherwise improper. Perhaps these distressing doubts were but the permitted buffetings of Satan, to preserve him from spiritual pride; the preparatory darkness, which enabled him more highly to appreciate, and more earnestly to recommend to others, " the Bright and Morning Star." Many of God's chosen servants have been disciplined for their work in darkness. Dr. Payson, during all the earlier part of his eminently useful ministry, and John Summerfield, when his sweet persuasive tongue was leading multitudes to the Cross, were constantly distressed with doubts of their own spiritual condition. Though it is certainly the privilege of every believer to know that he is " a new creature in Christ Jesus," we cannot thence infer that all such as have not constantly the direct witness of the Spirit are in an unregenerate state.

Labors in Leyn

In 1790, Mr. Evans attended the Baptist association at Maesyberllan, in Brecknockshire. Some ministers from North Wales persuaded him to accompany them on their return. He found the Baptist people at Lëyn, in Caernarvonshire, few and feeble. They earnestly besought him to remain with them, to which he at length consented. He was immediately ordained a missionary, to itinerate among several small churches in that vicinity.

Now he began emphatically to " live by faith on the Son of God." The burden which he had borne so long, rolled away like that of Bunyan's Pilgrim. He received " the oil of joy for mourning, and the garment of praise for the spirit of heaviness." From this time, a wonderous power attended his preaching. Many were gathered into the church, as the fruit of his labor. " I could scarcely believe," says he, " the testimony of the people, who came before the church as candidates for membership, that they had been converted through my ministry. Yet I was obliged to believe, though it was marvellous in my eyes. This made me thankful to God, and increased my confidence in prayer. A delightful gale descended upon me, as from the hill of the New Jerusalem, and I felt the three great things of the kingdom of heaven, righteousness, and peace, and joy in the Holy Ghost."

During the first year of his labors in Lëyn, he was united in marriage to Miss Catherine Jones, a pious young lady of his own church, and a very suitable companion. After this event, his duties were increasingly arduous. He frequently preached five times during the Sabbath, and walked twenty miles. His heart was full of love, and he spoke with the ardor of a seraph. Con-

stant labor and intense excitement soon wore upon his health. He
became feeble, and his friends were apprehensive of consumption.
Through the mercy of God, however, he was spared; gradually
recovered his strength; and performed, through the remainder of a
long life, an incredible amount of ministerial labor.

Visit to South Wales

Mr. Evans naturally felt a strong desire to see his friends in South
Wales. During his second year at Lëyn, thinking it might benefit
his enfeebled health, as well as refresh his spirit, he determined
to make them a visit. He was unable to procure a horse for the
journey, and the small societies to which he preached were too poor
to provide him one. So he set forth on foot, preaching in every
town and village through which he passed. His talents were now
developed, and he had received " an unction from the Holy One."
All who heard him were astonished at his power. His old acquaint-
ances regarded him as a new man. A great awakening followed
him wherever he went. Hear his own language :—

" I now felt a power in the word, like a hammer breaking the
rock, and not like a rush. I had a very powerful time at Kilvowyr,
and also pleasant meetings in the neighborhood of Cardigan. The
work of conversion was progressing so rapidly and with so much
energy in those parts, that the ordinance of baptism was administered every month for a year or more, at Kilvowyr, Cardigan,
Blaenywaun, Blaenffòs, and Ebenezer, to from ten to twenty persons each month. The chapels and adjoining burying-grounds
were crowded with hearers of a week-day, even in the middle of
harvest. I frequently preached in the open air in the evenings,
and the rejoicing, singing, and praising would continue until broad
light the next morning. The hearers appeared melted down in
tenderness at the different meetings, so that they wept streams of
tears, and cried out, in such a manner that one might suppose the
whole congregation, male and female, was thoroughly dissolved by
the gospel. ' The word of God' was now become as ' a sharp two-
edged sword, dividing asunder the joints and marrow,' and revealing unto the people the secret corruptions of their hearts. Preaching was now unto me a pleasure, and the success of the ministry
in all places was very great. The same people attended fifteen or

twenty different meetings, many miles apart, in the counties of Cardigan, Pembroke, Caermarthen, Glamorgan, Monmouth, and Brecknock. This revival, especially in the vicinity of Cardigan, and in Pembrokeshire, subdued the whole country, and induced people everywhere to think well of religion. The same heavenly gale followed down to Fishguard, Llangloffan, Little New-Castle, and Rhydwylim, where Mr. Gabriel Rees was then a zealous and a powerful preacher. There was such a tender spirit resting on the hearers at this season, from Tabor to Middlemill, that one would imagine, by their weeping and trembling in their places of worship, and all this mingled with so much heavenly cheerfulness, that they would wish to abide for ever in this state of mind."

The fame of this "wonderful work of God" spread through South Wales on the wings of the wind. An appointment for Christmas Evans to preach was sufficient to attract thousands to the place. In a very short time he had acquired greater popularity in Wales than any other minister of his day.

Ministry in Anglesea

On Christmas day, when Mr. Evans was forty-six years of age, he removed from Lëyn to the isle of Anglesea. According to his own account, "it was a very rough day of frost and snow." Unencumbered with this world's goods, and possessing the true apostolic spirit, he "commenced the journey on horseback, with his wife behind him," and arrived on the evening of the same day at Llangewin.

Whatever the motive of this removal, it was certainly not the love of money. His salary in Anglesea was only £17 per annum, and for twenty years he never asked for more. He had learned, with the apostle, "having food and raiment, therewith to be content." He found his reward in his work. The privilege of preaching Christ and saving souls, with him, was preferable to mountains of gold and silver.

On his arrival in Anglesea, he found ten small Baptist societies, in a lukewarm and distracted condition; himself the only minister, and no brother to aid him within a hundred and fifty miles. He commenced his labors in earnest. One of his first movements was the appointment of a day of fasting and prayer in all the preaching places. He soon had the satisfaction to realize an extensive revival, which continued under his faithful ministry for many years.

Powerful Sermons

In 1794, the South West Baptist Association was held at Velin Voel, in Caermarthenshire. Mr. Evans was invited, as one of the preachers on the occassion. It was a journey of about two hundred miles. He undertook it on foot, with his usual fortitude, preaching at different places as he went along. The meeting was to commence with three consecutive sermons, the last of which was to be preached by Mr. Evans. The service was out of doors, and the heat was very oppressive. The first and second sermons were rather tedious, and the hearers seemed almost stupefied. Mr. Evans arose and began his sermon. Before he had spoken fifteen minutes, scores of people were on their feet, some weeping, some praising, some leaping and clapping their hands for joy. Nor did the effect end with the discourse. Throughout the evening, and during the whole night, the voice of rejoicing and prayer was heard in every direction; and the dawning of the next day, awaking the few that had fallen asleep through fatigue, only renewed the heavenly rapture. "Job David, the Socinian," said the preacher afterwards to a friend, "was highly displeased with this American gale." But all the Socinians in Wales could not counteract its influence, or frustrate its happy effects.

Mr. Evans continued to visit the associations in South Wales for many years: and whenever he came, the people flocked by thousands to hear "the one-eyed man of Anglesea." It was on one of those occasions, and under circumstances somewhat similar to the above, that he preached that singularly effective sermon on the demoniac of Gadara. The meeting had been in progress three days. Several discourses had been delivered with little or no effect. Christmas Evans took the stand, and announced as his text the evangelical account of the demoniac of Gadara. He described him as a naked man, with flaming eyes, and wild and fierce gesticulation ; full of relentless anger, and subject to strange paroxysms of rage ; the terror and pity of all the townsfolk. They had bound him with great chains, but he would break them as Samson broke the withes. They had tried to soothe him by kindness, but he would leap upon them like a furious wild beast, or burst away with the speed of a stag, his long hair streaming on the wind behind him. He inhabited the rocks of a Jewish cemetery; and when he slept, he laid down in a tomb. The place was a little out of town, and not far from the great turnpike road, so that people passing often saw him, and heard his dreadful lamentations and blasphemies. Nobody dared to cross his path unarmed, and all the women and children ran away as soon as they saw him coming. Sometimes he sallied forth from his dismal abode at midnight, like one risen from the dead, howling and cursing like a fiend, breaking into houses, frightening the inhabitants from their beds, and driving them to seek shelter in the streets and the fields. He had a broken-hearted wife, and five little children, living about a mile and a half distant. In his intervals of comparative calmness, he would set out to visit them. On his way, the evil spirit would come upon him, and transform the husband and father instantly into a fury. Then he would run toward the house, raving like a wounded tiger, and roaring like a lion upon his prey. He would spring against the door, and shatter it into fragments; while the poor wife and children fled through the back door to the neighbors, or concealed themselves in the cellar. Then he would spoil the furniture, and break all the dishes, and bound away howling again to his home in the cemetery. The report of this mysterious and terrible being had spread through all the surrounding region, and everybody dreaded and pitied the man among the tombs. Jesus came that way. The preacher described the interview, the miracle, the happy change in the sufferer, the transporting surprise of his long afflicted family. Then, shifting the scene, he showed his hearers the catastrophe of the swine, the flight of the affrighted herdsman, his amusing report to his master, and the effect of the whole upon the populace. All this was done with such dramatic effect, as to convulse his numerous hearers with alternate laughter and weeping for more than half an hour. Having thus elicited an intense interest in the subject, he proceeded to educe from the narrative several important doctrines, which he illustrated so forcibly, and urged so powerfully, that the people first became profoundly serious, then wept like mourners at a funeral, and finally threw themselves on the ground, and broke forth in loud prayers for mercy; and the preacher continued nearly three hours, the effect increasing till he closed. One who heard that wonderful sermon says, that, during the first half hour, the people seemed like an assembly in a theatre, delighted with an amusing play ; after that, like a community in mourning, over some great and good man, cut off by a sudden calamity ; and at last, like the inhabitants of a city shaken by an earthquake, rushing into the streets, falling upon the earth, and screaming and calling upon God !*

Sandemanianism and Sabellianism

About this time arose among the Baptists of North Wales a bitter and distracting controversy, concerning Sandemanianism and Sabellianism, which had been introduced by the Rev. Mr. Jones, a man of considerable learning and influence in the denomination. Mr. Evans was at first inclined to fall in with these doctrines, and participated largely in the strife of tongues. He says :—

" The Sandemanian system affected me so far as to quench the spirit of prayer for the conversion of sinners, and it induced in my mind a greater regard for the smaller things of the kingdom of heaven than for the greater. I lost the strength which clothed my mind with zeal, confidence, and earnestness in the pulpit for the conversion of souls to Christ. My heart retrograded, in a manner, and I could not realize the testimony of a good conscience. Sabbath nights, after having been in the day exposing and vilifying with all bitterness the errors that prevailed, my conscience felt as if displeased, and reproached me that I had lost nearness to, and walking with God. It would intimate that something exceedingly precious was now wanting in me ; I would reply, that I was acting in obedience to the word ; but it continued to accuse me of the want of some precious article. I had been robbed, to a great degree, of the spirit of prayer and of the spirit of preaching."

Mr. Evans thus describes the effect of this controversy upon his people :—

" The Sandemanian spirit began to manifest itself in the counties of Merioneth, Caernarvon, Anglesea, and Denbigh, and the first visible effect was the subversion of the hearers, for which the system was peculiarly adapted ; intimating, as it did, that to Babylon the

---

* A part of this sermon, as delivered on another occasion, is given in the latter part of this volume.

crowd of hearers always belonged. We lost, in Anglesea, nearly all those who were accustomed to attend with us; some of them joined other congregations; and, in this way, it pulled down nearly all that had been built up in twelve or fifteen years, and made us appear once again a mean and despicable party in the view of the country. The same effects followed it in a greater or lesser degree in the other counties noticed; but its principal station appears to have been in Merionethshire; this county seems to have been particularly prepared for its reception, and here it achieved by some means a sort of supremacy."

Time of Refreshing

Mr. Evans had been a long time in this controversy, destitute of all religious enjoyment, or, to use his own expressive phrase, " as dry as Gilboa," when he experienced a remarkable refreshing from the presence of the Lord. The following account is extracted from his journal:—

" I was weary of a cold heart towards Christ, and his sacrifice, and the work of his Spirit—of a cold heart in the pulpit, in secret prayer, and in the study. For fifteen years previously, I had felt my heart burning within, as if going to Emmaus with Jesus. On a day ever to be remembered by me, as I was going from Dolgelley to Machynlleth, and climbing up towards Cadair Idris, I considered it to be incumbent upon me to pray, however hard I felt my heart, and however worldly the frame of my spirit was. Having begun in the name of Jesus, I soon felt as it were the fetters loosening, and the old hardness of heart softening, and, as I thought, mountains of frost and snow dissolving and melting within me. This engendered confidence in my soul in the promise of the Holy Ghost. I felt my whole mind relieved from some great bondage: tears flowed copiously, and I was constrained to cry out for the gracious visits of God, by restoring to my soul the joy of his salvation;—and that he would visit the churches in Anglesea, that were under my care. I embraced in my supplications all the churches of the saints, and nearly all the ministers in the principality by their names. This struggle lasted for three hours: it rose again and again, like one wave after another, or a high flowing tide, driven by a strong wind, until my nature became faint by weeping and crying. Thus I resigned myself to Christ, body and soul, gifts and labors—all my life—every day and every hour that remained for me ;—and all my cares I committed to Christ.—The road was mountainous and lonely, and I was wholly alone, and suffered no interruption in my wrestlings with God.

" From this time, I was made to expect the goodness of God to churches and to myself. Thus the Lord delivered me and the people of Anglesea from being carried away by the flood of Sandemanianism. In the first religious meetings after this, I felt as if I had been removed from the cold and sterile regions of spiritual frost, into the verdant fields of the divine promises. The former striving with God in prayer, and the longing anxiety for the conversion of sinners, which I had experienced at Lëyn, was now restored. I had a hold of the promises of God. The result was, when I returned home, the first thing that arrested my attention was, that the Spirit was working also in the brethren in Anglesea, inducing in them a spirit of prayer, especially in two of the deacons, who were particularly importunate that God would visit us in mercy, and render the word of his grace effectual amongst us for the conversion of sinners."

Covenant With God

Mr. Evans now entered into a solemn covenant with God, made, as he says, " under a deep sense of the evil of his heart, and in dependence upon the infinite grace and merit of the Redeemer." This interesting article is preserved among his papers. We give it entire, as a specimen of his spirit and his faith :—

I. " I give my soul and body unto thee, Jesus, the true God, and everlasting life—deliver me from sin, and from eternal death, and bring me into life everlasting. Amen.—C. E.

II. " I call the day, the sun, the earth, the trees, the stones, the bed, the table, and the books, to witness that I come unto thee, Redeemer of sinners, that I may obtain rest for my soul from the thunders of guilt and the dread of eternity. Amen.—C. E.

III. " I do, through confidence in thy power, earnestly entreat thee to take the work into thine own hand, and give me a circumcised heart, that I may love thee, and create in me a right spirit, that I may seek thy glory. Grant me that principle which thou wilt own in the day of judgment, that I may not then assume pale facedness, and find myself a hypocrite. Grant me this, for the sake of thy most precious blood. Amen.—C. E.

IV. "I entreat thee, Jesus, the Son of God, in power, grant me, for the sake of thy agonizing death, a covenant-interest in thy blood, which cleanseth; in thy righteousness, which justifieth; and in thy redemption, which delivereth. I entreat an interest in thy blood, for thy *blood's* sake, and a part in thee, for thy name's sake, which thou hast given among men. Amen.—C. E.

V. "O Jesus Christ, Son of the living God, take, for the sake of thy cruel death, my time, and strength, and the gifts and talents I possess; which, with a full purpose of heart, I consecrate to thy glory in the building up of thy church in the world, for thou art worthy of the hearts and talents of all men. Amen.—C. E.

VI. "I desire thee, my great High Priest, to confirm, by thy power, from thy High Court, my usefulness as a preacher, and my piety as a Christian, as two gardens nigh to each other; that sin may not have place in my heart, to becloud my confidence in thy righteousness, and that I may not be left to any foolish act that may occasion my gifts to wither, and rendered useless before my life ends. Keep thy gracious eye upon me, and watch over me, O my Lord, and my God for ever! Amen.—C. E.

VII. "I give myself in a particular manner to thee, O Jesus Christ, the Saviour, to be preserved from the falls into which many stumble, that thy name (in thy cause) may not be blasphemed or wounded, that my peace may not be injured, that thy people may not be grieved, and that thine enemies may not be hardened. Amen.—C. E.

VIII. "I come unto thee, beseeching thee to be in covenant with me in my ministry. As thou didst prosper Bunyan, Vavasor Powell, Howell Harris, Rowlands, and Whitefield, O do thou prosper me. Whatsoever things are opposed to my prosperity, remove them out of the way. Work in me every thing approved of God, for the attainment of this. Give me a heart 'sick of love' to thyself, and to the souls of men. Grant that I may experience the power of thy word before I deliver it, as Moses felt the power of his own rod, before he saw it on the land and waters of Egypt. Grant this, for the sake of thine infinitely precious blood, O Jesus, my hope, and my all in all! Amen.—C. E.

IX. " Search me now, and lead me in plain paths of judgment. Let me discover in this life what I am before thee, that I may not find myself of another character, when I am shown in the light of the immortal world, and open my eyes in all the brightness of eternity. Wash me in thy redeeming blood. Amen.—C. E.

X. " Grant me strength to depend upon thee for food and raiment, and to make known my requests. O let thy care be over me as a covenant-privilege betwixt thee and myself, and not like a general care to feed the ravens that perish, and clothe the lily that is cast into the oven; but let thy care be over me as one of thy family, as one of thine unworthy brethren. Amen.—C. E.

XI. " Grant, O Jesus! and take upon thyself the preparing of me for death, for thou art God; there is no need, but for thee to speak the word. If possible, thy will be done; leave me not long in affliction, nor to die suddenly, without bidding adieu to my brethren, and let me die in their sight, after a short illness. Let all things be ordered against the day of removing from one world to another, that there be no confusion nor disorder, but a quiet discharge in peace. O grant me this, for the sake of thine agony in the garden! Amen.—C. E.

XII. " Grant, O blessed Lord! that nothing may grow and be matured in me, to occasion thee to cast me off from the service of the sanctuary, like the sons of Eli; and for the sake of thine unbounded merit, let not my days be longer than my usefulness. O let me not be like lumber in a house in the end of my days,—in the way of others to work. Amen.—C. E.

XIII. " I beseech thee, O Redeemer! to present these my supplications before the Father: and O! inscribe them in thy book with thine own immortal pen, while I am writing them with my mortal hand, in my book on earth. According to the depths of thy merit, thine undiminished grace, and thy compassion, and thy manner unto thy people, O! attach thy name, in thine upper court, to these unworthy petitions; and set thine amen to them, as I do on my part of the covenant. Amen.—CHRISTMAS EVANS, Llangevni, Anglesea, April 10, 18—."

Mr. Evans, in speaking of this solemn transaction and its influence upon his spirit, subsequently observes: " I felt a sweet peace and tranquillity of soul, like unto a poor man that had been brought under the protection of the royal family, and had an annual settlement for life made upon him; from whose dwelling the painful dread of poverty and want had been for ever banished away."

Thus "strengthened with might in the inner man," he labored with renewed energy and zeal, and showers of blessings descended upon his labors. In two years, his ten preaching places in Anglesea were increased to twenty, and six hundred converts were added to the church under his care. "The wilderness and solitary place were glad for them, and the desert rejoiced and blossomed as the rose."

Studying the English Language

Mr. Evans made several visits to Liverpool, Bristol, and other parts of England. On these occasions he was frequently solicited to preach in English, to which he several times consented, to the great gratification of his English friends. These sermons evinced the same energy of thought, and the same boldness of imagery, as those which he preached in Welsh; but in the power of his peculiar delivery, they were inevitably far inferior. His brethren in England were much delighted with his performances, and said it was "no wonder the Welsh were warm under such preaching;" but his language was broken and hesitating, and they could scarcely have any conception of his animation and energy when he spoke in his vernacular tongue.

His success induced him to commence a systematic study of the English language, that he might be able to preach in it with greater freedom and effect. He could read English before, and was some-what familiar with the best English authors of his day; but never acquainted himself with the grammar of the language till he was thirty-three years of age. But read his own account of the matter :—

" The English brethren had prevailed upon me to preach to them in broken English, as it was; this induced me to set about the matter in earnest, making it a subject of prayer, for the aid of the Spirit, that I might be in some measure a blessing to the English friends, for there appeared some sign that God now called me to this department of labor in his service. I never succeeded in any thing for the good of others, without making it a matter of prayer. My English preaching was very broken and imperfect in point of language; yet, through the grace of Jesus Christ, it was made in some degree useful at Liverpool, Bristol, and some other places. I was about forty years old when I learned to read the Hebrew Bible and the Greek Testament, and use Parkhurst's Lexicons in both languages. I found that, had I studied the English language attentively and perseveringly, I should be able to overcome great difficulties; and also, that I could without much labor in the course of few years, even in my idle hours, as it were, understand all the Hebrew words corresponding with every Welsh word in the Bible; and so also the Greek. I had always before thought that it was impossible to accomplish this, for I had no one to encourage me in the undertaking; but I found it was practicable, and proved it in some measure, yet relinquished the pursuit on account of my advanced age."

New Troubles and Sorrows

Here we pass over several years of Mr. Evans' history, during which nothing of very special interest occurred, except the agitation of the Fullerian controversy. This is a matter which requires only a passing notice in this brief memoir. We let it sleep in silence.

Mr. Evans was now nearly sixty years of age. Infirmity, the result of his arduous labors and numerous afflictions, began to prey upon his system. The several congregations under his care had hitherto constituted but one church. But the number of preaching places had now become too great for him, in his enfeebled state, to continue his pastoral visits and labors among them as he had done. He therefore advised them to form themselves into separate churches, two or three stations uniting in one. This was the occasion of a dark and dreadful storm upon the apostle of Anglesea. Some of the churches refused the ministers he recommended, and called others whom he disapproved. Then arose a bitter party spirit, and a general contention, among the congregations. Mr. Evans was severely censured, and even assailed with the shafts of slander. Many of his former friends forsook him, and some of those who professed to feel for him in his troubles did nothing for his vindication. The severity of these public calamities was increased by private afflictions. His beloved wife had gone " the way of all the earth." He was himself brought very low by sickness, in which he nearly lost his only remaining eye, and seemed fast tending to his final home.

But though cast down, he was not destroyed. "I wonder greatly," says he, "that I did not sink into the grave under the weight of sorrows that came upon me in my old age, together with an accumulation of trials of all kinds; but the Lord sustained me. There was, in the midst of all, a strong persuasion in my mind, that there was yet much work for me to do for God in the world, as well as much to suffer, ere I died. If I only entered the pulpit, I felt raised as it were to Paradise—above my afflictions—until I forgot my adversity; yea, I felt my mountain strong, my mind was in such a heavenly frame, and as anxious as ever for the conversion of sinners. The truth appeared to me in its power like a hammer in its strength. The doctrine dropped as sweet as the honey, yea, sweeter than the honeycomb, and as comfortable as the best wine. I was now particularly wishful that all the ministers in Anglesea should join with me, according to the promise, 'If two of you agree to ask the *same thing*, it shall be given unto you of my Father which is in heaven;' for I had such confidence that then I should see prosperity attending the ministry, and that I should not die until I had finished my work. I said to a brother:—'Brother, the doctrine, the confidence, and strength which I feel, will make some persons dance with joy yet in some parts of Wales.' 'Yea, brother,' said he, with tears flowing in streams from his eyes.

"Every thing now contributed to remove me from Anglesea. The unbending disposition of those who were offended at me, and the ardor of my own spirit, believing that there was work for me to do in some other field of the harvest of the Son of man, and my having prayed earnestly for twelve months for the direction of Divine Providence, together with the visions of my head in the night seasons, appeared to unite together to lead in one direction. At length, the determination to leave Anglesea, afflicted as I was, preponderated. I was much like Jacob, leaving his father and his mother, going with his staff only over Jordan: so was I, leaving the church: I had prayed, yea, I had striven with God for its prosperity, and had labored nearly forty years with it—now leaving it—possessing nothing of this world's goods, save the horse upon which I rode, and a small amount of silver in my pocket; and scarcely could I say that these were mine."

Legal Prosecution

During the above-mentioned tribulations he received an insulting letter, threatening him with a civil prosecution. "They talk," said he, "of casting me into a court of law, where I have never been, and hope I shall never go ; but I will cast them first into the court of Jesus Christ, the source of law and authority." So saying, he retired to his chamber, and falling upon his knees, he wept and made supplication in the following pathetic strain :—

"O blessed Lord! in thy merit I confide, and trust to be heard. Lord, some of my brethren have run wild; and forgetting their duty and obligations to their father in the gospel, they threaten me with the law of the land. Weaken, I beseech thee, their designs in this, as thou didst wither the arm of Jeroboam; and soften them, as thou didst soften the mind of Esau, and disarmed him of his warlike temper against thy servant Jacob, after the wrestling at Penuel. So disarm them, for I do not know the length of Satan's chain in this case, and in this unbrotherly attack. But thou canst shorten the chain as short as it may please thee. Lord, I anticipate them in point of law. They think of casting thine unworthy servant into the little courts here below; but I cast my cause into the High Court, in which thou, gracious Jesus, art the High Chancellor. Receive thou the cause of thine unworthy servant, and send them a writ or a notice immediately—sending into their conscience, and summoning them to consider what they are doing. O, frighten them with a summons from thy court, until they come and bow in contrition at thy feet; and take from their hands every revengeful weapon, and make them deliver up every gun of scandal, and every sword of bitter words, and every spear of slanderous expressions, and surrender them all at thy cross. Forgive them all their faults, and clothe them with white robes, and give them oil for their heads, and the organ, and the harp of ten strings, to sing, for the trampling of Satan under our feet by the God of peace."

Having thus poured out his heart to God, he felt some confidence of security. But he was never satisfied in such cases without an inward assurance of acceptance and success. So he went again and again; and when, like Jesus, he had "offered up many prayers, with strong crying and tears," like Jacob "he had power with God, and prevailed." "At the seventh time," says he, "I came down in full confidence that Christ had taken my cause into his own hand, and would be my Savior. I felt as cheerful and happy as Bunyan's Pilgrim, when his load fell off and rolled into the grave of Christ; or as Naaman, when he came up from the waters of Jordan, cured of his leprosy."

It is scarcely necessary to add, the threat was never executed. The Throne of Grace is the good man's sure resort in every emergency. Jehovah "hides him in his pavilion from the strife of tongues."

Caerphilly

An invitation, which he received about this time, to take charge of the Baptist church in Caerphilly, Glamorganshire, South Wales, confirmed Mr. Evans in his determination to leave the scene of his recent trials. He set out alone, in his sixtieth year. The distance he had to travel was about two hundred miles. On the way, while dwelling on his past misfortunes, he found his heart melted within him, and drawn out in fervent prayer. His faith soon triumphed over his afflictions and his fears. He renewed his covenant with God, and went on his way rejoicing. This revival of his religious feelings had a powerful effect upon his ministry. He had not been long in Caerphilly, before the Spirit of God was poured copiously upon the people.

Previous to this time of refreshing, he had a remarkable dream, which he noted in his diary. He thought he was in the church at Caerphilly, and found many harps hanging about the pulpit, wrapped in coverings of green. Then, said he, "I will take down the harps of heaven in this place." In removing the covering, he found the ark of the covenant, inscribed with the name of Jehovah. Then he cried, "Brethren, the Lord has come to us, according to his promise, and in answer to our prayers." In that very place, he shortly afterward had the satisfaction of receiving one hundred and forty converts into the church, as the fruit of his ministry.

While at Caerphilly, he entered into a second marriage. He remained there only two years. He says: "I never spent a short time in greater comfort, for the ark of God had appeared there, and the harps of one hundred and forty souls had been tuned to the song of redemption." Happy years no doubt they were, and gladly would Mr. Evans have ended his life in Caerphilly; but troubles arose between him and some of his parishioners, and, receiving a call from Cardiff, a neighboring town, he went to take charge of a church in that place.

Another Covenant

Previous to his removal, and while he was meditating the matter, he made a new covenant with God. We extract again from his journal:—

"While returning from a place called Tongwynlâs over Caerphilly mountain, the spirit of prayer descended very copiously upon me. I wept for some hours, and heartily supplicated Jesus Christ, for the blessings here following. I found at this time a particular nearness to Christ, as if he were close by me, and my mind was filled with strong confidence that he attended to my requests, for the sake of the merits of his own name. This decided in favor of Cardiff."

I. "Grant me the great favor of being led by thee, according to thy will—by the directions of thy providence and word, and the disposing of my own mind by thy Spirit, for the sake of thine infinitely precious blood. Amen.—C. E.

II. "Grant, if I am to leave Caerphilly, that the gale (of the Spirit's influence) and religious revival I had there may follow me to Cardiff, for the sake of thy great name. Amen.—C. E.

III. "Grant thy blessing upon bitter things, to brighten, and quicken me more and more, and not to depress and render me more lifeless. Amen.—C. E.

IV. "Suffer me not to be trodden under the proud feet of members, or deacons, for the sake of thy goodness. Amen.—C. E.

V. "Grant me the invaluable favor of being, in thine hand, the means of calling sinners unto thyself, and of edifying thy saints, wherever thou wilt send me, for the sake of thy name. Amen.—C. E.

VI. "If I am to stay at Caerphilly, give me some tokens, as to Gideon of old, by removing the things that discourage me, and are in the way of the prosperity of religion in that church. Amen.—C. E.

VII. "Grant, Lord of glory, and Head of thy church, that the Ark of the cause which is thine, in Anglesea and Caerphilly, may be sustained from falling into the hands of the Philistines. Do not reject it. Aid it speedily, and lift up the light of thy countenance upon it; and by thy Spirit, word, and providence, so operate as to carry things forward in the churches, and neighborhoods, in such a manner as will produce changes in officers, and measures that will accomplish a thorough improvement in the great cause, for the establishment of which in the world thou hast died;—and by scattering those that delight in war, and closing the mouths of those that occasion confusion. Amen.—C. E.

VIII. "Grant me way-tokens by the time I begin my journey to Liverpool, and from thence to Anglesea, if it is thy will that I should go thither this year. Amen.—C. E.

IX. "O grant me succor beneath the shadow of the sympathy that is in thee towards them who are tempted, and the unbounded power there is in thee to be the relief of such. Amen.—C. E.

X. "Accept of my thanksgiving a hundred millions of times, that thou hast not hitherto cast me from thine hand, as a darkened star, or a vessel in which there is no pleasure; and suffer not my life to be extended beyond my usefulness. Thanks, that thou hast not given me a prey to the teeth of any. Blessed be thy name. Amen.—C. E.

XI. "For the sake of thine infinite merit, do not cast me, thy servant, under the feet of pride and injustice, of *worldly* greatness, riches, and selfish oppression of any men, but hide me in the secret of thy tabernacle from the strife of tongues. Amen.—C. E.

XII. "Help me to wait silently and patiently upon thee, for the fulfilment of these things, and not become enraged, angry, and speak unadvisedly with my lips, like Moses, the servant of the Lord. Sustain my heart from sinking, to wait for fresh strength from Zion. Amen.—C. E.

XIII. "Help me to wait upon thee for the necessaries of life; let thy mercy and goodness follow me while I live; and, as it hath pleased thee to honor me greatly, by the blessing thou hast vouchsafed upon the ministry through me, as an humble instrument, at Caerphilly, after the great storm had beaten upon me in Anglesea, like Job, grant that this honor may continue to follow me the remainder of my days, as thou didst unto thy servant Job. Amen.—C. E.

XIV. "Let this covenant abide like the covenant of salt, until I come to thee in the world of eternal light. I entreat aid to resign myself to thee, and to thy will. I beseech thee take my heart, and inscribe upon it a deep reverence of thyself, with an inscription that time and eternity cannot efface. O let the remainder of my sermons be taken by thee from my lips; and those which I write, let them be unto thee for a praise. Unto thee I dedicate them. If there should be any thing in them conducive to thy glory, and to the service of thy kingdom, do thou preserve it, and reveal it unto men; else, let it die like the drop of a bucket in the midst of the scorching heat of Africa. O grant, that there may be a drop of that water which thou alone canst impart, and which springs up to eternal life, running through all my sermons. In this covenant, which probably is the last that will be written between me and thee on the earth, I commit myself, my wife, and the churches amongst whom I have preached, to the protection of thy grace, and the care of thy covenant. Amen.—C. E.

XV. "Let this covenant continue when I am in sickness or in health, or in any other circumstance; for thou hast overcome the world, fulfilled the law, finished justifying righteousness, and hast swallowed up death in victory, and all power in heaven and earth is in thine hand. For the sake of thy most precious blood and perfect righteousness, note this covenant with thine own blood in the court of the memorials of forgiving mercy: attach unto it thy name in which I believe; and here I, this day, set my unworthy name unto it, with my mortal hand. Amen.—Christmas Evans. Dated, Cardiff, April 24, 1829."

Cardiff

"After having entered into this covenant," says Mr. Evans in his diary, "I came to Cardiff, heartily and unhesitatingly, like a merchant that should send his vessel to sea after it had been registered in the insurance office. I had nothing now to lose, for I had given myself up to the possession of Jesus, the Mediator of the New Testament, for time and for eternity; and so I have had to abide here in the secret of his tabernacle for these nine months."

He removed to Cardiff in the autumn of 1828, and remained there two years and a half. During this time, he received into the church about eighty converts. He was much in secret prayer, and enjoyed intimate communion with his God. He not only retired for devotion several times every day, but ordinarily rose at midnight to call upon the Lord. But the whole period of his residence was not a cloudless day. Some unpleasant matters arose in the church, which caused him much sorrow, as is evident from the following entry in his diary:—

" April 27, 1829. I earnestly entreat thee, blessed Jesus, for the sake of thine own name, to regard me in this request. * * * * Let things be ordered, O Lord, that they may not be impediments and discouragements unto me, and a hinderance to the progress of religion. O, interpose between me and these obstacles, O Lord, that I may have no occasion to dispute with any, and so embitter my spirit! Thy power is infinite, and thy wisdom is infallible. Stand thou between me and all contention, that no ill effect come upon me. I flee to hide myself under the shadow of thy wings. Permit nothing to blunt the edge of my talents, my zeal, or my success,—nor corrupt the church. Grant me this for the sake of thine infinitely precious blood. Set thy name to this request in the court of heaven, and let Satan's party grow weaker and weaker, and the cause of truth and righteousness become like the house of David, and the house of David like the angel of the Lord. Deliver me, that my spirit be not irritated, and I speak unadvisedly with my lips, as Moses did. Hide me in thy pavilion from the strife of tongues * * * *. I am as it were on the verge of eternity ; O save and preserve me by thy boundless power. Amen, Amen, Amen. Lord, regard, behold, hear, and spare.—Christmas Evans. Write this in thy book, O my Lord, and my God. Let none be disappointed that wait upon thee, gracious Lord.—Remember me."

He adds in another passage :—

" I have given my soul anew to Christ ; my body ; my talents ; my influence in preaching ; my name ; my character as a man, as a Christian, and as a preacher of the gospel ; my time, and the remnant of my opportunities ; my success ; my peace and comfort as a Christian and a minister. I have resigned all afresh into the hands of Christ. I have commended to his care, also, my wife, and all the circumstances of my family, and my friends and assistants in the work of the Lord, for whom I pray earnestly that they may be blessed, throughout Anglesea, Caernarvon, Caerphilly, Cardiff, and indeed in all the counties of Wales. There are many of them who were helpers to me in my day. I will say, in the language of Paul, and I hope with affectionate emotions of love to Jesus Christ, ' The Lord grant unto them that they may find mercy of the Lord in that day.' It is a great privilege to a minister to retain beloved friends, who have helped him with their prayers and sympathy. O bless those whom I have, and preserve the new race, the new generation of them that I have found in these parts. I committed to God, also, those who obstruct the progress of the cause here, and disturb the unity and brotherly love of the church. Let Christ, whose the church is, and let not me, remove every obstacle, either by changing and melting in the love of the gospel, or taking them somewhere else, where they shall not be a curse and an impediment to the cause—and by the means that shall seem fit in his sight. A word or a nod of thine shuts and opens heaven and earth, and all the locks of the land of *Hades*, or the invisible state. For the sake of the blood of thy covenant, grant the above things unto me, thine unworthy servant."

Sermons for the Press

During his sojourn at Cardiff, though now sixty-five years old, much debilitated, and almost blind, he wrote about two hundred sermons for the press, many of which have since been published. It is certainly very remarkable, that he should write, at his advanced age, with all the vigor and vivacity of his earlier years. Perhaps, of all the sermons he ever made, those composed at Cardiff are the best. Most of them were preached on the Sabbath, and written out during the following week. This circumstance, with their author's peculiar nearness to God, may account for their freshness and power.

Mr. Evans was in the habit of referring every important matter to God. We find in his diary the following paragraph :—

" Cardiff, February 2, 1829. Lord, I have been importuned by many of my brethren in the ministry, to prepare a number of my sermons, that have been in the course of my ministry the most useful in thine hand for the conversion of sinners, with a view to publication. I had no time when in Anglesea to engage in the work, because my circumstances required so much travelling every week. I left the work to lie by, the two years I was at Caerphilly; but here, at Cardiff, I have had a new impulse in my thoughts to enter upon it; and I come unto thee, my great Lord, to consult thee, who art the Head of the church, and the Head-Prophet and Teacher of thy people. Shall I proceed with the work or not? Is it a part of my duty, or is it a useless, foolish notion of my own? I entreat thy gracious direction in this matter, for the sake of thy great name. Suffer me not to afflict myself, when my eyesight is so weak, with a work that thou wilt not bless, but which shall be buried in the land of forgetfulness. If thou wilt not open a door—with thee are the keys of the house of David—in thy providence, that I may obtain subscribers, and bring the work through the press, without hazarding myself in such a way as will involve me in debt and disgrace : and also if thou, the great feeder of the flock, wilt not direct me to give the true gospel, not only without error, but with the savor and unction which accompanies the works of Bunyan and others, which thy Spirit is likely to make use of whilst thou hast churches in Wales : if they should not be for thy glory in the building up of thy church, and the calling of sinners,—if these objects should not be accomplished by the publication of the sermons, dispose my mind to relinquish the undertaking. But if thou wilt patronise the work, strengthen me to accomplish the design. Lord, thou knowest I feel my own insufficiency for such an important enterprise, and my unworthiness to solicit of thee such a favor : but I cannot refrain from making these requests : therefore, for the sake of thine infinite merits, according to thy manner unto thy people, grant unto me my request. Amen."

Welsh Jumping

In the autumn of 1829, Mr. Evans wrote in his diary extensive notes of a conversation which he had with several ministers in Bristol, on "the manner of religious rejoicing so remarkable among the Welsh." His friends condemned it in a sweeping sentence, under the name of " Welsh jumping." Mr. Evans attempted its vindication. We insert his own account :

"I observed that I could find no account of it among the Welsh until the time of Harris and Rowlands, Calvinistic Methodists, who flourished in Wales about the same time as Whitefield and Wesley in England. The preaching of these men was the means of producing a religious revival throughout all the principality, which had sunk into a state of deep lethargy, since the time of the great awakening under Vavasor Powell, about one hundred years before. At this period nothing was to be seen in almost every parish but young men and young women flocking together into the churches and church-yards, and engaging in different gambols and pastimes, such as ball-playing, foot-ball, leaping, fighting, and such like frolics, as if Wales had been changed into an Olympic mountain, and old paganism restored again. It is true, there were some preachers and churches, both Congregationalists and Baptists, then existing in the principality ; but their talents, their spirits, or their magnanimity could not storm such a fortress of impiety. And, besides, there was a dreadful prejudice still remaining in the country against all sects, since the days of Charles II. ; and they suffered persecution even unto blood, for about one hundred years previous to the appearing of these men. But from the ashes of those sufferers the revival by Harris and Rowlands sprung up, as did Luther from the ashes of Huss and Jerome of Prague.

" Mr. Rowlands and Mr. Harris were both of the communion of the Episcopal church, and, as such, there was not so much enmity against them at first; but after they had come out, and when the people understood that they were preachers of the cross of Christ, considerable persecution arose against them from the multitude ; but it was now too late—for the gates of the city were opened—the leaven was put in the meal—the fire had been kindled—the sword was drawn from the scabbard, and many had been wounded, (spiritually,) and were ready to open the door for the gospel in spite of every danger. Harris, Rowlands, and the two Williams's, had been clothed with power from on high, and the hammer of their ministry was sufficiently heavy to break in pieces the northern iron.* Several laymen of powerful minds were also raised up about this time ; such as Mr. David Morris, and others, who were valuable auxiliaries to carry on the work. By their ministry, this praising and jumping in religious enjoyment began in Wales, which has not wholly left it on certain occasions until this day.

" As an apology for them, granting at the same time the possi- bility of extremes even in a good cause in the present state; and that graceless persons may feel something from these excitements

---

* Jer. xv. 12.

as of the powers of the world to come, in the miraculous gifts of the Holy Ghost in the apostolic age; observe,

" 1. That it appears to me like the residue of the Spirit, and the powers of the world to come; which were necessary to open a way for the gospel through the darkness and obduracy of paganism in the days of the apostles.

" 2. It is no argument of importance against it, that many grace-less persons felt a considerable degree of influence at the time, as well as others; for so it was in the case of Saul, king of Israel, and some besides named in Scripture.

" 3. There is no essential difference between religious enjoyment in Wales and that which is now experienced in America; and that which accompanied the preaching of Whitefield in England, and even in Scotland: and that which also followed the ministry of President Edwards, in America, when whole towns and neighbor-hoods echoed with the sound of persons praying and praising God, as if a bursting cloud-shower of the Spirit of grace and prayer had descended upon them. Persons under the ministry of Whitefield wept, cried for mercy, and even fainted by the power of this influence.

" 4. And such gracious influences are necessary for the spread of the gospel in every country, and in every land: and therefore the Millennium is described in the Bible as a period remarkable for the outpouring of the Holy Ghost—'that a nation shall be born at once,'*—and 'the flowing of the nations shall be to the mountain of the Lord's house.'† It is this influence that has driven, as it were, the gospel into every nook of the mountains of Wales, as well as into its cities, towns, and villages; while in England, with all the advantages of education, the gospel, in a manner, is hid in a corner; and it has not run through the country, and searched out, and taken possession of all the inland parts of that spiritual Africa, and that for the want of these gales of divine influence, and powers peculiar to the gospel: and it can never be spread through every part of England as it is in Wales without these gifts. Common preaching will not do to rouse sluggish districts from the heavy slumbers into which they are sunk. Indeed, formal prayers and lifeless sermons are like bulwarks raised against these things in

---

* Isaiah lxvi. 8.   † Isaiah ii. 3.

England ; and this evil genius has also entered the principality under the pretence of order. Five or six stanzas will be sung as dry as Gilboa, instead of one or two verses, like a new song, full of God, of Christ, and the Spirit of grace, until the heart is attuned for worship. The burying-grounds are kept in fine order in Glamorganshire, and green shrubs and herbs grow on the graves, but all this is of little value, for the inhabitants of them are all dead—so is every form of godliness where its power is not felt. Order without life is exceedingly worthless. You exhibit all the character of human nature, leaving every bud of the flower to open in the beams of the sun, except in divine worship. On other occasions you appear to have as much fire in your affections as the Welsh have. If you are noticed in a court of law, the most efficient advocate, such as Erskine, will give you the greatest satisfaction ; but you are contented with a preacher, speaking so lifelessly and so low that you can hardly understand the third part of what he says ; and you will call this decency in the sanctuary. To-morrow, I shall see you answering fully to the human character, in your own actions. When the speakers on the platform will be urging the claims of missions, you will then beat the boards, and manifest so much life and cheerfulness, that not one of you will be seen to take up a note-book, nor any other book, while the speaker shall be addressing you. A Welshman might suppose, by hearing your noise, that he had been silently conveyed to the midst of one of the meetings of the ' Welsh jumpers,' with this difference, that you would perceive many more tears shed, and hear more ' calves of the lips'* offered up, in the rejoicing meetings of Wales. But you will use your heels well on such occasions, and a little of your tongues. But even in Wales, in certain places—that is, places where the fervent gales are not enjoyed which fill persons with fear and terror and joy in approaching the altar of God—you may see, while hearing a sermon, one looking into his hymn-book, another into his note-book, and a third turning over the leaves of his Bible, as if he were going to study a sermon in the sanctuary, instead of attending to what is spoken by the preacher as the mouth of God. If there is joy and gladness pertaining to many, the light of God's countenance in the sanctuary should develope it ; until a fire is kindled,

---

* Hos. xiv. 2.

and he speak with his tongue, making melody unto the Lord in his heart, and praising Him with his lips.

" 5. It is in vain to urge objections against these powerful gales of divine influence, and allege that it is under the ministry of the illiterate preachers of Wales only they are experienced. Harris, Rowlands, and the two Williamses were not so, for they had been brought up for the established church. Whitefield and Edwards were men of education, and they preached the doctrine which in England is considered evangelical.

" 6. It is also beside the point to affirm that only persons of no weight, that is, ignorant boys and girls, are in the habit of thus rejoicing and praising God in His temple ; for it is certain, that those who express their joy in this manner possess so much sound experimental knowledge, as to make them eminent in that respect. I have listened to many of them in the midst of their enjoyment, and have often been delighted while they repeated true, evangelical, and substantial stanzas, replete with profound sentiment : for in such seasons, they could find out the very best, which made impressions on their memories ; and these rapturous feelings developed them, as if the tongue were moved by the heat and force of the fire within. And many other things of an evangelical and gracious character they will utter on these joyful occasions, with such heavenly eloquence as would be inimitable, and impracticable even for themselves to utter with the same effect, without enjoying these meltings of spirit. This enjoyment is accompanied by many tears and much tenderness of heart : nor are persons of a dry spirit and hard heart ever regarded as fit subjects for this work of praise, in these blessed seasons of Christian enjoyment. It does not accord with any, but with him whose heart melts like wax, and runs in the form and mould of the gospel.

" 7. There is no way in which churches or particular persons may enjoy this heavenly ecstasy, but by walking with God, and by cultivating a spirit of watchfulness and prayer, which shows its pure and holy character. It awakens watchfulness against all evil tempers, improper expressions, and wicked actions, lest the sense of it should be lost. Such a frame of mind cannot be expected by living in sin. These individuals come to the house of God with an earnest desire for this enjoyment, and dreading lest there should be a something in them which would cause God to deny them this unspeakable privilege. It is an exceedingly easy matter for a minister to manage a congregation while Christian enjoyment keeps them near to God. They are diligent and zealous, and ready for every good work. But it is very easy to offend this joyous spirit—or give it what name you please, enthusiasm, religious madness, or Welsh jumping, (its English name,)—and make it hide itself. A quarrel and disagreement in the church will occasion it to withdraw immediately. Indulging in sin, in word or deed, will soon put it to flight. It is like unto the angel formerly, who could not behold the sin of Israel without hiding himself; so is the angel of the *religious* life of Wales, which proves him to be a holy angel, though he has the name of a ' Welsh jumper.' My prayer is, that this angel be a guard upon every congregation, and that none should do any thing to offend him. It is an exceedingly powerful assistant to accompany us through the wilderness. But the individual that has not felt its happy influences, has nothing to lose ; hence he does not dread a dry meeting and a hard prayer, for they are all the same to him ; but the people of this enjoyment pray before prayer, and before hearing, that they may meet with God in them.

" 8. The seasons when these blessings are vouchsafed to the churches of Wales, are to be noticed. It is generally at a time when the cause of religion is at a low ebb—all gone to slumber. This happy spirit of enjoyment, like the angel of the pillar of fire, appears when there is distress, and every thing at the worst. Its approach to the congregation is like the glory of God returning to the temple of old ; it creates a stir among the brethren,—they have a new prayer, and a new spirit given them to worship God. This will lay hold of another,—some new strength and light will appear in the pulpit, until it will be imagined that the preacher's voice is altered, and that his spirit is become more evangelical, and that he preaches with a more excellent savor than usual. Tenderness will descend upon the members, and it will be seen that Mr. Wet-eyes and Mr. Amen have taken their place among them. The heavenly gale will reach some of the old backsliders, and they are brought with weeping to seek their forfeited privilege. By this time the sound of Almighty God will be heard in the outer court, beginning to move the hearers like a mighty wind shaking the forest. In these seasons of refreshing from the presence of the Lord some churches will receive, in the course of a year, additions of one hundred, others a hundred and fifty, and some others upwards of two hundred new members. Sometimes, the gale seems as if it blew upon the outer court—upon the hearers, and the young people from ten to fifteen years of age—when nothing extraordinary appears in the light and effect of the ministry, nor in the church; but afterwards making its way through the outer court to rouse the inner court, until a great concern is awakened for the state of the soul. But observe: The revival that begins in the church, and proceeds from thence to the world, and not that which commences outside of the church, is more frequent, and more efficient in its converts, for the pangs of labor are to begin in Zion.

"9. Again, it may be remarked that the happy effects which follow these powerful revivals, evince their nature. They are certain, where they are strong, to bend the oaks of Bashan—men of strong and sturdy minds, and haughty hearts—to attend the ministry of the word. They will bring all the ships of Tarshish, the merchants of this world, into the harbor of hearing. The power of the day of the Lord will raze all the walls of bigotry to the foundations. The thoughts of eternal realities, and the spirit of worship, are by these blessings diffused abroad, and family worship is established in scores of families, where a few months before no regard was had unto it. The door of such a district, thus opened by the powers of the world to come, shall not be closed against the hearers of the gospel, until a goodly number of souls are there converted unto God. Where the living waters flow, dead fish are made alive by its virtues.

"10. Since the first appearing of these gracious gifts at Llangeitho, under the ministry of Mr. Rowlands, they have been showers of blessings, which are poured down on the congregations of the Baptists and Congregationalists as well as the Calvinistic Methodists; and sometimes one of these denominations is favored with them, whilst the others are destitute. These refreshing seasons were, at times, experienced in a very powerful manner at Llangeitho, for about fifty years; that is, all the period of Mr. Rowlands' ministrations in that church. About two thousand persons assembled there for communion once a month, from the several counties of Wales, even in winter, and about three thousand in the summer season; which rendered it the most extraordinary place in

Europe: and beyond a doubt, hundreds of those who assembled there, on such occasions, are now in heaven singing the new song. If to live on the merits of Christ, to fear God, and praise him, and lead a sober and righteous life, is an evidence of a godly state, then this was visible *at that time* at Llangeitho."

Caernarvon

Mr. Evans' next settlement was in Caernarvon. The Baptist interest in that town was in a feeble and languishing condition. The church numbered about thirty members, but they were chiefly of the lowest class, and sadly disunited. They had a decent house of worship, but it was involved in a debt of £800. "All things," said Mr. Evans, "seemed like a waste howling wilderness; yea, a habitation of dragons, where they made their rest night and day." Some advised the dissolution of the church, but he thought better to attempt its reformation. His coming produced quite a sensation through the town. His first congregation was very large, and for some time multitudes flocked to his ministry, but they were only accidental hearers, generally members of other churches, who, when they had satisfied their curiosity, returned to their own places of worship. His Welsh biographer mentions with commendation the sympathy and help which he received from the Wesleyan and the Calvinistic Methodists, and Mr. Evans himself calls them the Aarons and the Hurs that sustained his hands in Caernarvon.

His labors and zeal in this place were not less than in Caerphilly and Cardiff; but owing to many unfavorable circumstances, his success was far inferior. During the first year, however, he reduced the chaos around him to some incipient order; and was enabled, by the payment of a mortgage upon the church, to save it from sheriff's sale. He employed a Mr. Edwards to travel into England, Ireland, and Scotland, and make collections for this purpose. Mr. Evans was already known extensively, as the author of the celebrated Specimen of Welsh Preaching, which had been translated into English, and published in many of the periodicals, eliciting universal admiration. Mr. Edwards had this piece reprinted, and distributed the copies wherever he went, thus making known the pastor of the church for which he solicited pecuniary aid.

Though the aged servant of God saw few conversions from his

labors in Caernarvon, the seed which he sowed in tears upon that sterile soil has sprung up since his decease, and others have gathered the harvest. The Baptist church there has experienced a gracious revival, and many of the new converts attribute their salvation, under God, to Christmas Evans.

While in Caernarvon he penned in his journal the following pious reflections: "I have been thinking of the great goodness of the Lord unto me throughout my unworthy ministry, and now, in my old age, I see the work prospering wonderfully in my hand, so that there is reason to think that I am in some degree a blessing to the church, when I might have been a burden to it, or rather a curse, by which she might have been induced to wish me laid in the earth, that I might no longer prevent the progress of the work. Thanks be to God, that it is not so! though I deserve no better; yet I am in the land of mercy. This is unto me according to the manner of God unto his people. My path in the valley, the dangers, and the precipices of destruction upon which I have stood, rushes into my thoughts, and also the sinking of many in death, and the downfall of others by immorality, and their burial in Kibroth-Hattaavah, the graves of inordinate desire; together with the withering, the feebleness, and the unfruitfulness of some through the influence of a secret departure from God, and of walking in the hidden paths that lead to apostasy."

Pulpit Popularity

Mr. Evans' popularity in the pulpit was never greater than during the last few years of his life. His descriptive powers, which were transcendent from the first, improved to the day of his death. His services were always solicited at the anniversaries of the Missionary and Bible societies in Caernarvon, and the mayor of that town once made him a handsome present for a temperance speech which he delivered there.

In 1834, he preached at the Holyhead association. His text was Heb. vi. 18. There were many seamen present; and beautifully did the preacher describe the believer's hope, "the anchor of the soul;" and eloquently did he set forth the necessity of its having, not a bare rock, but a rock covered with clay—not abstract divinity, but "God manifest in the flesh,"—in order that its hold may be " sure and steadfast," securing the Christian against spiritual shipwreck amid the many storms of the world!

The last association he ever attended in Anglesea was held in the same place, in 1837. On that occasion he preached from Col. ii. 14, 15. This sermon was one of the most effective he ever delivered. " The powerful manner," says one of his friends " in which he described the enemies, who were like unicorns and strong bulls of Bashan, and all the little elves—the great roaring lion, together with all the hosts and principalities and powers of hell, death, and the grave, giving way when Christ cried, ' It is finished,' was indescribably grand and majestic: one might have thought that the scene was actually before the eye, and that Jesus could be then seen laying hold of the powers of darkness, casting them forth, and making a show of them openly."

Interesting Letter

We insert in this place an interesting letter written during Mr. Evans' residence at Caernarvon.

" Beloved Brother: * * * I write to you, August 5, 1836, in the seventieth year of my age, and in the fiftieth of my ministry, after conversing much with ministerial brethren, earnestly desiring to see our associational union brought into action by representatives of the churches, with a view to promote a determination,—1. To bear each other's burden more efficiently in the denomination to which we belong. I lament the deficiency in this point, and ardently wish to see it effectually remedied. 2. To watch over and promote a holy conversation among all the members and all the preachers in a more efficient manner, to prevent persons of unbecoming conversation from obtaining privileges in any church, when they have been excluded in another, for that would occasion spots and blemishes to appear on the bright countenance of the ministry. The associational union, in which all the churches of the same faith and order join, should be a defence of the independence of the churches through their representatives: it should also operate as a sort of check upon independency, lest it should become opposed to the general good, and frustrate the co-operation of the whole body. *That they may all be one*, is the motto.

" Respecting church discipline. We cannot be certain that we

are doing right by administering the same punishment to all offend-
ers, even for the same offence; for the general character weighs
heavily in the balance of discipline. Also a distinction should be
made between the seducer and the seduced; and between being
overcome, or falling into sin, and living habitually in sin, and following it as a slave following his master. The denial of Peter, from
weakness, and without previous deliberation, was very different
from the betrayal of Judas, and his intentional selling of Christ.
The different characters of Saul, king of Israel, and that of David,
required different treatment in discipline on account of their offences. The Lord's discipline upon Saul was that of a rod of iron,
but upon David the correcting rod of a father, for his good, that he
might be a partaker of his holiness.

" There are two things, brother, which we ought to avoid in the
exercise of discipline. 1. We should avoid too great severity on
the one part, and 2, too much leniency on the other part. Wisdom
is necessary here to distinguish the different characters, those who
require severity, and those who claim tenderness: the two are to
be found blended in the principle of evangelical discipline. A difference is to be made betwixt some who may have been companions
in the same crime; snatching some of them as brands from the burning. The ground of the distinction lies in the different amount of
guilt which subsists between the seducer and the seduced.

" I have witnessed danger, and have sustained some harm myself, and seen harm done in churches, by exercising tenderness
towards some persons, in the vain hope of their reformation. Receiving verbal testimony or mere fluent acknowledgments from their
lips, without waiting for fruit in action also: some having been
often accused, and as often turning to the refuges frequented by
them. I never exercised tenderness towards such as these, without being repaid by them afterwards, if they had opportunity.
Shimei-like, they would curse me after having shed the best oil of
tenderness on their heads. There are some in the Christian church
like Jezebel; and there are some in our congregations like Joab,
the son of Zeruiah, that you can scarce discipline them without
rending the kingdom, until they become ripe for judgment; for
they hardly ever repent, more than did Joab and Shimei; they are
ultimately suddenly broken, without any danger to the church from
their fall.

"I perceive that the Scriptures make a difference between one that falls into sin, and one wallowing in it; between one overtaken by a party of marauders, and dragged into the camp, and made drunk at supper, and one like Judas, going to the party, and being secretly one of them, having pistols as they had: such are hypocrites. I have many times been the advocate of the fallen, and in a variety of instances have observed this operating beneficially for the church. Sometimes I have found those who had been spared upon their own verbal contrition, blessing God for his long forbearance of them, and also their spiritual brethren, who had in a manner set their bones; as the Scripture hath it, 'Restore such an one in the spirit of meekness.'

"We should be careful that discretion and love be in exercise, though in strife and contention it be not always an easy matter to do this. When the beasts of dissension get loose from the caravan, Satan sometimes drives them through the streets of Zion, that they may enter the houses of the inhabitants; and like the lioness that escaped from the keepers at Shrewsbury, and attacked the foremost horse in the carriage;* so contentions frequently attack the leaders, in order to stop the carriage of the ministry as it travels on in the labors of the pulpit. In the midst of the noise of strife, the man of God must raise his voice to heaven for courage and tenderness, so that the oil of Christ's love to the souls of men may be found in the oil-flagon of reproof, which is poured on the head; for if anger and revenge enter in, they will drop, like the spider in Germany, into the pot, and that will prevent the salutary effect of the oil, because the poison of wrath is mixed with it. The righteousness of God cannot be fulfilled in this manner in the discipline. O! brother, who is sufficient for these things, without constant help from heaven? How awful is this place! This is the house of God and the gate of heaven—and here is a ladder by which we may climb up for help; and a school in which we may learn how to conduct ourselves in the house of God.

"You cannot but be conscious, brother, of the great difficulty there is not to speak unadvisedly with our lips, as did Moses whilst drawing water for the rebellious Israelites. The rebellion of the

---

* Such an accident is said to have occurred at Shrewsbury, in England, a few years ago.

people had imbittered his spirit, so that his obduracy stood like a cloud between the people and the tenderness of the Lord, when he was showing mercy upon them by giving them water. Moses upbraided their rebellion instead of showing mercy, as the dispensation of God now required; a dispensation which contained in it a secret intimation of the great mercy to be shown by the death of Christ on the cross. Their strife was the cause of imbittering the spirit of Moses, yet he should have possessed his soul in patience.

" There are two things, brother, which you should observe: First, you will be called upon to attend to causes of contention; and you will find persons so hardened, that you will not be able to obtain weapons in all the armory of God's word that will terrify them and make them afraid of entering their old haunts. Such are persons without faith, and without the fear of God and the love of Christ influencing their minds; and though you warn them of the consequences of their contentions, that they are likely to deprive them of the privileges of the house of God, and thus forfeit the promised land, yet they stand unmoved, nothing terrified, for they value the flesh-pots of Egypt and their livelihood there, more than the manna and the land of promise. You cannot frighten them by speaking of the danger and loss of the immunities of the church below, or that above; Esau-like, they will sell their birthright as Christian professors for a mess of pottage. A man who has no money is not afraid to meet with robbers in the wood; but the individual that has gold to lose will be cautious and watchful, lest he should be robbed of his property. On a night of great storm, when ships are broken to pieces and sinking, a person who has no share in any of them will not tremble or feel any concern on their account. Thus there are some men concerning whom it is impossible to make them dread going out among the rapacious beasts of backslidings, and no storms can keep them in fear. Their spirit is one with the marauders, and they have no care, for they have nothing to lose in the tempests that blow upon the cause of the religion of Christ. These are the tares, or the children of the wicked one, in the church.

" Secondly, for your own encouragement, brother, I remark that you will have to attend to the exercise of discipline, and to treat with persons that may be alarmed, and made to tremble at the word of God, and not rush on presumptuously in their evil course. These are professors who possess white garments, and the gold of faith, and eye-salve from the unction of the Holy One. These individuals are rich in faith. They are afraid of revolutions and upsettings of the constitutional order of the new covenant, for they have funds invested in the stocks of God's kingdom. They are afraid that any storm or rock of offence should come in the way of the gospel ship, for their treasure is on board of it, and they have an interest in it. They dread the thought of walking unwatchfully and licentiously, lest they should be robbed of their riches, and forfeit the fellowship of God in prayer, lose the light of his countenance, and his peace in the means of grace, and lest they should be deprived of their confidence in the merits of Christ and a good conscience. They have denied themselves, and have pulled out the right eye, lest they should not be acceptable before God. They dread harboring in their bosoms the old guilt and former doubts. They are cautious not to give a night's lodging to such miscreants as anger, revenge, lust, and things which are of the earth; for they know that these are robbers, and if they have any indulgence they will steal away the *title-deeds* of assurance to the inheritance. They are well aware, also, that they will sustain the loss of a pure conscience, which has been purged by the blood of Christ, and which, as a golden chest, is a preserver of our confidence immovable unto the end. It is possible, brother, to manage and discipline such professors. They have something to lose, consequently they will not flee from their refuge, lest they should be destroyed. *Keep that which thou hast.* David lost for a season the enjoyment of the above blessings; but he was cleansed with hyssop, had his spirit renewed, and his riches were restored to him by faith's view of the Messiah, for which he vowed to sing aloud for ever and ever. He prayed, after this, to be delivered from presumptuous sins, lest he should be imprisoned a second time by a party so wicked and detestable. May the spiritual gift be kindled in you, brother. Grace be with you for ever and ever.

" Affectionately,

" CHRISTMAS EVANS

" *Caernarvon, August* 5. 1836 "

Tour Through the Principality

In April, 1838, when Mr. Evans had been about four years in Caernarvon, the church under his charge received notice to pay up the £300 yet due on their house of worship. He took a tour through the principality, to collect money for this purpose. Before he set out, he wrote a circular to his brethren, which was published in the Welsh Magazine. We make the following extract :—

" The term of the lease of life has expired in my case, even three score and ten years, and I am very much afflicted. I have purposed to sacrifice myself to this object, though I am afraid I shall die in the journey, and fear I shall not succeed in my errand for Christ. We have no source to which we can now repair, but our own denomination in Wales, and brethren and friends of other communities that may sympathize with us. O brethren, pray with me for protection on the journey—for strength and health this *once*, on occasion of my bidding farewell to you all—pray for the light of the Lord's countenance upon me in preaching, pray for his own glory, and that his key may open the hearts of the people to contribute towards his cause in its present exigency. O help us, brethren,—when you see the old brother, after having been fifty-three years in the ministry, now, instead of being in the grave with his colleagues, or resting at home with three of them who are yet alive —brethren Lewis of Llanwenarth, Davies of Velin Voel, and Thomas of Aberduar*—when you see him coming, with the furrows of death in his countenance, the flowers of the grave on his head, and his whole constitution gradually dissolving ; having labored fifty years in the ministry in the Baptist denomination. He comes to you with hundreds of prayers bubbling as it were from the fountain of his heart, and with a mixture of fear and confidence. O do not frown upon him !—he is afraid of your frowns. Smile upon him by contributing cheerfully to his cause this once for all. If you frown upon me, ministers and deacons, by intimating an *irregular case*, I am afraid I shall sink into the grave before returning home. This is my last sacrifice for the Redeemer's cause."

---

* The three are since dead; the first two named died before Mr. Evans, and Mr. Thomas since.

In this journey, he was cordially received everywhere by the churches, and very successful in raising money. At no former period of his life was his popularity so great as now. Wherever he preached, the place was thronged at an early hour; and frequently multitudes remained without, unable to obtain admittance.

Monmouthshire Association

During this tour, he attended the Monmouthshire Association, and preached his last associational sermon. In his introduction, he described a man whom he had seen in Caernarvon, throwing a few beans to a herd of swine that followed him, and thus enticing them to the door of the slaughter-house, where they were to be slain; and said that, in a similar manner, with one temptation after another, Satan allures deluded sinners to the very gates of hell, where they are to be tormented for ever and ever. He spoke of the gospel on the day of Pentecost, as a great electrical machine; Christ turning the handle; Peter placing the chain in contact with the people; and the Holy Ghost descending like a stream of ethereal fire, and melting the hearts of three thousand at once!

Perhaps no sermon that Mr. Evans ever preached evinced more vigor of intellect, more power and splendor of genius, than this; and seldom, if ever, had he a more perfect command over the feelings of an audience. But the effort was too much for him, and he was afterward confined to his room by illness for a week.

Last Sermon, Sickness and Death

Following this indefatigable man of God, we find him, on Sunday, the fifteenth of July, notwithstanding his late illness, at Swansea, preaching like a seraph, on the Prodigal Son in the morning, and in the evening on the words of St. Paul—"I am not ashamed of the gospel of Christ," &c.

The next evening he preached in the church at Mount Pleasant. He said he had taken his pulpit model from the day of Pentecost. He described the event of that memorable day, as a great naval battle between Emanuel and the Prince of Darkness. "The captain of our salvation" sent out twelve little boats to engage the whole fleet of hell. For a time all was enveloped in fire and smoke, and the issue of the day seemed doubtful; but when the conflict ceased, and the cloud cleared away, it was ascertained that the twelve little boats had captured three thousand of Satan's ships of war.

When the preacher sat down, he said, "*This is my last sermon.*" And so it was. That night he was taken violently ill. The next day he lay in a partial stupor, taking but little notice of his friends. The third day he seemed somewhat better. On the morning of the fourth day, Thursday, he arose and walked in the garden. Toward evening he sunk again, and grew worse during the night. At two of the clock on Friday morning, he said to his friends:—"I am about to leave you. I have labored in the sanctuary fifty-three years; and this is my comfort and confidence, that I have never labored without blood in the basin"—meaning, evidently, that he had not failed to preach "Jesus Christ, and him crucified." After a few more remarks of a similar character, he repeated a Welsh stanza, expressive of his firm trust in the Redeemer; and then, as if he had done with earth, and desired to depart, exclaimed in English—"GOOD-BYE! DRIVE ON!" He now turned over, and seemed to sleep. His friends tried to rouse him. It was too late. The angelic postillion had obeyed the order. The chariot had passed over the everlasting hills.

Thus died Christmas Evans, at the house of his friend, Rev. Daniel Davies, in Swansea, July 19th, 1838, in the 73d year of his age, and the 54th of his ministry. His life was blameless, and his end was peace. "This honor have all his saints!"

Funeral Sorrow

His funeral took place four days after his death. Never before was there such a funeral in Swansea, never such a concourse of mourners. The people came in crowds, and wept their way to the grave as if they had been following the bier of their father. The melancholy tidings of his departure spread through the principality, and the fountains of sorrow were everywhere unsealed. In Anglesea, especially, the grief was deep and universal. There he had spent more than half of his ministerial life, and hundreds owned him as their father in Christ. The Baptist pulpits were all clothed in mourning, and funeral sermons were preached throughout the principality.

PORTRAITURE

Personal Appearance

MR. EVANS was a good-looking man, nearly six feet high, and well proportioned. His intellectual faculties, phrenologically speaking, were amply developed. He had lost one of his eyes in his youth, but the other was large and bright enough for two. It had a peculiarly penetrating glance; and when kindling under the inspiration of the pulpit, added wonderfully to the effect of his eloquence. All his features were expressive of intelligence and love; his whole bearing, dignified and majestic; and the blending of great and amiable qualities in his character commanded at once the reverence and the confidence of all who knew him.

Moral and Christian Character

From the time of his conversion to the day of his death, Mr. Evans exhibited a consistent and exemplary piety. Though he several times fell into darkness and doubt, and lost a portion of his burning zeal, he never forfeited his place in the church, or tarnished his Christian name. The uprightness of his deportment was acknowledged by all his neighbors; and those of other denominations, differing widely from him in creed and custom, always accorded to him the reputation of "a holy man of God." But his piety was never ostentatious or austere. Modesty and humility were among his most prominent qualities, and a high degree of Christian cheerfulness characterized his conversation. However low, at times, his religious enjoyment, he was always careful to walk with becoming circumspection before the world, that the cause of Christ might suffer no reproach through his imprudence.

Mr. Evans was naturally of a quick and irritable temper; but
Divine Grace subdued his constitutional impetuosity, made him
" gentle toward all men," and clothed him with " the ornament of
a meek and quiet spirit." He was eminently social in his feelings,
and took great delight in the company of his friends. It cost him
no effort to render himself agreeable in any society. In the cottage
and the mansion he was equally at home, and the unlettered peasant
and the erudite philosopher were equally interested by his conversation. He never had any children of his own, but was always
remarkably fond of the children of others. After discoursing for
an hour on the sublimest topics of the Christian faith, in a style
befitting their importance, to the great delight, and often to the
amazement of all who heard him, he would descend to the relation
of some pretty story, in a manner so affectionate and familiar as at
once to win the hearts and enlighten the minds of half a dozen
bright-eyed little creatures, grouped around him like Peter Parley's
scholars in the picture.

Reading and Study

Mr. Evans was a great lover of books. He seized and devoured
with avidity every interesting volume that fell in his way. He
never resorted to reading, however, as a mere pastime. He sought
for mental and spiritual treasures to enrich his sermons. For this
he beat the fields and dug the wells of knowledge. Every thing
was made subservient to his holy calling. Every thing was pressed
into his preparations for the pulpit. His authors were selected
with prudent discrimination, and perused with earnest attention,
indicating an intense desire to be thoroughly furnished for his work.
He studied what he read. He was extensively acquainted with
the best theological writers of the age, and quoted them frequently
in his discourses. But there is one volume to which he referred
more frequently than to all the rest, " the book of books divine."
He was emphatically " a man mighty in the Scriptures." From
the word of God he derived the principal matter of his preaching.

Even that lofty imagery which constituted the peculiar charm of his ministry, was ordinarily but an amplification of scriptural tropes and descriptions. In theology, next to the Bible, Dr. Owen was his favorite author. He paid considerable attention to Oriental manners and customs; was well read in history, ancient and modern; and particularly fond of tracing the rise and fall of empires.

Devotional Habits

Mr. Evans was eminently a man of prayer. Prayer was his daily bread, the very breath of his spirit. He considered himself entitled, through Christ, to all the blessings of the gospel, and came boldly to the throne of grace in every time of need. During his whole ministerial life, much of his time was spent in the closet. It was his custom for many years, to retire for devotion three times during the day, and rise regularly for the same purpose at midnight. The disorders of the church, the slanders of his enemies, and the various afflictions of life, all drove him to the mercy-seat, and made him peculiarly earnest and importunate in supplication. After these seasons of agony, he came into the church, or the social circle, as an angel from the presence of God, and " all his garments smelt of myrrh and aloes and cassia from the ivory palaces."

He never undertook a new enterprise, without first asking counsel of the Lord. When he had a call to another field of labor, he could not decide upon the matter till he had spread it repeatedly before the throne. When he was about to preach at an association, or on any important occasion, he wrestled for hours with the angel of the covenant, nor relinquished his hold till he felt himself " endued with power from on high." Then he came forth to the congregation, as Moses from the Tabernacle, when he had communed with God. Just before leaving home on his tour of collection for the Caernarvon church, the last labor of his life, he penned in his book of appointments the following paragraph :—

" O Lord, grant me my desire on this journey, for thy name's sake. My first petition ;—Comfort in Christ—the comfort of love—the bowels of love and mercy in the denomination—the fellowship of the Spirit.—Amen. My second petition ;—That the sermons I have prepared for this journey may increase in their ministration, like the five loaves and two fishes.—Amen. C. E."

Christian Beneficence

Mr. Evans was a poor man, but " rich in good works." Suffering poverty always excited his pity, and opened his purse. Wherever he beheld distress, he was " ready to distribute, willing to communicate," according to the ability which God had given him. His salary in Anglesea, for twenty years, was only seventeen pounds per annum; and afterward, only thirty. With so small an income, he could not be expected to bestow much upon the various objects of charity. But he gave annually one pound to the Bible Society, one pound to the Missionary Society, and ten shillings to the Baptist Education Society, besides contributing liberally to the relief of the poor and the sick in his neighborhood.

Sometimes his liberality was larger than his purse. Once, when a Protestant Irishman, poorly clad, told him that he spent much time in reading the Scriptures to his illiterate countrymen, he pulled off his own coat, and gave it to him. At another time, he presented a poor Jew, who had recently been converted to Christianity, a new suit of clothes, the best he had in his wardrobe. While in Anglesea, he visited a brother in the church, who had been reduced by protracted illness to a condition of great distress; and finding the family almost in a state of starvation, emptied his pocket of the only pound he had. His wife remonstrated with him, told him she had not bread enough in the house to last twenty-four hours, and demanded what he would do now he had given away all his money. His only answer was: "Jehovah-jireh; the Lord will provide!" The next day he received a letter from England, enclosing two pounds as a present. As soon as he had read it, he called out to his wife;—"Catherine! I told thee that Providence would return the alms-pound, for it was a loan to the Lord; and see, here it is, doubled in one day!" It is evident from this incident, that Mr. Evans' liberality was the fruit of his faith in God; and the good man's confidence is never put to shame. " There is that scattereth, and yet increaseth."

Spirit of Forgiveness

" Be ye merciful, even as your Father who is in heaven is merciful." There is no virtue more beautiful in its character, or more important to the Christian, than that thus enjoined by the Son of God. The spirit of forgiveness infinitely transcends all the effects of mere human philosophy, and allies man to his Maker. In this amiable quality, Christmas Evans was never wanting. He took a thousand times more pleasure in pardoning the offender, than the offender in asking his pardon. " It was only," says his Welsh biographer, " for the person who had given offence to make some sort of acknowledgment, to say there had been a misunderstanding Mr. Evans would anticipate him with :—' O, say nothing about it! let it be buried! very likely I have been in fault myself!' " The spirit of Mr. Evans' diary everywhere corroborates this description of his character. We extract a single paragraph :—

" I trust that by the grace of God, I have overcome my natural disposition to anger and revenge. I have been enabled to forgive my greatest enemies, and pray that they may be forgiven of God. I can say from my heart, with Stephen ; ' Lord, lay not this sin to their charge!' I have no wish that any of them should suffer for their attempts to injure me, but that they may all be led to repentance, and settle their matters at the mercy-seat, where I hope also that the multitude of my own trespasses will be covered and forgotten."

His mercy was as impartial as it was cordial. He had held a controversy with a minister of another sect, who, forgetting the rules of Christian courtesy, treated him very unkindly before the public. This minister was afterward arraigned and imprisoned on a very serious allegation. If he had been convicted, degradation from the ministry would have been the smallest part of his punishment. Mr. Evans, learning the fact, and believing the prosecution unjust and malicious, felt greatly distressed for his polemical opponent. On the day of trial, he retired to his room, and poured out his heart to God on his behalf, for a long time, and with peculiar fervor. Then he waited with great anxiety for the issue. As he sat at the table, with several friends and brethren, a minister, who had been at court, entered the room, and said : " Mr. ―――― is acquitted!'' Mr. Evans instantly fell upon his knees, with tears streaming down his face, and exclaimed:—'' Thanks be unto thee, O Lord Jesus! for delivering one of thy servants from the mouth of the lions!'' He then arose, saluted his friend, and joined in the mutual congratulations of the company.

Catholic Generosity

That Christmas Evans was no bigot, might be inferred from the above anecdote. But we have other and ampler evidence of his Christian catholicity. He was a Baptist ; and, with the rest of his brethren, a strenuous advocate for exclusive immersion. He was a Calvinist, and thought it very important to vindicate against Arminian views what are sometimes called ''the doctrines of grace.'' But he was also a Christian, and held all other Christians as brethren. He did not repudiate the sincerely pious, because they could not say his '' Shibboleth.'' Kind, candid, and ingenuous, he judged of things according to their real value and importance, and appreciated true talent and virtue wherever he found them. His creed was not; ''I am of Paul ;'' nor, ''I am of Apollos ;'' nor, ''I am of John the Baptist ;'' but, '' We are all of Christ!'' He was not blinded by the senseless prejudice of sect. He was influenced less by the peculiarities of his denomination than by the love of Christ. Many of his warmest friends were ministers of other orders; and of the Methodists and Congregationalists at Caernarvon, he made honorable mention in his diary.

The most despicable reptile of the moral world is envy, the spirit that prompted revolt in heaven, and hurled archangels down to hell. Yet it is often found among Christians; among the ministers of a religion whose very principle is charity. Some men, like king Saul, can never bear a rival. If the thousands of Israel raise the voice and tune the lyre in honor of some victorious David, the evil spirit comes upon them, and they launch their javelins at the young anointed, and seek '' to smite him even to the wall.'' From such feelings Mr. Evans was always free. His large heart was utterly incapable of any thing of the kind. He esteemed others better than himself, and in honor preferred his brethren. Wherever he discovered talent and sanctified ambition in a young preacher, he never exerted an influence to hinder him, but heartily bade him

God-speed. He did not deem it necessary to smite him on the head with a cudgel to keep him in his place. He was not afraid that others would outshine him in the pulpit. He would gladly have taken his place at the feet of any of Christ's ambassadors. He was willing to accord due praise to merit, not only in the dead, but also in the living; not only in those of other countries and other denominations, but also in those of his native principality and the Baptist church. His immediate contemporaries and neighbors were often the subjects of his highest encomiums. His heart was as large as the world!

Ingenuous and Honest

A late American writer has said of insincerity, that it is the most detestable of all vices for which men go unhung. Yet it must be admitted, there is no vice more prevalent, even among the professed followers of Him, " who knew no iniquity, neither was guile found in his lips." The sentiment, that it is right to deceive for the good of the church, is not peculiar to the Papists. Perhaps the enlightened Protestant can scarcely be found, who would verbally avow such a doctrine; but it is often practically avowed, even by the messenger of truth; and ecclesiastical elevation is sometimes attributable more to dishonesty than to real virtue or talent.

Christmas Evans' popularity, however, could boast a better origin. It was the spontaneous fruit of his graces and his gifts. He was never indebted to unfair and underhanded measures for his success. His conduct was always open and ingenuous. Of deceit and secret design he was incapable. He never attempted to build up his own church by proselyting the converts of other churches. In one instance, when a young man, who had been educated for the ministry in the established church of England, came to him, desiring baptism by immersion, instead of eagerly seizing upon so valuable an acquisition to the Baptists, as some doubtless would have done, he endeavored to dissuade him from his purpose, and yielded at length only to his fervent importunity.

He deemed the slightest departure from truth, in any instance, a crime, and a deep disgrace to the Christian character. He was innocent and unsuspecting as a child. His frank and confiding disposition was unquestionably the occasion of most of his heavy trials. Jealous and malicious men took advantage of his Christian simplicity, and made one of his sweetest virtues a poison to his peace.

He once employed a person to sell a horse for him at a fair. After some time, he went out to see if he was likely to succeed. There was a man bargaining for the animal, and the contract was nearly completed.

" Is this your horse, Mr. Evans?" said the purchaser.

" Certainly it is," he replied.

" What is his age, sir?"

" Twenty-three years."

" But this man tells me he is only fifteen."

" He is certainly twenty-three, for he has been with me these twenty years, and he was three years old when I bought him.'

" Is he safe-footed?"

"Very far from that, I assure you, or I would not part with him, and he has never been put in harness since I have had him either."

" Please to go into the house, Mr. Evans," whispered the man whom he had employed to make the sale, " for I shall never dispose of the horse while you are present."

The frank manner, however, in which Mr. Evans told him all the truth, induced the dealer to make the purchase at a very handsome price ; while it procured for Mr. Evans a good name, which is better than gold.

Sarcastic Rebukes

In conversation he was always careful of the feelings of others. He would never employ a sarcastic remark, but for the purpose of merited rebuke. "It is better," said he, " to keep sarcasms pocketed, if we cannot use them without wounding the feelings of a friend." But he was capable, when occasion required, of wielding this weapon with terrible effect. Take the following instances

Just before his removal from Cardiff to Caernarvon, he was conversing on the contemplated change in a circle of several ministers. His labors had been solicited in two or three other places, and the company were canvassing the comparative claims of the different churches. A feeble-minded young man present, who " thought more highly of himself than he ought to think," said :—" It is my opinion, Father Evans, that you had better go to Caernarvon. It is not likely your talents would suit either of the other places, but I think you might do very well at Caernarvon." Mr. Evans opened his large eye upon the speaker, and replied;—"And hast *thou* peeped? When didst thou creep from the shell?"

Once, two ministers, of different sects, were disputing in his presence on what he deemed an unimportant matter of ecclesiastical discipline. One of them asked:—"What say you, Mr. Evans?" Mr. Evans replied:—"I saw two boys quarrelling over two snails. One of them insisted that his snail was the better, because it had horns; while the other as strenuously argued for the superiority of his, because it had none. The boys were very angry and vociferous, but the two snails were friends." The disputants burst into a hearty laugh, and the debate ended.

A shallow atheist was ridiculing the idea of a God, because, as he alleged, he had no sensible evidence of his being. Mr. Evans answered:—"My friend, the mole in the meadow has never seen a king; shall he therefore say there is no king? O thou atheistic mole! thou hast never travelled out of thy own narrow field; and if thou hadst, thou hast no eyes to see with; and wilt thou dare to say there is no God? Dost thou think all others as blind as thyself? All that thou canst say is, that thou dost not see God, and dost not wish to see him. How dost thou know that the being of a God is not so manifest on the other side of the river of death, that no doubt is entertained concerning it throughout all the expanse of eternity? Can the earth-mole say there is no grand Lama in Thibet? Poor worm! thou must travel through the gates of death, and fathom the bottomless pit, and measure the land of destruction, and scale the very heaven of heavens, and surround all the borders of time and eternity, before thou canst assure thyself there is no God!"

Pulpit Talents and Labors

As a preacher, Mr. Evans was very peculiar. No translation of his sermons can give the English reader an adequate idea of their force and beauty in the original.

He was exceedingly methodical and perspicuous. His arrangement was never loose and vague; his thoughts never confused and mingled together. He was a "wise master-builder," who took care to lay a broad and firm foundation, and then "built thereon gold, silver, and precious stones." The several parts of his discourse bore a mutual relation of dependence, and each would have been incomplete without the others. His order was so natural, that it was very easy to follow him; and his manner so impressive, that it was nearly impossible to forget him.

He never spoke on a subject that he did not understand. Before entering the pulpit, he invariably measured his text in all its extent, and considered it in every possible aspect. "He had a wonderful method," says one, "of making the most abstruse passages appear easy and plain. He interpreted scripture by scripture, and exhibited the component parts of his subject in a clear and beautiful manner, and illustrated them by the most appropriate and striking metaphors; and forging link by link, united them together, and bound the whole up in one glorious chain. His talents were such as to enable him to cast a ray of light upon the darkest points of the Christian system."

Mr. Evans' descriptive powers were altogether unique. He abounded in allegories of the most forcible character. In this respect, he was equalled by none of his contemporaries; transcended by none of his predecessors. Passages of this kind will be so frequently met with in the following selection from his sermons, that it is not necessary to point them out to the reader.

His happy art of description is attributable chiefly to a very remarkable imagination. This is one of the primary qualities of an orator. When it is lacking, no depth of learning, no graces of delivery, can compensate for its lack. True, argument is important. There is no eloquence without argument. Argument must constitute the bone and the sinew of every good discourse. But the bone and the sinew constitute only the skeleton. Imagination must supply the muscle and the nerve. Imagination must clothe it with beauty, and inspire it with life; give expression to the features, animation to the eye, and to the tongue motion and melody articulate. Argument is the John Baptist of eloquence, after whom there cometh a mightier, baptising with fire!

"Logic," says Carlyle, "is good, but not the best. The irrefragable doctor, with his chain of inductions, his corollaries, dilemmas, and other cunning logical diagrams and apparatus, will cast you a beautiful horoscope, and speak you reasonable things; never-theless, the stolen jewel which you wanted him to find you is not forthcoming. Often, by some winged word, winged as the thunder-bolt is, of a Luther, Napoleon, Goethe, shall we see the difficulty split asunder, and its secret laid bare; while the irrefragable, with all his logical roots, hews at it, and hovers round it, and finds it on all sides too hard for him."

Mr. Evans had feeling as well as fancy. This in a preacher is even more important than the other. Here, we conceive, lies the principal distinction between the orator and the poet. Poetry is the language of fancy; eloquence, the language of feeling. The preacher who operates only on the judgment and the fancy may instruct and please, and thus prepare the way for persuasion. Per-suasion itself requires a warm and glowing heart. Eloquence has been defined, " the power of imparting one's feelings to others." " If you want me to weep," said Horace, " you must weep your-self." The preacher who is himself unmoved, will toil in vain to move his hearers. His sermon may be as beautiful as the moon-beams on the snow; but it will be as powerless and as cold. As saith Longinus:—" The orator must have a vehement and enthusi-astic passion, a certain madness, or divine phrensy, breathing into his thoughts, and inspiring his speech." To use the language of another:—" Truth must be planted in the hot-bed of feeling, if we would witness its flowery development, and enjoy its fruit. The orator must be roused and inflamed by the majesty of his theme; not wrought up into an unmeaning fury, like a tempest in a tea-pot; but influenced and agitated by solemn considerations of truth, duty, interest, and moral grandeur."

If this description of eloquence was ever realized in the pulpit, it was in the preaching of Christmas Evans. He spoke what he felt, and because he felt. The fountain was in his own soul, and it flowed out upon his audience in streams of living water. He was always full of his subject, and his ordinary manner was exceedingly ardent and pathetic. Sometimes he seemed quite overwhelmed with the magnitude and grandeur of his theme, and then he spoke with such impassioned earnestness as to storm the hearts of his hearers. Thus inspired, it was scarcely possible that any man of ordinary sensibilities should be otherwise than eloquent. But Mr. Evans talents were of a superior order; and when kindling with the enthusiasm of his message, he became peculiarly energetic and impressive. "His words came out," as Longinus says, "as it discharged from an engine," and their influence rested like a spell upon the ear and the heart. He transported his hearers beyond the region of argument, and leaving all their cavils and prejudices immeasurably behind, rapt them away to the third heaven of ecstasy!

The secret of all this power is found in the preacher's piety. He was a man of eminent faith and holiness. The " things new and old" for the edification of his hearers, he " brought forth out of the treasure of his own heart." The love of God within him imparted to his preaching a wonderful unction. His splendid mental creations were instinct with the inspiration of sanctified feeling. This divine anointing often rendered him superior to himself, clothed him with a superhuman energy, till he seemed a messenger from the other world. The man was lost in his theme. Art was swallowed up in the whirlpool of excited feeling. The audience were swept irresistibly along by the current of the discourse; acknowledging, by tears and groans, the preacher's hold upon their hearts; and sometimes losing all self-control, and bursting into the most extravagant expressions of wonder and delight. On this subject take the language of one, who, from personal acquaintance with Mr. Evans, was qualified to form a correct estimate of his character as a Christian minister:—

" He was also an experimental preacher. That a preacher feel his subject, constitutes one of his excellencies; but that his sermon be deeply imbued with the spiritual experience of the preacher, is the crowning point of his excellency. It is true, a person may speak well of the distress of other people, but he will speak more powerfully of his own distress. Persons may expatiate very eloquently on the pleasant fragrance of the herbs and flowers of foreign lands, but those who have themselves participated in the fragrant odors, in the soft breezes of those countries, can describe them in an infinitely superior manner, and to much greater advantage. Many may speak fluently of the mercies of God, in providence and grace—protecting, preserving, pardoning sinners, &c.; but those who have experienced a sense of the divine mercy in their own souls can speak much better of it. Mr. Evans had an experience of the things of God. Not only had he heard of Calvary, but in Calvary he lived ; not only had he heard of the bread of angels and of the corn of heaven, but this bread and this corn were his daily food; not only had he heard of the river of life, the streams whereof make glad the city of our God, but the crystal waters of this river were his constant drink; not only had he heard of the renewing influences of the grace of God, but he himself had been made the subject of these influences. He had experienced the operations of the Spirit renovating his own heart, and therefore he could speak of them, not as a matter of hearsay, but with the apostle—' And what our hands have handled of the Word of life, declare we unto you.' "*

Mr. Evans' preaching was highly evangelical. " Jesus Christ and him crucified," was the alpha and omega of his ministry. The character of the following sermons fully justifies that remarkable saying upon his death-bed : " I have never labored without blood in the basin." Every one of them is illustrative of some important point in the economy of salvation. Every one of them tends to humble the sinner, and exalt the grace of God. Every one of them abounds with lofty views of the Divine Justice and Mercy.

" It is generally allowed," observes his friend " that the people who are trained by a minister, and moulded by his instructions, are a good evidence of the tendency of his doctrine and ministry. In this view then, it is observed, the church where he more statedly labored in Anglesea, and where the most of his care and efforts were bestowed, were a people mighty in the Scriptures; that they would converse well and readily on most of the doctrines of the Christian faith; that they labored much to improve in knowledge, and were active in the cause of religion. These nearly all were Mr. Evans' own people ; they were nurtured by him, and upon his ministerial food they grew to be men, and were wholly according to the mold of his doctrine. It has been remarked, ' that if volumes upon volumes were written upon the subject of the tendency of his ministry, it could never be exhibited to greater advantage than has been done by himself, in those bright, clear, and golden letters, which he has inscribed upon the people of his charge at Llangevni.' "

---

* 1 John i 1—3.

The following extracts from Mr. Evans contain his views of the evangelical over the legal style of preaching :—

" While a preacher inculcates duties in any way but with a view to the promises of mercy, and of undeserved strength, he is more like to a moral philosopher, than to the apostles and preachers that have been a blessing unto men, such as Whitefield, and hundreds who have been in a degree blessed in the same doctrine, and by the same Spirit. It is not in the duties we are to rest, but in Christ. ' Blessed are the dead which die in the Lord—that they may rest from their labors, *and their works follow them.*' It was not in reliance upon their works they passed through the river of death, as if presumptuously on a bundle of rushes, but their works will meet them in the judgment day, to be weighed there in the balance of the faith and love of Christ ; and they will be there as witnesses on the part of the saints, bearing testimony that the love of Christ constrained them to live to him that died for them and was raised again."

Again :—" By endeavoring to avoid the bog, you sink in the quicksands—while you are hiding the system of grace, and casting it, as it were, into the shade—duties without faith are not acceptable, for ' without faith it is impossible to please God.' I compare you to a dry-goods merchant, who should hang up a piece of white cloth over the shelves of his store, where the cloths, fine linen, silks, &c., are kept, and thus hiding every article in his store, without exposing any thing to the view of his customers, yet he would stand at the counter, and address them in the language of surprise, Why do you not buy here, for I know you have wherewith ? So some preach, standing like the store-keeper at the counter, saying, while the doctrine of grace is kept out of sight, Why do you not buy here ? for we know that you have the money of ability ; but you spend your money in the shops of the lusts of the flesh, the lusts of the eye, and the pride of life. But they reply, What shall we buy, sir ? you tell us that there is salvation in your store—and fine linen wrought out from Bethlehem to Calvary, and white raiment ; gold and pearls, and food and drink indeed ; but you hide them under the vail : bring them to the counter, and open them before us ; show us, carefully and plainly, whence this salvation proceeds, and by what means it has been procured ;—has it been expensive to some one, seeing it is free for us ?''

Once more:—"I compare such preachers to a miner, who should go to the quarry where he raised the ore, and taking his sledge in his hand, should endeavor to form bars of iron of the ore in its rough state, without a furnace to melt it, or a rolling-mill to roll it out, or molds to cast the metal, and conform the casts to their patterns. The gospel is like a form or mold, and sinners are to be melted, as it were, and cast into it. 'But ye have obeyed from the heart that form of doctrine which was delivered you,'* or into which you were delivered, as is the marginal reading, so that your hearts ran into the mold. Evangelical preachers have, in the name of Christ, a mold or form to cast the minds of men into; as Solomon, the vessels of the temple. The Sadducees and Pharisees had their forms, and legal preachers have their forms; but evange-lical preachers should bring with them the 'form of sound words,' so that, if the hearers believe, or are melted into it, Christ may be formed in their hearts—then they will be as born of the truth, and the image of the truth will appear in their sentiments and experi-ence, and in their conduct in the church, in the family, and in the neighborhood. Preachers without the mold, are all those who do not preach all the points of the gospel of the grace of God."

Christmas Evans was in labors more abundant than any of his Welsh contemporaries. We have stated in the memoir, that while in Anglesea, he frequently preached five times a day, and walked twenty miles. During his ministry, he made forty journeys from North to South Wales, and preached one hundred and sixty-three associational sermons. It is wonderful that his extensive travels and arduous labors did not hurry him to the grave before he had lived out half his days. But he had a firm and vigorous constitu-tion; and having borne the burden and the heat of the day, the Master sustained him in the vineyard till the setting of the sun.

And his labors were as successful as they were extensive. "The sound of heaven," remarks his friend "was to be heard in his sermons. He studied his discourses well; he 'sought to find out acceptable words, even words of truth;' and the Holy Ghost attended his ministry in an extraordinary manner."

Few men of modern times have had a more numerous spiritual family than he. Wherever he went, throughout all Wales, multi-

---

* Rom. vi. 17

tudes claimed him as their father in Christ. "In his day the Baptist associations acquired their great popularity, and in his day arose a number of the most respectable ministers ever known in the principality." Some of them were his own converts, and many of them had their talents inspired and their zeal inflamed under his powerful ministry. "Life and evangelical savor," said one of them, "attend Christmas Evans, wherever he is." "None of us," said another, "understand and comprehend the full extent of his usefulness." The celebrated Robert Hall mentioned his talents in terms of high commendation, and ranked him among the first men of his age. A Congregational clergyman, who was well acquainted with him, speaks of him as follows:—

"He is a connecting link between the beginning and the ending of this century.* He has the light, the talent, and the taste of the beginning, and has received every new light that has appeared since. He was enabled to accompany the career of religious knowledge in the morning, and also to follow its rapid strides in the evening. In this he is unlike every other preacher of the day: the morning and evening light of this wonderful century meet in him. He had strength to climb up to the top of Carmel in the morning, and remain there during the heat of the day, and see the fire consuming the sacrifice and licking up the water; his strength continued, by the hand of the Lord, so that he could descend from the mount in the evening, and run without fainting before the king's chariot to Jezreel."

We conclude this brief and somewhat imperfect portraiture with the following characteristic paragraph from the pen of Mr. Evans, illustrative of his views, not only of the right kind of pulpit ministration, but also of the injurious influence and tendency of the principal theological controversies which during his day agitated the Baptist churches in the principality of Wales:—

"I consider that a remarkable day has begun upon Wales. The dawn of this day was with Vavasor Powell and Walter Caradork; the former amongst the Baptists and the latter amongst the Independents (Congregationalists). Several churches were gathered in both denominations in the twilight of morning. But when Rowlands and Harris rose—it was the sunrising of this revival day.

---

* The eighteenth.

Mr. Jones, of Pontypool, was one of the sons of the sunrising. About ten or eleven o'clock, a host of Baptists, Calvinistic Methodists, and Congregationalists, arose; and among this class I had the honor of entering the field. The day was warm—the sermons and prayers were short, and the doctrine was evangelical. But I have reached the evening, and the day is greatly cooled. Power, tenderness, and the cross of Christ, marked the sermons in the morning; but length and tediousness are the distinguishing features of the prayers and sermons in the evening. It was too warm to preach two hours in the heat of the day. It appears, also, that talents are become much weaker and more effeminate as the evening spreads its shades. Beyond a doubt, the preaching of intricate points—something like questions concerning the law, and endless genealogies, have been the means of cooling the work and the workmen in the evening of the day. They will now lift up their heads and talk to every traveller that passes the field; and towards Merionethshire, they will inquire, 'Dost thou know any thing about Sandemanianism?' and in other districts they will ask, 'Dost thou know something about Williamsism* and Fullerism?' and in consequence you may see young doctors many, springing up, talking like learned Lilliputians. 'Some say that Christ died for all, and others that it was for his church he died; but the truth is this,' said the Lilliputians: 'he did not die for any man, *but for the sin of all men*.' I was there also on the great platform of this period, but I dared not condemn all systems by a sweeping sentence of infallibility, and take the bagpipe under my arm, as some were disposed to do, and cry down every new voice without proving it. 'Prove all things.' "

* Dr. Edward Williams, of Rotherham, author of some abstruse inquiries on the Divine Sovereignty.